# Walking with Presidents

# Walking with Presidents

## Louis Martin and the Rise of Black Political Power

ALEX POINSETT

ROWMAN & LITTLEFIELD PUBLISHERS, INC.
*Lanham • Boulder • New York • Oxford*

ROWMAN & LITTLEFIELD PUBLISHERS, INC.

Published in the United States of America
by Rowman & Littlefield Publishers, Inc.
4720 Boston Way, Lanham, Maryland 20706
http://www.rowmanlittlefield.com

12 Hid's Copse Road
Cumnor Hill, Oxford OX2 9JJ, England

Copyright © 1997 by the Joint Center for Political and Economic Studies
First Rowman & Littlefield edition published 2000

The poem "Evil," by Langston Hughes, which appears on pages 1 and 7, is from *Selected Poems of Langston Hughes* (Vintage Books, 1959), reprinted by permission of Random House, Inc. / Alfred A. Knopf, Inc. Excerpts from editorials by Louis Martin published in the *Michigan Chronicle* and the *Chicago Defender*, which appear on pages 11, 12, 19, 25, 27, 28, 30, and 33, are reprinted by permission of the *Chicago Defender*.

The Joint Center gratefully acknowledges the John D. and Catherin T. MacArthur Foundation and the Ford Foundation for their support of the research that underlies this volume, as well as Helene Berinsky for her generous donation of photographs.

British Library Cataloguing in Publication Information Available

The hardback edition of this book was previously catalogued by the Library of Congress as follows:

    Walking with presidents : Louis Martin and the rise of Black political power /
Alex Poinsett : introduction by David Garrow
       p.    cm.
  Includes bibliographical references and index.
    1. Martin, Louis 1912–1997  2. Afro-Americans—Biography
3. Afro-Americans—Politics and government.  4. Educators—United States—
Biography.  5. Afro-American journalists—Biography.
I. Title.
E185.97.M37P65  1997
973'.0496073'0092—dc21                     97-1997
[B]                                         CIP

ISBN 1-56833-093-6 (cloth : alk. paper)
ISBN 0-8476-9741-X (pbk. : alk. paper)

Distributed by National Book Network

Printed in the United States of America

♾™ The paper used in this publication meets the minimum requirements of American National Standard for Information Sciences—Permanence of Paper for Printed Library Materials, ANSI/NISO Z39.48–1992.

*Dedicated to the memory of
Louis Emanuel Martin,
the "Godfather of Black Politics."
1912–1997*

# CONTENTS

# FOREWORD

This biography is a testimony to the enthusiasm, wisdom, and optimism with which Louis Martin approached politics. For more than half a century he was an indefatigable participant in America's political affairs. After helping FDR with reelection in 1944, he went on to serve as advisor and assistant to Presidents Kennedy, Johnson, and Carter, and along the way initiated generations of black people into the leadership ranks of the American political system.

For me he not only was a teacher and a mentor but remained a steadfast friend and a constant source of inspiration. Louis was always immensely generous with his time, and I—like so many others—knew that I could call him any time and hear that familiar greeting, "What's up?" by which he meant "fill me in and let's see what needs to be done."

I am delighted that *Walking with Presidents* will give students of politics and others interested in the rise of black political power the opportunity to read about Louis Martin and his many accomplishments. It also gives me a chance to pay homage to a truly great American.

Vernon E. Jordan, Jr.
Senior Partner
Akin, Gump, Hauer & Feld

# PREFACE

The Joint Center is pleased to sponsor this first biography of Louis Martin, one of its founders, its first board chairman (1970–78), and a truly outstanding American.

Louis Martin profoundly influenced the course of recent American history and the development of black political power, so much so that the *Washington Post* once dubbed him "the godfather of black politics." Martin served as an advisor to three Democratic presidents—John F. Kennedy, Lyndon B. Johnson, and Jimmy Carter—and in that way remained near the center of power during the critical years of the civil rights revolution. Prior to that time, he had worked arduously to increase and intensify black political participation and to build progressive alliances between blacks and the labor movement.

Surprisingly, Martin has remained relatively unknown to the American public. One reason for this is that in Washington, he was the consummate political insider. He traversed the corridors of power for many years without calling attention to himself or his achievements, a rather remarkable feat. As the principal black advisor to Presidents Kennedy, Johnson, and Carter, he influenced their actions on a wide array of political and civil rights matters. He was especially effective in promoting the appointment of blacks to prominent positions throughout the federal government, thereby helping to break barriers and set precedents that laid the foundations for today's involvement of African Americans in the executive and judicial branches of government.

Among the many black presidential appointments for which Martin's aid was crucial were: Thurgood Marshall to the U.S. Supreme Court, Andrew Brimmer to the Federal Reserve Board, and Robert Weaver to the cabinet as secretary of Housing and Urban Development. In addition to these prominent firsts for black Americans, Martin promoted numerous other appointments throughout the federal government, including subcabinet positions and ambassadorships. His remarkable success in breaking down discriminatory barriers was the result of his deep commitment to the advancement of blacks in every aspect of the American political and economic arenas.

*Walking With Presidents* fills a major gap in political history by bringing Louis Martin out of the shadows and onto center stage where he belongs.

# WALKING *with* PRESIDENTS

We are pleased that Alex Poinsett, former writer-editor for *Ebony* magazine, was able to undertake this biography. Poinsett had not only covered the civil rights and political reform movements, but had also observed and written about Martin's activities as a journalist and businessman in Chicago. We hope that this book will encourage further study of Louis Martin's remarkable influence on major events of his day.

A large number of individuals made major contributions to this study. Dr. Eleanor Farrar, first as senior vice president and later as project consultant, shepherded the work through its many phases. Dr. Milton Morris, vice president for research, provided intellectual guidance for the study. Pulitzer prize-winning historian David Garrow served as a valuable reviewer of the manuscript and prepared a thoughtful and eloquent introduction; Marc DeFrancis and Kitty Garber applied their considerable skills as Joint Center editors; and Theresa Kilcourse carried out text design and extensive photo research. We are indebted to them and the many others whose contributions helped make this book possible.

Finally, we are grateful to the John D. and Catherine T. MacArthur Foundation, the Ford Foundation, and other funders for their support of the research for this book.

Eddie N. Williams
President
Joint Center for Political and Economic Studies

# INTRODUCTION

Journalism and history habitually reward self-promoters at the expense of those who are self-effacing. Whenever photos are about to be taken or a television news crew appears on the scene, there are those who literally will use their elbows to insure that they are in the front line—and at the center of that front line. Political figures often focus more on whether their efforts are being "covered" than upon the import and impact of their actions.

These dynamics not only regularly poison potential cooperation between political and organizational allies, they also distort contemporary journalism's chronicling of important developments and historians' later rendering of crucial events. Students of history—like viewers or readers of contemporary media—can be left with a highly misleading view of both the real wellsprings of political influence and what actually constitutes public leadership.

The as-yet underappreciated life and career of Louis E. Martin is just one poignant illustration of these larger dynamics. But Louis (pronounced "Louie") Martin is far from alone; the long history of the black freedom struggle is replete with examples, both individuals and organizations. Recent film and television treatments have rescued from relative obscurity one American martyr, Mississippi's Medgar Evers, who was murdered in 1963. Fresh histories of the southern movement, such as Charles M. Payne's wonderful *I've Got the Light of Freedom,* have drawn attention anew to the crucially creative but sometimes undervalued work in the early 1960s of the Student Nonviolent Coordinating Committee's young organizers.

A critical contribution to twentieth century black political activism that has been repeatedly overlooked is that which for decades was made by what was then called "the Negro press." Readers of this biography will quickly realize that once he reached adulthood, Louis Martin was first and foremost a black journalist. Martin's early years as an editor and columnist were not only formative for his own personal political outlook and social vision; they were also the years when the black press became a powerful, indispensable force for social change, creating the awareness and cultivating the convictions that would undergird the activism of the 1950s and 1960s.

Martin no doubt will be best remembered by history as the most influential black political advisor to both Presidents John F. Kennedy and Lyndon B. Johnson, but his voice and influence within the Kennedy-Johnson White House should not be thought of as the voice of one lone individual. Rather, his impressive behind-the-scenes involvement in the central political events of the 1960s ought to be viewed through a wider lens. Martin was a well-versed representative of the black protest tradition that African-American newspapers nurtured and sustained both before and after Robert S. Abbott's founding of the *Chicago Defender* in 1905. In his roles at the White House, Martin felt he was speaking up for a whole race.

Martin's journalistic experiences in Chicago and Detroit prepared him for the role he would play between 1960 and 1968 in the uppermost reaches of two Democratic presidencies as perfectly as anything any black American could have experienced during those preceding decades. As editor of the *Michigan Chronicle*, he gained a profound appreciation for the tremendous promise that Franklin D. Roosevelt's New Deal programs held for black Americans. Likewise, he achieved a deep understanding of the importance that industrial unionism, exemplified in Detroit by Walter Reuther's flourishing United Auto Workers union, would have for a progressive, biracial coalition. Above all, however, his Detroit editorship taught Martin—as he in turn would teach thousands of others—that the struggle for equality and justice was unceasing and that *protest* was the essence of black life in America.

Martin made the *Michigan Chronicle* an explicitly pro-Roosevelt paper, in marked contrast to its local black competitor, the *Detroit Tribune.* Indeed, his crusading journalism played a major role in turning black Detroit away from traditional Republican loyalties and toward a new Democratic coalition. Equally important, for Martin as well as Detroit, were the pivotal affiliations and linkages that grew up between black progressives on the one hand and the tough young leadership of the United Auto Workers on the other. The *Chronicle* was outspokenly pro-labor, and its willingness to attack Henry Ford, the ultraconservative automaker who was Detroit's most dominant citizen, marked both Martin and his newspaper as courageous voices.

Michigan State University historian Richard W. Thomas, whose splendid *Life for Us Is What We Make It: Building Black Community in Detroit, 1915–1945* draws upon a 1939 Louis Martin editorial for its title, credits Martin and his paper with playing a vital role in black Detroit's political modernization. "Without Martin and the *Chronicle*," Thomas writes, "black social consciousness would not have been able to take the ideological leap from

# INTRODUCTION

what many blacks considered the old tried and tested political orthodoxy, with its heavy dependency upon the Republican party... to the Democratic party and industrial unionism."

Any careful perusal of Martin's *Chronicle* editorials also underscores, powerfully and repeatedly, how Martin saw his post as a platform from which he could rally black readers to greater mutual dedication and commitment to community betterment and racial justice. Richard Thomas stresses that the *Chronicle* "had a knack for using bad news to raise the consciousness of the black community and inspire it to struggle on," and in the 1939 editorial earlier referred to, Martin instructed his readers that "we cannot permit ourselves any pessimism in considering either our present or our future." Martin's prose was often movingly elegiac, as that 1939 essay well represents: "We inhabit no vale of tears despite the fact that we represent the most oppressed minority in America.... To some extent, at least, life for us is what we make it."

Making black life better required a nonstop crusade for racial justice, and Martin pursued that quest with energy and forthrightness. Rejecting calls in early 1943 for black workers to "cool off" in their efforts to win better jobs in Detroit's wartime factories, he declared that "if we fall victims to this cooling off technique, we can kiss all of our gains against industry goodbye. Instead of cooling off, we need to get hot and stay hot until effective machinery is established to guarantee equal job opportunities to all Americans regardless of color, creed, or national origin. Let the stooges of Hitler and the Negro-haters do the cooling."

Louis Martin was "hot" in 1943 and still just as "hot" two decades later in 1963, when he vehemently told John and Robert Kennedy that federally mandated desegregation of all public accommodations had to be included in the legislation that a year later would emerge from Congress as the landmark Civil Rights Act of 1964. Martin's voice was an important and unique one within the councils of the Kennedy White House, but students of the civil rights policies of the Kennedy and Johnson administrations need to appreciate how Louis Martin had perfected his voice during his earlier years of service to the black citizens of Chicago and Detroit. Evaluating Detroit politics in the early 1940s, Richard Thomas concludes that the *Chronicle* "played a leading role in directing black moral indignation and protest against racist forces bent on keeping blacks from benefiting from the prosperity of the war years." Martin was especially outspoken about the widespread racist violence that characterized Detroit's race riots during the summer of 1943. Martin was steeped in black journalism's legacy of protest, and as Thomas strikingly notes, "few black papers fulfilled this honorable mandate as well as the *Michigan Chronicle*" during Louis Martin's editorship.

The political education Martin received in Detroit during the 1930s and 1940s was not limited to black protest and progressive activism, however. His work there featured the same deeply held, altruistic principles that prompted him later to refrain from seeking personal publicity or rewards during his years of service to Presidents Kennedy, Johnson, and Carter. Martin understood that self-promotion and credit-claiming work to the detriment, not the benefit, of any cause one might hope to advance. Writing in the *Chronicle* as early as 1939, Martin pointedly asserted that "public men who are doing their utmost for the common good do not have the time to seek personal applause nor indulge in petty jealousies." Five years later, speaking wishfully of how America's and the world's goal ought to be "a unity which stems from the hearts and minds of the great masses of the people," Martin sharply decried how too many citizens leave "the business of shaping the future to those aggressive egotists who lust for power and the glory it brings."

Louis Martin's lifelong vision was of a democratic society where racial and ethnic discrimination no longer held sway. "We of the rank and file," he told his Detroit readers in 1944, "must resolve to take a new view and a new responsibility" for making a better America. The betterment of black America was always Martin's uppermost task, but even when he became a political and personal intimate of successive American presidents, he never stopped speaking for "we of the rank and file." Influence and importance never went to his head, and he never felt a need, or saw any good reason, to advertise his successes and accomplishments to a wider public.

Louis E. Martin's name thus has little of the public resonance that accompanies those of Martin Luther King, Jr., or Thurgood Marshall, or even lesser-known black leaders such as A. Philip Randolph and Bayard Rustin, but Louis Martin's name belongs on the same page with these better known and more celebrated compatriots. Martin's contributions to the historic civil rights triumphs of the Kennedy and Johnson administrations guarantee him a place in the history books of the future, but Martin's entire public career, in journalism as in politics, stands as an even larger monument to how much one person can do when fame and glory are *not* a part of his purpose.

David J. Garrow
Presidential Distinguished Professor
Emory University

# .1.

## LEARNING ABOUT RACE

*Looks like what drives me crazy*
*Don't have no effect on you—*
*But I'm gonna keep on at it*
*Till it drives you crazy, too.*

*—Langston Hughes*

The receptionist in the medical office on West Bolton Street hurried to waken the doctor, who was napping in a back room. "You've got to get up!" she said excitedly. "It's a white man." Louis E. Martin, Sr., did not rouse himself quickly enough for the anxious black woman. She repeated, "It's a white man!" Jolted awake, Dr. Martin rushed to the waiting room up front.[1]

The doctor's seven-year-old son, Louis, stopped playing with his toys in a corner of the back room. From the receptionist's tone he realized, for the first time, that being white conferred a special status. It had not occurred to the boy that skin color would make a difference to his proud Cuban father, who had a smattering of white patients and counted a white police officer among his friends. As elsewhere in the Deep South, the social and economic life of Savannah, Georgia, in the year 1919 was rigidly segregated. Nevertheless, whites and blacks sometimes lived on the same street, and at St. Mary's Catholic School, which young Louis attended, some black students could barely be distinguished from whites—a telltale reminder that segregation did not always keep the races apart.

For Louis, the experience that day at his dad's office was a peek through a clouded window at a world in which nonwhites were subordinate. Seven decades later, he would look back and say, "I always regretted that my old man got up. It struck me that just being a white man made a hell of a lot of difference. It impressed me so much that I became a civil rights advocate at age seven. From that time forward, I kept looking for signs and studying people closely as I began to understand how crazy this society is."

Only craziness could explain why Louis's father, a well-educated, locally prominent physician, was sometimes called a "monkey-chaser" because of his black Cuban ancestry. He had been around the world twice as a merchant sailor, then at age sixteen jumped ship in San Francisco and decided to study medicine. Slated to get his medical degree there at the University of California in 1906, Louis Martin, Sr., interrupted his studies when the San Francisco earthquake hit, and he and his classmates were pressed into service to treat victims of the disaster, which killed more than 500 people. He later graduated from Meharry Medical College in Nashville, Tennessee, where he also interned. There he met and married Willa Hill of nearby Shelbyville. The eldest child in a large farm family, she was very different from her husband—he emotional and fiery, she shy and retiring. She doted on Louis, Jr., their only son. When the boy was four, the family moved to Savannah, where the climate reminded the doctor of his hometown, semitropical Santiago, Cuba.

Dr. Martin opened an office on the first floor of a three-story building on West Bolton Street, near one of the city's commercial strips. On each of the two big windows that framed the entrance, the doctor had hired an artist to paint a pair of American and Cuban flags with their staffs crossed, surmounting a pair of hands, one brown, one white, clasped in a handshake. Dr. Martin, who applied for U.S. citizenship late in life but died before it was granted, drilled into Louis his conviction that the greatest tribute the boy could ever receive was to be called a great American. It was an appellation the son would use with a flourish throughout his life as a grand way of saying thank-you.

Looking back, the doctor's son would come to see his father as a man whose idealism often blinded him to the facts of American life. "My father had some illusions that because of his Cuban citizenship, he could at least transcend the rigid color bar," he recalled. "Occasionally some incident involving whites in the community led him to believe that he had carved out a unique place for himself in the rigidly racist social structure." Young Louis did have both white and black playmates, and his father had a few white patients in the neighborhood. One of them, a policeman, kept his father regularly supplied with scotch and bourbon during those Prohibition years.

But society's mixed messages prompted the doctor's son to remember, years later, a telling incident. Louis's father had decided to beautify their front lawn and had mentioned this to his good friend Mr. Murphy, an Irish-American whose wife and children rarely spoke to the Martins, though they lived just across the street. Soon after, Dr. Martin announced to his family that Mr. Murphy would be coming by to plant two palm trees. The next day a large truck pulled up to the house with two tall palms and a load of black chain-gang workers, supervised by Mr. Murphy himself. No one in the Martin household, apart from the doctor, had known that their neighbor was a prison officer.

After the gang completed the planting, Mrs. Martin told her husband that their black friends would be outraged and that she was frankly disgusted. Her husband assured her that he had shaken hands with each prisoner and given him a tip and that they seemed happy enough to do the job. The doctor's son recalled it all years later: "The palm trees were a growing reminder for all of us of the murky area of race relations in a culture built on the color line."

In the meantime, Louis had come across the stories buried on the back pages of the *Savannah Morning News* about young blacks escaping from white lynch mobs. The escapees usually hid out in Yamacraw, a black neighborhood in town, until some of the better-off black residents could help them flee on one of the coastal ships that sailed regularly to New York. Louis knew that his father had helped some of these men, and it made him proud.

When Louis was twelve, two black men were hanged by a mob in Darien, thirty-five miles from Savannah. The trumped-up charge was that they had attacked a white woman. A black photographer took pictures of the giant, moss-draped tree, then sawed off the limb from which the men were hanged and brought it to Savannah. He placed it on the front steps of a black Baptist church just two streets away from Louis's home. Nearly seventy years later, Louis Martin still could close his eyes and see that limb, an image that, among many others, fueled his lifelong passion for social justice.

ᴈ▪ ᴈ▪ ᴈ▪

Until Louis attended St. Benedict's in grade seven, he had not been a particularly good student. But one of the nuns, Sister Mary Finbar, thought so well of an essay he wrote on St. Francis of Assisi that she read it aloud in class. The encouragement inspired Louis to buckle down. His teachers urged the promising student to be more disciplined about his schoolwork, and when he displeased them, they slapped his palm with a ruler. A real whipping was in store at home if his father heard of any misbehavior. Louis began to see the wisdom of following the straight and narrow, and he graduated from the ninth grade as valedictorian of his little class.

Dr. Martin wanted his son to become a doctor, but the boy could not stomach the sight of blood. Louis was also more contemplative than his father, even at a young age, content to sit for hours on the family's third-floor porch reading his books and observing the world below. As he grew older, he began to chafe at parental authority and balked at having to wash and wax his father's two cars. Feeling that he should at least make some money for the work he did, Louis entered a cosmetics-selling contest staged by two black drugstore owners to whom his father sent his patients for prescriptions. Searching out neighborhoods that lacked drugstores, Louis went from house to house selling the merchandise and discovered that he had a talent for sales, something that would prove valuable to him later in life. He won the contest, which brought him a new bicycle.

Because Savannah had no accredited high school for blacks, his parents decided to enroll him at Fisk Academy in Nashville, a high school associated with Fisk University. Although his Catholic schooling had been rigorous, he had learned nothing of black history or the magnificent literature that was just emerging from the Harlem Renaissance. At Fisk, Louis not only read the seminal work of W.E.B. Du Bois, the philosophy and criticism of Alain Locke, the novels of Claude McKay, and the poetry of Langston Hughes, but saw many of these leading black intellectuals at campus engagements.

Along with other Fisk students, he was especially impressed with the intellect of Fisk undergraduate Malcolm Nurse, from Kingston, Jamaica. Nurse was widely read and spoke with more authority on public affairs than even most Fisk faculty members, and Louis was certain he would achieve a leadership position in the world. Louis would lose track of Nurse for the next thirty years until one day in 1960, when he was working in Nigeria and heard Ghana's prime minister, Kwame Nkrumah, announce on the radio that George Padmore, formerly called Malcolm Nurse, had died. Throughout the 1940s and 1950s, Nurse had attacked British colonialism in Africa in articles under the pen name Padmore, many of them published in the columns of the *Chicago Defender*. Louis Martin, who by then was working for the *Defender*, had admired Padmore's brilliant writing without ever suspecting that the author was his former classmate.

During his high school years, Louis grew to love the English language, particularly its poetry, which inspired him to digest the entire set of the Harvard Classics. In addition he regularly read the local newspapers as well as the *New York World,* to which his father subscribed. "I learned about the whole world," he recalled. "I had my mind straightened out early about who I was and where I was, and I found that the United States was not the end of everything."

A lack of funds forced Fisk Academy to close at the beginning of Louis's final year in high school, so his parents transferred him to Pearl High School in Nashville, where he lived with his maternal grandparents. There his lifelong interest in journalism and social reform began to emerge. Because Pearl High had no newspaper, Louis and a fellow senior launched the *Pearl High Voice*, not only to publicize their school but also to crusade against segregation. With Louis as editor-in-chief, they secured ads from local black businessmen, producing the paper out of a small office that the principal, impressed by their work, set aside for them. Meanwhile, during his senior year in high school, Louis took afternoon courses at Fisk University until a serious case of psoriasis kept him out of school for an entire semester.

He started college work at Fisk, but at the end of his freshman year decided not to return there. He had never felt quite sure whether an "A" at Fisk matched an "A" at predominantly white universities, such as nearby Vanderbilt University in Nashville. Troubled by the isolation of the white and black worlds, he sought relief at the integrated University of Michigan in Ann Arbor. A friend in Savannah was a student there, and several Fisk faculty members were among its alumni. Louis had not bothered to apply for admission beforehand, nor had he shared his impulsive decision with his parents. But he had saved from his earnings on a summer job as night watchman on a steamship that sailed between Savannah and Boston, and he had enough money to pay the $127-per-semester tuition and to meet his other expenses, at least for a while.

Though passengers were segregated on the train to Ann Arbor, Louis knew that when he crossed the Mason-Dixon line, Jim Crow laws would not apply, and he looked forward to living in an integrated community for the first time in his life. The train did take him away from the harshest realities of southern oppression, but he soon discovered that racism was not a strictly southern disease. Multiple social codes segregated the races in housing, education, and work in the North as well.

Arriving at the University of Michigan, Louis met with the dean to discuss his enrollment. "Where is your transcript?" the administrator demanded. "You mean you came all the way from Savannah without applying?" Louis sheepishly replied that he didn't know he had to have that sort of thing. "You've done everything wrong," the dean continued. "I'll let you enroll here, but only if you pass the entrance exam." He passed the exam and became one of only five black undergraduates and fifty black graduate students in a student body of 15,500. The University of Michigan was a new world for the ambitious youth, but Louis was confident that he could compete on equal terms with his white classmates, a conviction confirmed as he came to know them better. Being black only added to his determination to excel. He was set on becoming a journalist, but chose to major in English composition instead after some friction with one of the journalism instructors. One especially challenging English course required him to produce a 3,000-word composition each week. Here and elsewhere, Louis sought to develop a writing style that was simple and clear.

Lectures by renowned writers and other public figures at the university's Hill Auditorium supplemented Louis's formal education. He was seated in the front row when Winston Churchill, then a member of the British Parliament, addressed a full house. "Churchill symbolized for black students the British Empire and the 'white man's burden' around the world," Louis later recalled. "I came to hear him, fully conscious of all the reasons to dislike him. I wondered how he would attempt to justify British colonialism." Churchill began speaking with the accent and deliberation that later became familiar worldwide, but he did not follow the script Louis had expected. With wit and charm, the British legislator extolled the English language and spoke of its history and the intrinsic unity of English-speaking persons. All who claimed English as their mother tongue were brothers, Churchill declared. Their common legacy of Shakespeare, Milton, and other English literary giants provided a cultural link stronger than caste, race, or color. His message was not about white supremacy but about the supremacy of the English language. Already sharing Churchill's passion for the beauty of English, Louis was impressed.

Although Louis heard most of the speakers who appeared at Hill Auditorium, he was sorely disappointed that none was black. That glaring omission was just one more piece of evidence that true integration did not exist, not even at the University of Michigan. Each experience was another element in the evolution of his political consciousness. A fellow student from Detroit, Willis Ward, had been the first black to make the varsity football team at Michigan, and at one game, Louis heard a white student shout to Ward from the stands, "Run, nigger, run! Come on, darkie!" Another outstanding campus athlete, Olympic sprinter Eddie Tolan, objected to news stories that focused on his skin color and described him as the "midnight express."

Throughout his college years, Louis lived according to his conviction that racial inferiority was, in his words, "a sham, a fraud perpetrated by whites on blacks." He was determined not to conform to segregation's dictates or accept someone else's restricted definition of his humanity. Part of that determination stemmed from his father's example. Dr. Martin had refused to let his children ride Savannah's segregated streetcars. Rather than have them humiliated, he directed that they proudly and defiantly ride their bicycles instead.

An acquaintance on campus told Louis one day that he would classify him as an "antiestablishmentarian," a rebel. "That was the first time I found out what I was—just a contrary Negro," he later mused. "I guess that and the fact that I couldn't stand the sight of blood were the reasons I didn't study medicine. That would have been the established route for me." Louis began to develop a sense of his mission in life, a persistent sense that he had to fight the system. It was a much angrier attitude than that of fellow black students from the North. Yet he made friends with whites easily enough, hobnobbing and shooting pool with them on campus. These close associations gave him firsthand experience of his white peers' characters, their weaknesses and strengths, and their intellectual tools.

It seemed to Louis that the society around him was mad and that sometimes he had to be just as irrational to cope with it. A favorite Langston Hughes poem, "Evil," came to mind as capturing this side of his life perfectly:

Looks like what drives me crazy
Don't have no effect on you—
But I'm gonna keep on at it
Till it drives you crazy, too.

Forty years later, he quoted these same lines in his address when receiving an honorary degree from Harvard.

Louis was still in college when he met Gertrude Scott at a party in Savannah, where she also lived. The daughter of a highly successful black businessman, she found the tall, handsome young English major amusing and very bright, even if somewhat cynical. He found the petite, pretty young lady with the gentle demeanor irresistible. Right off, he told her he was going to marry her. She laughed, thinking it all a big joke, but Louis continued to write letters to her at Ohio State University, where she was studying French and Spanish. When they both graduated in 1934, Louis instructed the University of Michigan to mail his diploma to him, while Gertrude—a Phi Beta Kappa honoree—attended Ohio State's graduation ceremonies, receiving her bachelor's degree with honors in romance languages. She went on to teach for a semester at Shaw University in Raleigh, North Carolina, then accepted a fellowship at Ohio State to earn her master's degree.

Meanwhile, in the fall of 1934, Louis traipsed off to Cuba after telling his father that he *might* study medicine at the University of Havana. Thinking his son might follow in his footsteps after all and pleased that his son would also learn something about his native land, Dr. Martin had given Louis the fare and agreed to send him fifty dollars a month to cover his expenses.

The Cuban ancestry of his father had a profound influence on Louis's decision. Cuba had always been a lively subject of conversation in the Martin household, and as a young boy Louis had met many Cuban visitors, a number of whom enjoyed the Martin home as a stopover as they traveled up the Atlantic coast. Louis marveled at the stories about Fulgencio Batista, a lowly sergeant in the Cuban military who had recently overthrown dictator Gerardo Machado in a bloodless coup. Machado and key members of his regime had been attending a huge banquet at Havana's Hotel Nacional when Batista and his armed cohorts simply surrounded the hotel and forced all of the government officials to surrender.

After arriving in the island nation, Louis tried to land a job as a Havana correspondent for U.S. newspapers. His romanticized image of Batista changed abruptly when he confronted the reality of the new leader's regime. Batista's response to a student and faculty strike against him was to close down the University of Havana, preventing Louis's enrollment. Thereafter, Louis, who dreamed of writing the Great American Novel, spent most of his time playing table tennis at the Havana YMCA and talking with students in Antonio Maceo Park, named for the mulatto hero of an earlier revolution. He was startled to hear young Cubans, some only sixteen, actually plotting yet another revolution to relieve the poverty that forced families to live in shacks and kept children naked and undernourished. The embarrassing contrast between himself, an "Americano" with money, and the penniless Cubans around him drained Louis of any desire to remain on the economically depressed island beyond a year. But he had learned two important facts about Cuban attitudes toward the United States: many ordinary Cubans, including students, were outraged by the arrogance of American tourists and retirees, and many Cubans, of mixed ancestry themselves, resented the rigid U.S. color line. While on the surface relations between Cubans and Americans seemed ideal, beneath the polite facade unexpressed resentment seethed.

Very late one night, a student rapped on Louis's door to awaken him. Louis listened to his obviously distressed friend tell him how a drunken American woman from a cruise-ship tour had slapped a Cuban policeman without provocation in the middle of the street. Like a spanked child, the policeman walked away, afraid to arrest the woman. Bystanders looked the other way. Louis apologized to his friend and explained that the woman was not a typical American. But he realized that to many Cubans this Ugly American epitomized what they perceived as the Yankee attitude.

In early 1935, Louis returned from Cuba determined to document the pain and misery of his fellow human beings. In addition, his experience among the students in Havana had further strengthened his resolve to do something about the inequities he saw around him. He landed his first real job as a journalist with the *Savannah Journal*, a black weekly owned by Walter Scott, president of the Guaranty Life Insurance Company and father of his future wife, Gertrude. In the fall of 1935, Louis returned to the University of Michigan to begin graduate work in English and hone his writing skills.

Louis's father was the attending physician for the Savannah branch of the family of Robert S. Abbott, the distinguished publisher of the *Chicago Defender*, and in 1936 Louis was invited to a New Year's Day dinner at Abbott's Chicago mansion. At that time, the *Defender* was the nation's most widely circulated black newspaper. In his quest for nationwide readers during the 1930s, Abbott had ignored charges of sensationalism and applied the journalistic techniques made famous by William Randolph Hearst: bold headlines, exciting graphics, hard-hitting editorials, lively coverage of sensational news, and campaigns against social and political evils.[2] Louis showed Abbott copies of the *Savannah Journal*, a newspaper for which he had worked. Impressed by his writing, the ailing publisher referred the young man to his nephew, John Sengstacke, who was also among the dinner guests and was assuming increasing responsibility for his uncle's paper.

"Look, I need a job," Louis told John, who was his own age. "I want to write." The two made a deal and shook hands on it. "I'm going back to Ann Arbor, but when the semester is over in February," Louis proposed, "I'll come to Chicago." Sengstacke agreed. This casual conversation initiated the relationship that would be the crux of Louis Martin's career. His association with the *Defender*, with some breaks, was destined to span more than fifty years.[3] His work as a journalist allowed him not only to develop his skills as a reporter and columnist, but also to enter the fray of politics and campaigns, develop a network of black contacts beyond Chicago and Detroit, and become fully informed about the circumstances, needs, and opinions of African Americans. From this forum he addressed an ever wider audience and, in time, came to the attention of national leaders.

ะ

# .2.

## CRUSADING IN DETROIT

*I got into the press because of my own feelings about race in this country. It wasn't just a job with me. I looked upon it as a lever, to move this mountain of racism.*

*—Louis Martin*

When Louis Martin signed on with the weekly *Chicago Defender* in February 1936, he joined not just a newspaper but a tradition of protest that stretched back to 1827, the year John Russwurm and Samuel Cornish published the first black-owned paper in America, *Freedom's Journal*. "We want to plead our own cause. Too long have others spoken for us," the maiden editorial of *Freedom's Journal* proclaimed. Other black-owned publications, including Frederick Douglass's *North Star*, were the first newspapers in the country to advocate—well before slavery was abolished—that blacks receive full equality as citizens.[1]

After emancipation, Reconstruction brought a fleeting moment of political enfranchisement to southern blacks. When Reconstruction ended and Jim Crow segregation settled into place, a militant civil rights tradition took hold within the black press. Joining this effort were the *Chicago Defender*, founded in 1905, and the *Crisis*, launched in 1910 as the organ of the newly formed National Association for the Advancement of Colored People (NAACP). During World War I, the black press grew in importance and militancy, condemning the contradiction between the war aim of making the world safe for democracy and the domestic reality of the undemocratic treatment of black Americans. The editorial policy of the *Defender* fit squarely within this protest tradition. In a June 15, 1935, editorial offering a civil rights plank for the Republican party, the *Defender* articulated its long-standing demands:

> Simply stated, we want the same rights and privileges accorded every foreigner and every WHITE native of this country. We want EQUALITY—FULL equality with all the term implies. We want the right to work whatever

job we find ourselves FITTED for. We want the right and the privilege to VOTE for whatever candidate we deem best suited to carry out the policies and interests of ALL the people. We want the right and the privilege to be VOTED FOR and to be seated if we win.... We want to be able to ride from Chicago to Raleigh, N.C., and from there to Texas without being insulted and humiliated.... We want the protection of the laws of the land against mobs and against prejudiced, vicious courts.... What is it the Negro wants? Just ask yourself, "What is it I want?" [2]

The *Defender* preached its message well beyond the Chicago area. Through a network of Pullman-car porters, it was distributed across the nation, particularly in the South. The founder of the paper, Robert Abbott, had grown up in Savannah and aimed many of his editorials at the wretched economic conditions and horrible abuses of black Americans in the South. From its inception, the paper publicized and campaigned against lynchings. While the *Defender* gradually gained national prominence among blacks, it was not popular with everyone. Bundles of the papers, shipped south on the Illinois Central Railroad toward New Orleans, were often confiscated and burned. It was said that in some places, merely possessing a copy of the *Defender* could get a black man arrested.[3]

Race relations in 1936, when Martin joined the *Defender*, were appalling throughout the nation. Jim Crow laws were strictly enforced in the eleven states of the old Confederacy. Lynchings were relatively common, running at two to three a month in the South, according to NAACP records.[4] As far as the mass media in both the North and the South were concerned, blacks were never born, never married, and never died. In the North as well as the South, racial discrimination and hostility were widespread.

It was in this context that Martin launched his lifelong battle for civil rights. His initial assignment with the *Defender* was an apt beginning: he was sent to cover the first meeting of the National Negro Congress at Giles Armory on Chicago's South Side. The congress was a federation of major black organizations—the NAACP, the Urban League, and the Brotherhood of Sleeping Car Porters, among others. Among the people Martin first met at the armory were the poet Langston Hughes; A. Philip Randolph, the head of the Brotherhood of Sleeping Car Porters and at that time the only black man to head a national union; Congressman Oscar DePriest of Chicago, the first black U.S. representative in the twentieth century; and Lester Granger, head of the National Urban League. The encounter with Granger grew into a friendship that lasted more than three decades.[5]

## CRUSADING IN DETROIT

By 1935, the Great Depression had decimated the *Defender*'s circulation, prompting some of its national advertisers to demand cash rebates for readership that the paper had promised but not delivered. Instead of paying rebates, the *Defender* agreed to give free national advertisements in a new paper. After surveying cities with growing black populations, the *Defender* publishers focused on Detroit as one of the most promising locations for the new paper. They calculated that starting up another paper would finally solve their down-time problem at the printers by keeping idle pressmen busy. The earlier founding of the *Louisville Defender* had already helped absorb some of the down time.

Lucius Harper, the *Chicago Defender*'s executive editor, went to Detroit in April 1936 to start the project rolling. The new paper was to be called the *Michigan Chronicle*. The automotive city's existing dailies, the *Free Press*, the *Times*, and the *Daily News*, carried little news about blacks other than crime reports and an occasional church-related story. The black community in Detroit kept up with news from the black weeklies—the Detroit editions of the *Pittsburgh Courier* and *Chicago Defender*, as well as two locally printed weeklies, the *Tribune* and the *Independent*.

In June, John Sengstacke sent Martin, then only twenty-three, to Detroit as editor and publisher of the *Chronicle*. They agreed that he would earn twenty dollars a week for the first six months, after which he would be expected to make the paper pay his salary and expenses. He had landed the job in part because he had attended college at Ann Arbor, only twenty-eight miles from Detroit, and Sengstacke assumed he knew more about the city and state than anyone else on the Chicago paper's staff. Harper warned that he had to produce a paper that would sell, that he was not in the business of giving papers away. The veteran editor added that as long as people bought the paper, Martin should not be alarmed by criticism; nearly everyone thought he could do a better job than the editor.

As Harper prepared to return to Chicago, he gave Martin the keys to the *Chronicle*'s one-room office and its roll-top desk. "If you want some help, kid, drop me a line," he said, adding, "From now on, it's your baby." He presented Martin with all the *Chronicle*'s cash—seventeen dollars and some change in a cloth bag.[6]

Publication of the *Chronicle* was somewhat complicated. After writing the news, Martin sent it to the *Defender* printers on Mondays and Tuesdays, driving down to Detroit's main post office to speed it on its way. Printed copies of the paper were shipped to Detroit on Wednesday nights for distribution on Thursdays. In the beginning, Martin himself picked up the baled papers at the railroad station on Wednesday, loaded them in his car, then distributed them the next day. During the time the eight-page publication was being printed, Martin sold advertisements and wrote copy for the following week's issue.[7]

After nine weeks, the *Chronicle* had not yet sold more than a thousand copies a week. Martin's entire staff at first consisted of himself and any literate person who happened to be in the neighborhood on Tuesday, the printer's deadline. He had learned that while newsmen and money were scarce, he could always scratch a preacher, doctor, or lawyer and find a would-be journalist.[8]

Russ Cowans, a *Defender* sports editor who was also secretary for heavyweight boxer Joe Louis, agreed to write for the *Chronicle*. Martin also hired Larry Chism, a man employed by the writing project of the Works Progress Administration (WPA). Because Chism was already getting a WPA salary, he could afford to accept the meager six-dollar-a-week salary that was all Martin could pay.

Martin quickly learned that in the newspaper business everything rides on the first year of publication—the toughest, most frustrating, most critical period. Some advertising agencies would not even grant a new publisher an interview until he had completed a full year of continuous publication. So after a few weeks of rewriting the notes he found on the blotter at police headquarters, covering civic affairs, and rounding up "journalists" to write what he described as "reams of wind," he began a methodical study of reader appeal. With a few carefully selected newsstands as his laboratory, he sought to determine the relative sales value of various news headlines.

The *Chronicle* was usually sandwiched between several other weeklies on the stands, and customers typically looked them all over before making the decision that was so crucial to Martin's fledgling enterprise. He found that a boldface headline of a murder was worth twenty headlines on such matters as the opening of the membership drive at the local YMCA. He also discovered that all the world loves a pretty girl, set three columns wide.

Murders were running at three a month in Detroit that first summer, and Martin found it profitable to devote at least one of his three or four headlines to what he called "life in the raw or death in the afternoon." He often wound up his stories with the implicit moral that crime did not pay. To attract readers who insisted on good news, he printed a mix of stories. He carried at least one story of black advancement—usually the first black to get some coveted municipal post or the first black to sit on a jury in a particular county. These experiments boosted circulation to 4,000. Nevertheless, when he asked people on the streets during this first year what they thought of the *Michigan Chronicle*, many said they had never heard of it.[9]

During the *Chronicle*'s first months of publication, Martin discovered the value of street speakers, men who spent their days speaking on busy corners in big cities. Some sold patent medicine or jewelry; others championed social causes and were often denounced as radical agitators. Several came to Martin's rescue by promoting the *Chronicle*, but the one who helped most was Arthur Caruso. A veteran street speaker from Harlem, Caruso always spoke from a ladder and built a crowd by baiting his listeners. Though lacking formal education, he was a student of current affairs. Before taking on the task of publicizing the *Chronicle*, he questioned Martin about the paper, his background, and his views on a black newspaper's responsibility. Caruso proposed that Martin give him copies of the *Chronicle* to sell at his sidewalk forums.

Martin had no money for promotion, so he agreed. Caruso set up his ladder at a busy intersection. Positioning himself above the heads of pedestrians, a copy of the *Chronicle* in hand, he questioned passersby in a provocative, sometimes insulting manner: "Can you read and write? Have you ever voted? Are you really free, or are you still in slavery?" Caruso continued the questioning until he found someone who appeared ready for an argument. Occasionally, he held up the paper to read the headline about a story protesting racial discrimination. "You didn't know that, did you?" He pointed his finger at someone. "How could you know if you can't read?" he continued. "Are you too dumb to get a copy of the *Michigan Chronicle* and find out what is happening to you?" Caruso's taunting harangue invariably worked. Before the furor subsided, he had sold copies of the *Chronicle* for twice the newsstand price, while insisting: "Knowledge is power; ignorance is a curse. Don't be a fool; don't be dead." [10]

In September 1937, some fifteen months after Martin came to Detroit, the *Chronicle* was incorporated under Michigan statutes. Although still printed on the *Defender* presses, it was now legally independent of the Chicago paper. As the *Chronicle* grew, Martin and Sengstacke formed a corporation, which gave Martin a minority ownership interest in the paper. His affiliation with Sengstacke Newspapers (formerly the *Defender* newspapers) would sustain him for the next forty-two years, apart from the eight-and-a-half years he served the Kennedy and Johnson administrations and the two years and four months with the Carter administration.

In those early years with the *Chronicle*, Martin's introduction to some black newsmakers came through an unusual source. John Roxborough, a numbers racketeer who handled thousands of dollars in numbers bets each day, occupied a suite of offices on the second floor of the building where the *Chronicle* was published. Roxborough also managed Joe Louis, who would soon regain his world heavyweight boxing title and was already a heroic figure to black Americans. Martin met many of the black sports and entertainment celebrities who trooped up to see Louis's manager and quickly discovered that Roxborough was handing out cash retainers to sportswriters who came to get hot copy for the media buildup of Louis. All of this activity in his building put Martin's newspaper operation in an unusual light. "Everyone in that building was a numbers king but my place," he would later say. "They were all gamblers. We had the only legit, so-called, operation going." Martin's paper was viewed as a scholarly oddity. "I got put in a category— they called me 'schoolboy.' I was one of the few people in that area who had any college training."

Roxborough, who saw Martin as a decent young man, said to him one day, referring to all the shady deals going on, "Leave these people alone, and leave their money alone. Just don't do anything involving yourself with those and you'll be all right." Martin took this to heart when, one Christmas season, he watched a pile of envelopes filled with cash at Roxborough's quarters disappear. "For two days, the entire police department of Detroit came in to get those envelopes." [11]

Meanwhile, Martin had continued to water his relationship with Gertrude Scott, writing to her while she pursued a teaching fellowship at Wilberforce University in Ohio. In January 1937, they eloped, precluding any family opposition to the fact that he was Catholic and she Episcopalian. Since she was still teaching at Wilberforce, it was not until the end of the semester that she permanently joined her husband in Detroit. A year later, Trudy, the first of their five daughters, was born. The Martins were not well off, but his weekly salary of twenty-five dollars put food on the table and kept a roof over their heads during the continuing economic depression, which had hit Detroit especially hard. Things were so bad at the time that Martin liked to joke about the Detroit River running only three days a week. Yet the young couple knew if they ever became ill or needed financial aid, their parents would help them. After all, Gertrude's father, Walter Scott, was president of an insurance company and owner of a newspaper, a funeral home, and two black movie theaters. Dr. Martin, too, was a man of means. When he came to visit the couple in 1939, he gave his son seven one-hundred-dollar bills, which the younger Martin used for a down payment on the house that became the *Chronicle* office.

Both Martin and his wife worked feverishly to develop the fledgling paper. Gertrude kept the books, billed advertisers, wrote weekly book reviews, even wrote editorials when necessary, and occasionally covered news events. Martin built up the paper's circulation with heavy doses of labor and church news that, on occasion, induced pastors to buy stacks of 150 or more of the weekly.[12]

With the *Chronicle,* Martin straddled journalism and politics. He recognized that merely seething with repressed rage—his chronic mindset in college—would in itself do nothing to attack either poverty or racism. He believed that ultimately, racist laws could be changed if blacks and other minorities were included in policy making with whites. The black community had to be mobilized before this could become a reality, however. In his editorials and elsewhere, he not only advocated full citizenship rights for blacks but also insisted that blacks fulfill their obligations as citizens to address the problems they confronted. He reminded readers that resolving long-standing grievances over unemployment, police brutality, and housing discrimination required enlightened use of the ballot, self-help, and articulate, forceful protest.

Martin used his paper to vigorously support black candidates for the city council and to boost the candidacy of Charles C. Diggs, Sr., for the state senate in 1936. Diggs, a prominent undertaker, won the seat to become the first black member of the Michigan legislature. "Diggs didn't have to spend a nickel," Martin recalled proudly. "I gave him all the publicity he needed. He beat the hell out of everybody. His victory was our victory." (In 1954, the legislator's son, Charles C. Diggs, Jr., carried on the tradition and became Detroit's first black member of Congress.) Diggs Sr. would become an important ally to Martin in the struggle for equal rights for Detroit's black citizens.[13]

Martin hoped that Diggs's electoral success would animate black voters. The *Chronicle* promoted the idea that each vote counted and that black citizens up North had a special responsibility to register and vote since those down South could not. Two years after Diggs's election, the *Chronicle* praised the legislator for his service and particularly for helping to make a reality one of the major planks of the *Chronicle* platform, namely, creation of a black unit of the Michigan National Guard. In an editorial, Martin reminded readers of the importance of black representation throughout city government and on state, county, and city boards of education. He concluded with a reminder to vote: "The ballot," he wrote, "is the tool which has been demonstrated to be the one most effective instrument for the attainment of these ends within our power." [14]

When the *Chronicle* started, Roosevelt's burgeoning New Deal was also big news. Martin and his wife had embraced New Deal programs wholeheartedly while still in college. FDR had not only put money in the hands of millions of the unemployed through new forms of public assistance, but with programs like the WPA and the Civilian Conservation Corps, he had also restored the dignity of the jobless as they built and repaired the nation's roads, bridges, airports, sewers, and post offices. Martin was convinced that Roosevelt's extensive reforms and social programs had saved the nation from revolution.[15]

In the 1932 election, most blacks in the North had continued to support the Republican party and voted for Herbert Hoover. Even four years later, many black ministers still preached the gospel of loyalty to Lincoln the Emancipator. In Detroit, many of the most powerful black ministers were allied with auto company officials to promote Republican politics and oppose labor unions. Company hiring bosses often demanded that black job applicants produce endorsement letters from these ministers before they could be hired. Companies even monitored employees' political activity. Workers who wore company badges or were otherwise identifiable were certain to be reported to their companies if they attended Democratic party meetings.[16]

Nevertheless, Martin proclaimed in *Chronicle* editorials that the time had come for blacks to turn away from the party of Lincoln and to support FDR. Blacks across the nation had been hit hardest by the Depression. Even though continuing discrimination limited the jobs available to them in New Deal work programs, they still benefited from the overall improvement in the economy and from the new federal social assistance. In the end, blacks in Detroit and other northern cities deserted the Republican party in droves, helping Roosevelt win the 1936 election by a landslide.

❧ ❧ ❧

The New Deal notwithstanding, during the middle and later thirties, millions remained unemployed, and unemployment actually began to rise again. For black people, traditionally last hired and first fired, conditions became extreme. In the summer of 1939, Martin warned in a *Chronicle* editorial that the army of unemployed was a threat to the continued existence of the political and economic system:

> We who shout save democracy and praise our economic system may find that we are faced with an army of hungry, dispossessed men and women who are asking in unison, "Where are my opportunities, where are my jobs?"... Congress cannot dismiss the plight of ten million people with a shrug of the shoulder, and the ten million are increasing their numbers.[17]

In the *Chronicle* and other venues during this period, Martin paid considerable attention to the rise of industrial unions. He saw the labor movement as a catalyst for broad social change, recognizing that unions were already bringing white workers better job security, higher wages, shorter hours, special overtime rates, a rational seniority system, and the machinery for handling work grievances.[18]

A momentous change in the labor movement had occurred the year before the *Chronicle* was launched, when United Mine Workers (UMW) president John L. Lewis and other labor leaders established the Congress of Industrial Organizations (CIO) for workers in the auto, steel, rubber, glass, textile, packinghouse, and other mass production industries. The CIO organized workers by plant instead of by crafts and skills as the more traditional American Federation of Labor (AFL) had done. Most important, the CIO was committed to worker solidarity regardless of race. This was a daring move at the time, in marked contrast with the AFL's history of excluding blacks or restricting them to Jim Crow units. The new union's stance on equal opportunity would help avoid the vicious labor strife that had sparked race riots in East St. Louis in 1917 when factory owners used blacks as strikebreakers.[19]

Because of the new union's promise of equal treatment for blacks and whites, Martin became one of labor's most influential supporters within Detroit's black community. Three black men would become crucial in linking the fortunes of the black community with those of organized labor: Martin, Horace White (a Congregationalist minister), and Senator Diggs. Of the three, only Diggs was over thirty. In allying themselves with the fledgling United Auto Workers (UAW), they found a critical supporter for the rights of black citizens in the coming decades.[20]

Largely because of the AFL's past discriminatory practices, both rank-and-file black workers and leaders of black advancement organizations were skeptical of unions. In addition, many blacks were grateful to their employers and remained loyal to them, even though they were not treated as well as whites. This was especially true at Ford Motor Company, Detroit's largest employer of black workers. Because the income of Ford's black workers had such a large impact on the prosperity of the larger black community, many in the black middle class believed that what was best for Ford was best for them.

The Ford Motor Company reflected the interplay of all the tensions and contradictions at work in industrial America during the late 1930s and early 1940s. Although Henry Ford himself was openly and vehemently hostile to Jews, his attitude toward blacks was more benevolent: the superior "Anglo-Saxon and Celtic race" had an obligation to help inferior races. Thus even though he believed in innate racial differences and in racial separation, he also believed that blacks should enjoy economic opportunity. Blacks did have more job opportunities at Ford's River Rouge plant than at other auto plants. Ford actually sought out black workers, sending recruiters down South to induce blacks to come to Detroit and work for the company. No doubt he also saw that greater opportunities and better treatment would produce an extremely loyal group of workers.

In 1937, as the CIO-affiliated UAW geared up its organizing drive in Detroit, the NAACP held its annual convention in the Motor City. At that time the NAACP's Detroit chapter was the wealthiest and largest in the country. The local chapter, along with prominent black ministers, the local Urban League, and black businessmen in the city, favored the company over the union, even though the union promised equal treatment of black workers. Many of the ministers had in fact been on the Ford payroll for years.

To address important economic and labor issues, the NAACP's assistant secretary, Roy Wilkins, who was in charge of planning the conference, invited UAW president Homer Martin to speak to the convention. The invitation stirred up a hornet's nest. Several of the ministers who had been screening employees for Ford for many years denounced the decision. To make matters worse, in his speech to the delegates, Homer Martin said he came to represent the poor and oppressed, whether white or black, "just like Jesus Christ." A firestorm of criticism erupted, nearly tearing the convention apart. Black ministers who sided with Ford were greatly offended that the UAW leader had compared himself to Jesus, thereby suggesting that God was on labor's side.

# CRUSADING IN DETROIT

The labor resolution that the national office of the NAACP had prepared, an innocuous statement that merely echoed the one adopted at the previous year's convention, went down to defeat, even though it simply affirmed the importance of labor unions to the economic future of blacks. Angered by the conduct of Detroit's black leaders and stung by the personal criticism, Wilkins wrote a scathing editorial in the NAACP magazine, *Crisis*. To those who had suggested that the NAACP was interfering with Detroit business, he pointed out that improving the economic well-being of black people *was* the business of the NAACP. He further suggested that those who supported Henry Ford look at his other plants across the nation, where blacks were treated as badly as anywhere in the industry. But he saved his sharpest barb for the ministers: "The spectacle of poor preachers, ministering to the needs of poor people whose lot from birth to death is to labor for a pittance, rising to frenzied, name-calling defense of a billionaire manufacturer is enough to make the Savior himself weep." [21]

The editorial reignited controversy, as the ministers defended themselves and denounced both the UAW and the NAACP, singling out Wilkins for personal attacks. In this melee, neither the leadership of the local NAACP nor any of the leaders of Detroit's black advancement organizations came to the defense of Wilkins or the NAACP national office. But Louis Martin and Horace White did take up their defense—Martin from the pages of the *Chronicle* and White from his pulpit. In doing so, Martin began to forge a strong relationship with the national civil rights organization and, in particular, with Roy Wilkins. [22]

Despite Martin's editorials, most of Detroit's black leadership continued to back the company against the union. Meanwhile, infighting within the UAW led a group headed by Homer Martin to split off and form a competing union affiliated with the AFL. In 1939, Louis Martin again played an important role in cementing the relationship between black workers and the UAW-CIO. As a result of a labor dispute, in November Chrysler locked out all 24,000 workers from its Dodge Main plant, and the UAW-CIO called a protest strike at all Chrysler plants. Although Chrysler did not treat its black workers nearly as well as Ford did, it was still the second largest employer of blacks in the area, many of whom had little sympathy for white co-workers who could advance to higher-level jobs that they were locked out of. Aided by a number of other organizations, including the breakaway UAW-AFL, Chrysler called a back-to-work meeting for black employees at its Detroit plant. Since these workers were only a tiny fraction of the plant's total workers and were limited to lower-level jobs, the plant could not have resumed production even if every black worker had returned. The striking UAW-CIO concluded that what the company wanted was to incite interracial violence so that the National Guard would be sent in, thereby breaking the strike.

On November 24, about sixty black workers attempted to force their way through the picket lines. In the ensuing violence, two policemen and six blacks were injured. The UAW called on the trio of young black leaders— Martin, Diggs, and Horace White—for help. Alarmed by the near inevitability of rioting, White and Martin sent telegrams to two dozen local black leaders urging them to attend a meeting at the Lucy Thurman YWCA the next day. Those who arrived at the meeting included not only union supporters but also company loyalists and others for whom this would be their first official encounter with representatives of the UAW-CIO. Martin particularly noted the presence of Beulah Whitby and Geraldine Bledsoe, members of Horace White's congregation who were leaders of the Detroit Urban League and wielded considerable influence in the black community. Whitby was the highest-ranking black social worker in Detroit's welfare department, and in 1941 Bledsoe would become head of Michigan's placement office for black state employees.[23]

Representing the UAW-CIO was a liberal white Southerner named Emil Mazey, who spelled out the difference between the older, craft-oriented AFL and the newer CIO approach of industrywide organization and, when necessary, action. "He was eloquent," Martin recalled, "and showed the kind of respect for his audience that many white speakers never seemed to learn." One of the notable results of the meeting was the change in attitude of Father Malcolm Dade, who commanded great respect and great influence through his Episcopal church on Detroit's west side.[24]

No doubt hundreds were deterred by the efforts that came out of that meeting, but still, the next morning several hundred black workers assembled to march through the picket line of more than 6,000 mostly white strikers. Leaders from the UAW locals, a number of them black, walked through the crowd telling them that it was a setup, that the company was trying to provoke interracial violence in order to break the strike. Although the black strikebreakers were jeered as they passed through the line, there was no violence. The next morning the strikebreakers were again allowed passage. Foiled in its efforts to spark a riot, Chrysler capitulated, and the federal labor conciliator managed to reach an agreement ending the strike. The UAW was profoundly grateful to the young black leaders who had helped it avert a catastrophe. For special praise, UAW leaders singled out Louis Martin and the other signers of the leaflet.[25]

The *Chronicle's* prolabor platform won the paper thousands of new readers among the auto workers. Many had never regularly read a black-owned paper. By 1940, with *Chronicle* circulation safely above 15,000, Martin enlarged his staff and moved to larger quarters.[26]

❧ ❧ ❧

In April 1941, Ford's River Rouge plant was the scene of another major strike. Like Chrysler, Ford attempted to use blacks as strikebreakers, not only encouraging them to stay inside the plant but arming them and sending them out periodically to attack white workers on the picket line. With a full-fledged race riot almost sure to erupt, the UAW-CIO appealed to Martin to help mobilize influential blacks in a campaign to persuade black workers to leave the plant. Quick to help, Martin invited black clergymen and leaders of black organizations to a luncheon conference with the union representatives. At the end of the conference, the group issued a statement condemning Ford's exploitation of blacks as strikebreakers and supporting the UAW-CIO. A few days later, NAACP executive secretary Walter White flew into Detroit from New York to personally urge black workers to leave the plant. Many did. The National Labor Relations Board called for an election, and the union won by a decisive 70 percent.[27]

The outcome of the 1941 strike was a victory not only for the auto union, which succeeded in organizing the Ford plant, but also for black workers. In the NAACP's *Crisis* magazine, Martin hailed the new contract, which stated that all of its terms would apply to all workers regardless of race or national origin, as a dramatic victory. The most significant gain for black workers, he felt, was job security: "[T]housands of Negro workers... may now plan their own future without fear. It is freedom from the eternal threats of layoffs for cause or no cause." Martin also touted the union's democratic process of selecting leaders as a means for blacks to advance: "Within the democratic processes of the union, the Negro worker can fashion a new place for himself in American labor and develop a new relationship between the races. White and black workers meet in the union hall on terms of equality, and they will of necessity educate each other." [28]

Urging black workers to take advantage of the many opportunities offered by the Ford contract, Martin summed up its significance:

Already many Negro workers at River Rouge have shown that they possess the capacity for leadership... a number of... unionists in the plant are giving leadership to thousands of whites as well as to members of their own race.... White workers have shown a willingness to accept and follow strong and sure leadership with little regard to color. If the black worker earnestly seeks to integrate himself into the union life, he has unlimited opportunity.[29]

Martin concluded that "within the framework of industrial unionism, there is an opportunity for the kind of democracy that gives status to all regardless of color or national origin."[30]

Addressing the UAW annual convention that year, the union's president, R.J. Thomas, thanked black leaders for mobilizing their community behind the strike and defeating the attempt to use race to divide the workers. He singled out for praise Louis Martin, Horace White, Charles Diggs, Malcolm Dade, Charles Hill, and James McClendon, as well as Walter White of the NAACP.[31]

As a result of the coalition that Martin and other young black leaders nurtured with the UAW during the late 1930s and early 1940s, black and labor union solidarity became a reality in Detroit. Likewise, the NAACP fashioned an alliance with labor that lasted for many decades.[32] During the quest in the 1940s for equal treatment in wartime jobs and housing and against police brutality, the coalition would prove useful. Indeed, two decades later, at the 1963 March on Washington, the largest single contingent of black workers would come from the UAW. Its president, Walter Reuther, addressed the crowd and was among the march organizers.

Nevertheless, even with UAW support, progress in job opportunity was slow and uneven during the next decade. After the unionization of the Ford plant, the company radically changed its attitude toward black workers. Indifference was replaced by outright hostility, and by the end of 1942 Ford's hiring practices had become the most discriminatory in Detroit. Black workers had little choice but to turn to the union to improve their job opportunities and working conditions. While committed to solidarity among black and white workers, the union faced two problems in carrying through on its promises: discriminatory employment practices continued unabated, and many white workers within the union remained as prejudiced as ever.[33]

These problems had become pronounced as plants converted to wartime production in advance of the country's entry into World War II. With five million whites still unemployed in 1941, blacks had great difficulty securing anything but the lowest paying, most menial jobs at what had now become weapons plants. In August 1940, a statement by the National Defense Advisory Committee condemned the exclusion of blacks from jobs in defense plants. A month later, in his message to Congress, Roosevelt spoke out against discrimination. To help blacks find jobs, the federal Office of Production Management established a Negro Employment and Training Branch in its Labor Division.[34] This office was now headed by Robert C. Weaver, a distinguished black economist who had already served as an advisor to the U.S. Housing Authority and the Interior Department. Weaver's new office dispatched field representatives to investigate complaints that blacks were being shut out of defense jobs. His office's options, however, were limited. Although Weaver could complain to his superiors in the Office of Production Management (later the War Production Board and then the War Manpower Commission), their mission was to recruit sufficient manpower to operate the new industries, not to ensure equal opportunity.[35]

The threat of a march on Washington by stalwart union leader A. Philip Randolph finally brought action from President Roosevelt on the problem of job discrimination. Randolph, at that time the only black union president in the United States, had organized a mammoth rally of blacks from all over the country, scheduled for July 1, 1941, to demand an end to discrimination in both the wartime job market and in the armed services. Eleanor Roosevelt and New York mayor Fiorello La Guardia, two of the nation's most prominent white progressives, warned that the march would do little good and might even provoke reprisals against blacks. But Randolph and fellow organizer Walter White determined to go ahead. Days before the target date, Martin expressed his strong support for the protest in a *Chronicle* editorial:

> Several thousand determined Negro citizens… will invade Washington, D.C., the nation's capital and the fountainhead of racial prejudice…. They will come from the voteless South and the jobless North, united in a protest over a way of life which offers neither freedom nor opportunity. They will make articulate the demands of the oppressed people who have been caught in the vise of racial intolerance and economic slavery. The Negro people seek a way out…. The Negroes of America are tired of the pussy-footing, double-dealing, lying traitors of democracy who cover their cloven hoof in a silken boot. The President by executive order must strike at the cancerous roots of racial discrimination in this social order, which is neither Christian nor democratic. And he must strike now.[36]

Faced with the prospect of many thousands demonstrating in the nation's capital against racial tyranny at home while the country waged war against fascism abroad, Roosevelt summoned Randolph to Washington and promised to issue an executive order if he would call off the march. Randolph accepted the offer, and the president immediately produced Executive Order 8802, which banned employment discrimination in defense industries and in the federal government. The order also made employers and labor organizations alike responsible for seeing that all workers were able to compete equally for new jobs and established the Fair Employment Practices Committee (FEPC) to monitor compliance.[37]

The FEPC and Weaver's office inevitably clashed over their areas of responsibility, but during the first few months the new agency continued to use Weaver's field representatives to conduct its investigations, since its own funds were meager. The new agency held public hearings to induce companies to comply with the president's order, a contrast with Weaver's more aggressive approach. Weaver's office conducted investigations, negotiated with companies and unions, and pushed officials in his agency and in the War Department to take further action where warranted.[38]

In October 1941, Louis Martin was regularly briefing Walter White of the NAACP about the mounting crisis of black unemployment and the rise in racial tensions: "The economic pinch has led a lot of whites to seek scapegoats. Negroes are more belligerent and the whites see jobless days ahead.... This general tension is evident in the acute school situation here. Student race riots are growing and this week a serious racial situation has developed in Ferndale, a Detroit suburb."[39] Martin told White that although auto production was being cut back, blacks were not being transferred to the defense jobs. At Chrysler, on more than one occasion black workers walked out to demonstrate their anger over not being allowed to transfer to Chrysler's Tank Arsenal plant.

Despite the UAW's public commitment to equal opportunity in defense jobs, the union faced formidable opposition from its white workers, many of whom had recently moved to Detroit from the South. Wildcat "hate" strikes broke out among white workers who were opposed to blacks being promoted to semiskilled jobs. Union officials hoped the federal government would take a lead that they could follow. Weaver later acknowledged that he worked closely with the UAW. Often after negotiating an agreement with a company to rehire or transfer black workers, Weaver sought the cooperation of union officials in getting the white work force to accept black employees.

## CRUSADING IN DETROIT

Martin and Gloster Current of the local NAACP were dissatisfied with the limited extent of union support for black workers. Martin told the union leaders it was their responsibility to protect blacks from discrimination in job transfers. After continued pressure from black union members and black leaders including Martin, the UAW International Executive Board adopted a resolution announcing to companies and union locals that the UAW was opposed to discriminatory treatment in job transfers, and it set up an Interracial Committee to monitor compliance with the FEPC.

With the *Chronicle*'s public prodding, the auto union's support, Weaver's skillful negotiating, and the threat of FEPC hearings, many Detroit companies were forced into compliance, and blacks found it easier to secure jobs in defense industries that were under federal contract. Employment opportunities for blacks expanded considerably. However, many industries stonewalled attempts by blacks to advance, and quite a few skilled positions, such as electrician and tool-and-die maker, were still out of reach. Meanwhile, throughout the war the armed forces remained segregated.[40]

ⓔ ⓔ ⓔ

The most explosive issue in Detroit during the war years was housing. As the nation geared up to produce war machinery, both blacks and whites flooded into Detroit, looking for jobs in the emergency industries. The available housing was vastly outsized by the expanding population, and large numbers of people had to make do sleeping in railroad cars and open fields. Ongoing tensions between newly arrived blacks and whites from the Deep South and whites from the mountains of Tennessee and Kentucky eventually triggered disturbances. The presence of entrenched ethnic European neighborhoods only intensified the volatility of the mixture.

By 1940, Martin's editorials had become increasingly strident as he discovered that New Deal federal housing policy actually enhanced existing discrimination. Discussing the outcome of a housing conference organized by State Senator Diggs, Martin wrote in the *Chronicle*:

> Just as in the years of slavery, we today live in communities which might easily be compared to slave quarters.... Our only expansion comes from occupying homes and districts that whites, for one reason or another, have abandoned.... We were told that even the federal government will not attempt to change the status quo. The federal government is willing to help, but its financial aid works within, not beyond the restrictions that already

chafe us.... In short, we may eventually have bigger and better ghettoes, but our right to be free to buy and live where we please is not recognized. This right is not recognized by private capitalists, nor is it recognized by the federal government.[41]

Martin went on to condemn the New Deal's federal housing policy of accommodating segregation—what some blacks had begun to call the "Dirty Deal":[42]

It is an affront to democracy. It is a damnable insult to twelve million Negroes and a disgrace to all America. We have heard and read much of social justice in the last few years. We have heard the often-repeated line that "The time has come when social changes are necessary if we are to preserve democracy." Yet all of these new concepts and all this new liberalism vanishes as if by magic when the American Negro stands up. America wishes to change everything else except the status of the Negro. Why should the federal government be a party to the perpetuation of housing restrictions? Will Federal aid really help us if it at the same time perpetuates a policy which has brought on the condition of which we complain.

Martin also made a pointed reference to the war in Europe against fascism:

It is idle in the face of these burning realities to speak of preserving our democracy. We cannot preserve what we do not have. We have a tyranny imposed by the majority, and as this tyranny is lessened, we approach democracy.[43]

In early 1942 racial tensions escalated into violence in Detroit at the Sojourner Truth Housing Project, which the federal government built as an all-black residential development. But Sojourner Truth bordered a Polish community, and many whites resented the project and wanted to keep blacks out of the area. After the Federal Public Housing Authority (FPHA) reversed itself, ruling that the project would be for whites rather than blacks, black Detroiters, including Martin, formed a coalition called the Sojourner Truth Citizens Committee. Initially all-black, the committee became interracial as Jewish groups, unionists, and white liberals joined. UAW Local 600 (River Rouge plant) was a major supporter of the group, providing money and organizing a postcard campaign that resulted in 5,000 postcard petitions to President Roosevelt from black workers.

# CRUSADING IN DETROIT

After a massive campaign by the committee, including nightly picketing at City Hall and the Detroit Housing Commission as well as the sending of a delegation to the FPHA in Washington, the federal housing authority reversed itself again and approved blacks' moving into the project, setting the occupation date for February 28. The evening before, 150 whites burned a cross and picketed at the site. Reportedly, the Ku Klux Klan, in league with the "White Improvement Association," helped to organize the protest. Black tenants who arrived the following morning were met by hundreds of angry whites. When the police arrived, they arrested blacks but not whites. News of the confrontation brought hundreds of blacks to fight against both the police and the white mob. More than 200 blacks, but only a few whites, were arrested.

Again the UAW was an important ally of the black community. The general council of Local 600 called for an FBI investigation of Klan involvement. R.J. Thomas demanded that blacks be allowed to occupy the project immediately, under police protection. The union was so united on this issue that even its white Catholic members sided with blacks against a number of Polish community and church leaders.

A final mass demonstration supporting black occupancy ended in a rally at Detroit's Cadillac Square. Martin worked with other members of the committee to organize, publicize, and lead the historic protest that attracted approximately 20,000 citizens, both black and white. At Cadillac Square, Martin was one of the speakers and read to the crowd the resolution adopted by the committee. With blacks and union members in accord, the federal government stood by its promise to blacks, and they moved into the project.[44]

Not all of Martin's crusades were so successful. The FPHA and the National Housing Agency issued a decision in February 1943 to bar blacks from the sprawling Willow Lodge housing project. Willow Lodge was built in a wilderness between Dearborn and Detroit in the shadow of the giant Willow Run Ford plant. Government officials suggested that a project would be built for black workers somewhere, some time. The NAACP reacted by forming an interracial delegation that included Martin and other prominent black leaders and representatives from the Willow Run and other UAW locals. The group met with FPHA officials to challenge the basis for the agency's decision. The agency denied that it deliberately segregated public housing and insisted that it merely adhered to local residential patterns, putting blacks only in black areas and whites only in white areas. The delegation pointed out that the as-yet-unoccupied project was on undeveloped land and that therefore no local pattern existed.[45] The officials in Washington refused to budge, and ruled against allowing blacks to reside in Willow Lodge. Martin wrote of his outrage in an editorial titled "Jim Crow Must Go":

> This travesty upon the freedom of the Negro people has its origins in the febrile brains of the conspirators against democracy in Congress and the Federal Housing administrators who have joined them in a crusade to abrogate the citizenship of the Negro people as the first step toward a fascist America.... Reaction has set in on Capitol Hill. Negroes, organized labor and all minority groups have come under heavy fire and the social gains of the last decade have been called into question.... There is no segregation or discrimination in the payment of taxes and there must be none in the spending of those taxes.... Between equal citizens the federal government must not discriminate, and when it does, as is being done here in public housing, it sows the seed of Fascism. We are at war against Fascism, and this is a total war.[46]

Martin repeatedly pointed out in his editorials that the government's policy of establishing segregated housing encouraged local racists and exacerbated local tensions. The year before he had warned that agitators in Detroit were fanning the embers of racial strife. Their actions, he argued, reflected a larger reactionary politics throughout the nation that had set in among those opposed to the progressive New Deal policies that benefited labor and minorities. Writing for the National Urban League's magazine, *Opportunity*, in June 1943, Martin boldly identified the culprits as the Republican party, which undermined New Deal policies for partisan reasons and because of its own alliance with big business; big business, whose moguls despised Roosevelt's interference with their prerogatives and claimed that the work programs and welfare benefits of the New Deal smacked of socialism; and white southern Democrats, who felt that welfare and work programs threatened their control over blacks. Through their lock on key chairmanships in Congress, southern congressmen could, and sometimes did, subvert Roosevelt's programs by withholding funds and influencing federal bureaucrats.[47]

᠊᠊᠊᠊ ᠊᠊᠊᠊ ᠊᠊᠊᠊

The housing crisis and job inequities led the organ of the Motor City's Association of Catholic Trade Unionists to warn city officials in 1942: "The ugly truth is that there is a growing, subterranean race war going on in the city of Detroit which can have no other ultimate result than an explosion of violence unless something is done to stop it." [48] In August of the same year, an article written by Martin and fellow journalist Earl Brown exposed the racial tensions in Detroit to a huge national audience through the pages of *Life* magazine. "Detroit Is Dynamite," which appeared anonymously, predicted that Detroit was bound for terrible racial violence.

The prediction came true in 1943. During the spring, three black workers at the Packard Motor Car Company plant in the city were upgraded to the position of metal polisher. At the time, virtually all the company's black workers were trapped in the lowest-pay categories, many of them as foundry workers. Outraged by the promotions, in June a group of white workers at Packard engineered a week-long strike. As a consequence, Martin recalled, "Tensions spilled over or combined with other waves of unrest arising from the housing and other issues to make the city a tinderbox." [49]

A few days after the Packard hate strike, the tinderbox exploded. Martin was home sound asleep when a close friend telephoned him to let him know that fighting had broken out at Belle Isle park, a nearby segregated beach, and it seemed to be spreading. As the *Chronicle*'s editor drove out of his racially mixed neighborhood early the next morning, he noticed his neighbors watering their lawns as usual. Only as he got closer to the downtown area did he see black residents gathered at the entrances to their buildings, looking as if they were waiting for a parade.

Violence was erupting in and near the black ghetto that ran alongside the business district, just blocks from the *Chronicle* office. From his office, Martin saw white mobs attacking cars along Woodward Avenue, overturning one of them. In front of his own office he saw the white driver of a milk truck try to pull away from a mob of black youths. A slender black girl in her teens was urging her comrades to pull the driver out of his truck, but he was able to escape. "I suddenly realized what it means to lose one's mind in blind hatred," Martin recalled. "An insane passion seemed to have seized the girl, contorted the features of her little face, and literally transformed a slender little teenager into a monster."

Twenty-four hours later, the toll was staggering. Federal troops had brought calm, but the worst riot in the city's history had left thirty-four people dead, at least seventeen of them blacks killed by the police. Even at the height of the rioting, there were no racial incidents anywhere outside the ghettos. Yet Martin had been in a position to witness the chaos firsthand, and he later remarked that "perhaps no single experience in my life made a greater impact on my outlook and philosophy than observing the rioters." The experience shook him deeply.[50]

Before the rioting ended, a gathering of local black ministers and UAW leaders was urging Mayor Edward Jeffries to take action—to stop armed white gangs and to bring in federal troops—but to no avail. Then and afterward, the city's white political leaders and industrialists took no action, leaving the UAW's R.J. Thomas as the only leading white person in the city to take black grievances seriously and to push for changes to prevent future outbreaks. Thomas and others asked for a grand jury to investigate charges of police brutality, but Mayor Jeffries, Wayne County prosecutor William Dowling, and Detroit police commissioner John Witherspoon rejected the idea. Instead, they issued their own report, in which Dowling named Martin as one of the black "agitators" responsible for instigating the violence through his editorials in the *Chronicle* and blamed the NAACP as well for raising black demands for change. A furious Walter White responded, "When did it become a crime to ask that all Americans be treated fairly in a democracy?"[51]

In the governor's report, to which Dowling again was a key contributor, the Detroit police were again vindicated and the chief blame laid on the black community. (It was admitted, however, that the black rioters interviewed had never read the *Michigan Chronicle.*) Walter White decided that the NAACP should undertake its own investigation, to be headed by the organization's chief counsel, a Howard University Law School graduate named Thurgood Marshall. Marshall's report contradicted Dowling's. It found that the Detroit police had responded to reports of looting by shooting blacks in stores, that "on several occasions, persons running were shot in the back" by police, that the police did not attempt to disperse armed white mobs on Woodward Avenue, and that indeed a number of officers were involved in attacking or encouraging attacks on blacks.[52]

Nevertheless, white Detroiters seemed too eager to believe that blacks were entirely to blame for the trouble, and quite a few still considered the mere presence of blacks in the city an affront to their way of life, a view reflected in the response that one white cabdriver made to a local newspaper reporter one day after the rioting. Asked what he thought about the story that white hoodlums had taken over the city by the time federal troops arrived, the cabbie replied: "Don't believe that, brother. I was in that mob last night, and I killed one of those niggers myself! I've got the iron bar right with me, too. A lot of good American citizens were in there fighting, mister."

The white driver went on to say that recent mayors were to blame for "catering" to black voters.[53]

In the wake of the riot, Mayor Jeffries rejected almost every proposal that Thomas and a group of black union and church leaders presented to ameliorate the city's racial problems. He did agree to appoint a biracial commission and included Martin as a member, but the commission was never granted the authority to challenge Jeffries's municipal government, in which many racists held high positions.[54]

Martin had responded swiftly and angrily to Dowling's charge that somehow he had helped foment the violence. He later said, "I was deeply hurt to think that I could be portrayed as anything but a constructive citizen and an editor always fighting to right the wrongs of society."[55] In a *Chronicle* editorial a few weeks after the riot, he pointed to the rash of anti-black attacks that had been launched well before the conflagration:

> We want to know who stirred up the hate strikes against Negroes in the Hudson Naval Arsenal, Dodge Truck, Timken-Detroit Axle, Vickers, Inc., U.S. Rubber, and where are the guys who led over 20,000 white workers at the Packard Motor Car Company to stop war production for a week because three Negroes were upgraded?[56]

Martin denounced Dowling and most of Detroit's public officials for failing to address the problems of black citizens. He charged that the riot resulted from their official anti-black and do-nothing policies. But the entire incident, particularly Dowling's scapegoating of him, had given Martin a new status, one he did not relish and had not sought: a status as an alleged "agitator," an activist, a newsmaker. "Somehow as an editor I had looked upon myself not as a maker of news but rather as a reporter and interpreter of the news," he later explained.

Martin got his revenge a few months later when Dowling ran for reelection to his post as county prosecutor. He not only actively editorialized against Dowling's reelection but also refused to carry campaign ads that Dowling sought to have printed in the *Chronicle*. Dowling publicly complained that the *Chronicle* was unfair and threatened to sue. "I did not consider myself as brave," Martin recalled, "but I got many phone calls from readers who asked me was I not afraid to fight the county prosecutor so vehemently. Somehow it never occurred to me that it took courage to buck the prosecutor.... The sweetest election result in my life came with Dowling's defeat."[57]

ﾀﾙ ﾀﾙ ﾀﾙ

Martin had missed the military draft in 1942 because of his age (he turned thirty that year) and because he had two children at home. In addition to publishing the *Chronicle*, by this time Martin was also occupied with political duties. He obtained his first political position when he was appointed to the 165-member Wayne County Board of Supervisors that year. The *Chronicle*'s associate editor, William Sherrill had run in the 1939 primary election, attempting to become the first black on the city council. Although he lost, Sherrill garnered a considerable portion of the vote. In exchange for Sherrill's support in the general election, one of the eighteen white candidates who won offered to appoint Sherrill to the county board of supervisors. Realizing that he would have to give up his county job to take the appointment, Sherrill suggested Martin for the position. Later Martin was appointed again to the board by a white councilman, George Edwards, a labor lawyer and close friend of the Reuther brothers. The experience on the board further whetted Martin's interest in politics, as he learned more about the workings of local government and got to know important public figures.[58]

Martin's hectic schedule did not stop him from taking on another challenge—trying to end flagrant racial discrimination in the armed services. Focusing on racial segregation at nearby Selfridge Field during the early 1940s, the *Chronicle* aroused the ire of Brigadier General Benjamin O. Davis, the Army's only black general. Davis finally asked Martin to come see him to discuss the matter. When he arrived, Martin was confronted by Davis, a stenotypist, and three other army personnel. The general, who had once announced to black troops, "I'm your color, but not your kind," insisted that the charge of segregation was untrue.

Throughout the war, the *Chronicle* and other black newspapers exposed the rampant racism in the armed forces, but the "double-V" goal of victory over both fascism abroad and racism at home was not achieved. Racial turmoil continued throughout the war years and not only in Detroit. A rash of postwar incidents against black military personnel, some horrifyingly brutal, led in 1946 to the formation of the National Emergency Committee Against Mob Violence. After reading the committee's report, President Harry Truman established a presidential commission to study the entire matter of civil rights and civil liberties and to make recommendations to him. A year later the commission's report, "To Secure These Rights," cited the significant gap between the American political creed and the nation's practice and made thirty-three recommendations. These included passage of an anti-lynching law, abolition of the poll tax, abolition of segregation in the military, establishment of a Civil Rights Division in the Justice Department, institution of home rule for the District of Columbia, establishment of D.C. residents' right to vote in presidential elections, and passage of a law for a permanent FEPC. President Truman ended segregation in the armed forces by executive order on July 26, 1948, but more than twenty years passed before most of the commission's other goals were achieved. The commission, which came to be known as the U.S. Commission on Civil Rights, continues to advise presidents.[59]

ì. ì. ì.

In its first five years, Martin had molded the *Michigan Chronicle* into a potent force for economic, social, and political justice for Detroit's black community. Through his editorials, articles, and civic activities, Martin was a rational, ardent, and courageous spokesperson for black candidates, black suffrage, the newly emerging industrial unions, and the New Deal and the Democratic party. At the same time, he challenged discrimination and injustice in whatever guise they appeared.

The crusading editor could be found everywhere on the firing line, working with the Detroit and national offices of the NAACP, the Detroit Urban League, and the fledgling UAW, and serving on the Sojourner Truth Citizens Committee and in other activist coalitions as well as on the Wayne County Board of Supervisors. He even managed to assist a young poet, Robert Hayden, who had worked briefly for the *Chronicle*, by publishing his first book of poetry, *Heart Shape in the Dust*. Hayden later taught at the University of Michigan and received the prestigious Hopwood Award for his poetry. During these years, Martin also founded Patrons of the Arts with Nellie Watts, a public school teacher. The group, which grew in popularity, brought outstanding artists such as Dorothy Maynor and Paul Robeson to Detroit.

While the *Chronicle* prospered, Martin himself labored at some personal sacrifice and risk. Subjected to the invective and name-calling that were directed at all those who challenged the entrenched white establishment of the day, he also faced the physical risks involved in going into riot areas to cover the news and in keeping the *Chronicle* open during the 1943 riots after curfews had been imposed. On more than one occasion he had to run for his life. His efforts to secure civil rights, like those of other black leaders in the North during the 1930s and 1940s, foreshadowed the civil rights revolution of the 1960s. In the process, Martin formed a network of relationships with some of the most eminent black leaders of that time and of the future—including Walter White, Lester Granger, Roy Wilkins, Thurgood Marshall, and Robert Weaver.

ఇ

# .3.

## DRAWING A LARGER CIRCLE

*FDR could handle any difficulty with some humor, by drawing a bigger circle and putting that problem inside the circle.*

*—Louis Martin*

Martin was completing his eighth year as copublisher and editor of the *Michigan Chronicle* in 1944 when he received the telephone call that propelled him into national politics. The call came from Congressman William L. Dawson of Illinois, the sole black member of Congress and vice chairman of the Democratic National Committee (DNC). Dawson had been assigned to mobilize the black vote for Roosevelt's reelection campaign. Martin had never met the distinguished black Democrat, who was now on the telephone asking him, "Would you be interested in helping us reelect the President?" [1]

At a time when political party bosses wielded considerable power, Bill Dawson was the lone black political boss on the national scene. His first serious competitor in that regard, New Yorker Adam Clayton Powell, Jr., had recently emerged in Harlem and was campaigning for his own seat in Congress. A close associate of Chicago's mayor, Ed Kelly, Dawson was an essential black cog in the city's well-oiled Democratic machine. Younger blacks had already begun to snipe at him as an Uncle Tom, an appellation that infuriated Dawson and his supporters. A retiring, diffident, even conservative figure, he nevertheless was solidly established. "Dawson had 200,000 votes that he could count on," Martin recalled. "You can be brilliant and make a hell of a speech, and get a big picture and a write-up in the paper, but when it comes down to it, if you ain't got no votes you ain't got no power. That is what Adam Clayton Powell learned, too." [2]

Dawson had good reasons for choosing to call Martin. By this time, Martin was well known not only as a journalist but also as an important figure in Michigan political and labor circles. The *Michigan Chronicle* had published reams of Democratic party news, and Martin, who avidly supported

Roosevelt's New Deal, had become friends with many important Democrats. Through his close friend Earl Brown, a senior editor at *Life* magazine and the first black to hold such a position, Martin had met most of the Democratic party's key staff at its national conventions. The notoriety attached to Martin and the *Chronicle* in the aftermath of the 1943 riot by the slanderous Dowling report also played a role in Dawson's phone call. For with that episode, many had come to think of Martin as an activist, and among black readers his name was now known around the country. White readers also had seen his name, generally in favorable contexts, in many of the big stories on the Detroit disturbances. Finally, over the last few years he had come to know several of the leading members of Washington's unofficial "Black Cabinet." This unheralded but influential group of distinguished black experts had been appointed to high positions in the administration and had organized themselves into a working group to advocate for equal opportunity and other black interests. Martin later discovered that his name had been given to Dawson by several members of this Washington circle, who let the congressman know what Martin had been accomplishing in Detroit.[3]

Dawson's phone call took Martin by surprise, and he was both delighted and anxious about the invitation. True, he had been pushing the New Deal all these years in his own paper, but he also had some misgivings. Aware of Dawson's reputation as a machine ward boss, Martin worried about risking an alliance with a corrupt political crowd whose goals were at odds with those of civil rights organizations. On the phone, he told Dawson that his own political work had been limited to Michigan. Dawson responded in kind: he had never worked on a national campaign either. "We'll learn together," he told the journalist.[4]

Overcoming his initial hesitation, Martin agreed to join the effort and travel to Chicago to talk over the assignment with Dawson. When he arrived at the congressman's Ward 2 headquarters, he found constituents filling the benches in the outer office. Dawson saw everyone on a first-come, first-served basis. Naturally, every visitor wanted help of one kind or another, and as Martin watched each petitioner enter and then leave with a new list of names to contact, it seemed that Dawson was running a referral office. "I saw quickly that he took pains to identify himself with the masses rather than the bourgeois blacks," Martin later recalled. "I could see immediately that Dawson lived in quite a different world than most of the rich black professionals."[5]

## DRAWING A LARGER CIRCLE

Dawson welcomed him warmly. He certainly did not come across as a political boss jealous of his prerogatives but rather as a thoughtful, unpretentious man who would be easy to work with. Martin's feelings about the older congressman might have been shaped by his resemblance to Martin's father. He even seemed to have the same sense of humor as the elder Martin. Martin described himself to Dawson as first and foremost a journalist, with little political experience apart from his two terms on the Wayne County Board of Supervisors. But he added that he believed strongly that climbing the political ladder was the most promising way for blacks to gain full citizenship rights.[6]

The congressman told him frankly that he didn't like newspapermen, but he found Martin different from the rest. The discussion wandered and never came close to dealing with the specifics of FDR's campaign or Martin's role in it. Of their conversation, Martin would later admit, "All I could remember were the stories, some hilarious, of his rise to power, of the infighting of ward politics, and of his relations with Robert Hannegan, who had been named chairman of the Democratic National Committee and put in full charge of the campaign." Dawson's stories fascinated the journalist, who returned home from Chicago even more inspired than when he had arrived. "He knew how to take an eager young man to the mountaintop," Martin later commented.[7]

ea ea ea

His enthusiasm over entering FDR's campaign could be traced not only to his faith in New Deal policies but also to his personal conviction that the Roosevelts were heroes worth fighting for. During FDR's first term, Martin had made special efforts to hear the president when he came to the Michigan campus to speak. "His assault upon the 'robber barons,' and his consistent demand for a new deal for the fifth of the nation that was ill-clothed, ill-housed, and ill-fed lifted my spirits more than anything I learned in college," Martin later said. Just after starting up the *Chronicle*, Martin had his first meeting with a public figure of national importance—Eleanor Roosevelt. Far more outspoken than her husband on the matter of civil rights, Mrs. Roosevelt had made numerous visits to black neighborhoods since entering the White House, and it was on one such visit to Detroit that Martin first met her. At the Lucy Thurman YMCA, the "colored branch," Martin was introduced to her as the editor of the only newspaper in Detroit that supported her husband's candidacy. "She was warm and gracious and assured me, and all others within hearing distance, that her husband meant what he said about a New Deal for all Americans.... The brief meeting with Mrs. Roosevelt touched me deeply; she seemed genuine and sincere, interested and concerned."[8]

He was impressed, as were many blacks of every station, by the first lady's willingness to come to the poorest ghettos to speak with people there. In Martin's experience, most whites in positions of power learned whatever they knew about blacks secondhand, often from academic studies, special reports, and the like. "Obviously Mrs. Roosevelt wanted to see for herself and observe firsthand the people and the conditions which caused unhappiness and unrest," he noted. Reflecting on the situation, Martin acknowledged that their elite background and position of power gave people like the Roosevelts freedom to defy convention, including the conventions of racism, though of course most of the wealthy did not employ that freedom. "A prejudice of many southern blacks which, perhaps unconsciously, I shared, involved a deep distrust of poor whites," he later wrote. "Associating with blacks, eating with them and socializing with them, might have some adverse political repercussions in the 'white trash' bloc, but she and FDR were secure enough in power, wealth, and prestige to ignore the political-racial risks. Blacks understood and appreciated noblesse oblige as the attribute of true aristocrats."[9]

As the New Deal took shape, Martin's position in Detroit and his advocacy of FDR brought him into frequent contact with several members of the Black Cabinet. Publicly, the most prominent member of this group was Mary McLeod Bethune, a sharecropper's daughter who had gone on to found Bethune-Cookman College and the National Council of Negro Women. Bethune had become friends with Eleanor Roosevelt well before FDR entered the White House, and it was largely through this friendship that she wielded her influence on the administration. Indeed, FDR's concern for issues of black rights as such was minimal, and throughout his four terms he rarely took any action on behalf of blacks that would place his New Deal or war initiatives at risk by alienating prosegregation Democrats. The first lady, however, pressed her husband frequently on race matters, and in many instances her pressure led to action.

The other dozen or so top members of the Black Cabinet, including Robert Weaver, were generally unable to get an audience with the president, and working within their departments they had to pass their ideas upward through an often hostile ladder of white superiors, so they devised other, more effective means. Frank Horne, who started as an aide to Bethune and then moved on to the U.S. Housing Authority, recalled how Bethune had advised him to tell her "what needs to be done" and that she would see that Mrs. Roosevelt knew about it.[10]

In addition to Robert Weaver, other members of this group with whom Martin came into contact included William H. Hastie, a Harvard Law School graduate and former dean of Howard University Law School who held several federal positions during the New Deal, initially as assistant solicitor in the Interior Department; Booker T. McGraw, an assistant to Robert Weaver in the federal housing authority; William J. Trent, Jr., a Wharton School business graduate and advisor in the Public Works Administration; and Ralph J. Bunche, a scholar who consulted for the Library of Congress and would later have a sterling career in international relations that would earn him a Nobel Prize. Martin's most extensive contacts were with Weaver during the battles over discrimination in job transfers to war industries. Weaver held posts of increasing influence as racial advisor to the Works Progress Administration (WPA), the Housing Authority, and finally the War Manpower Commission. He gradually became the Black Cabinet's unofficial policy chief, while Bethune, whose moral stature and grassroots appeal were unsurpassed, remained the group's spokesperson.[11]

Several other members of this group came to know Martin quite well, passing through Detroit en route westward from New York or Washington and often stopping in at the *Chronicle*, whose reports and editorials they found useful for their purposes. They also relied on Martin as their eyes and ears in Detroit and Michigan generally. "I was thrilled by the news they brought of inside operations by the government on the black front, and was anxious to cooperate with their programs," Martin recalled. Staying in close touch with black opinion makers like Martin and organization leaders like Walter White of the NAACP was essential to the Black Cabinet members in their efforts to achieve reform. They often made use of church and labor organizations as well as the black press to route their own advocacy positions back to the White House, creating the appearance of spontaneous, widespread black concern that carried far more weight than their own single voices. This took careful planning. When they discovered discrimination in the WPA, for example, they reported it to the NAACP rather than to the president, and the NAACP in turn raised hell with the White House. Soon afterward the black advisor to the WPA, who had started the chain of messages, was firmly instructed by the head of the WPA to propose changes to put an end to discrimination.[12]

Martin also talked often with Horne and McGraw about Detroit's housing problems and the need for action by the administration, particularly during the crisis over the Sojourner Truth Housing Project. From these two Black Cabinet members Martin learned as well how bureaucrats could be employed to political advantage. When the time came to choose a site for a large housing project designated for black residents, the black New Dealers carefully chose a location in a congressional district then represented by a Republican— "the theory being that the blacks in the project would vote Democratic and help bring an end to GOP domination of the district," Martin recalled. He saw the results: the plan worked. The Black Cabinet also saw that they could use their leverage occasionally to increase black political power, which also meant more votes for Democrats. Martin recalled how they sometimes made voter registration a prerequisite to employment on any of the New Deal projects. "Registering to vote was evidence of good citizenship," Martin later explained, "and who could argue against requiring public employees to meet the elementary test of good citizenship?" [13]

By 1944, the group included another member with whom Martin worked closely: Ted Poston, a reporter for the New York *Post*, who joined the administration during the war years as an advisor in the Department of War Information. Poston thought that some of the highbrow, Ivy League Black Cabineteers took themselves a little too seriously. "A few were echoing left-wing views, and some considered themselves radicals," Martin recalled. "Ted Poston used to make fun of the latter… because these black radicals loved the bourgeois lifestyle and had only an intellectual interest in the so-called working class." [14]

꒐ꜚ ꒐ꜚ ꒐ꜚ

When Martin received the phone call from Bill Dawson in 1944 inviting him to join the campaign, he had all of this experience with the New Dealers to go on, as well as his work in local and state politics. But the most recent episode that had sparked his interest in working for Roosevelt's reelection was a meeting he had attended at the White House just a few months earlier. Angered by the continuing discrimination against blacks in the armed forces, Martin and twenty-four other representatives of the Negro Newspaper Publishers Association (NNPA) filed into the White House to petition Roosevelt. Their plan was to read aloud a memorandum on the matter and leave it with the president. William Hastie had already resigned in protest from his prestigious position as civilian aide to Secretary of War Henry Stimson after

.42.

it became clear that his objections to segregated training, such as that designated for the black airmen at Tuskegee Institute, would be ignored.[15]

For many of the president's visitors, anger and solemn purpose mingled with awe. They were about to speak to the man who had led their nation through the Great Depression and was leading the allied nations to victory over fascism in Europe. Moreover, black journalists had rarely been in the same room with Roosevelt. Before 1944, no black reporter had been accredited to attend either the president's or Mrs. Roosevelt's press briefings, on the grounds that only daily newspapers merited a White House press pass. The black *Atlanta Daily World* finally was awarded a pass for its reporter Harry McAlpin, with the understanding that he would be representing not only the *Daily World* but also the NNPA.[16] "This meeting was the first time any of us had an opportunity to see FDR in action, exhibiting the wit and charm for which he had become so famous," Martin recalled. He recorded his impressions of the meeting in detail:

> Sitting like a grinning white Buddha, Roosevelt wore that broad uplifting smile as we filed before him and shook his hand. His touch and presence seemed electric enough to light up the darkest room anywhere, at any time.... He took us by storm, talking and laughing as we were warned he would.... Roosevelt seemed to have anticipated everything we had on our minds as he held forth in high spirits, answering questions before they could be asked. [He] wanted us to know that he was fully aware of the grievances which concerned us and he wanted us to know they also concerned him.... He told us that the most powerful and effective weapon for the social changes we sought was "the white light of publicity." Playing on this key had great appeal for us because as black newsmen we had always operated on that principle.

The president spoke to the NNPA delegates as if they were old friends. No one interrupted as he talked about his recent trip to Casablanca to meet with British Prime Minister Winston Churchill. On the way there, he said, his plane had stopped in Gambia, a small West African country about which he had known nothing before being briefed by his aides. Roosevelt said that when he met Churchill, he told him that the British had taken $110 out of Gambia for every single dollar they had invested in the colony. Jokingly, Roosevelt warned Churchill that when the war was over, he was going to call an international commission to investigate Britain's exploitation of its colonies. "What do you think Winston said to that?" the president asked his

NNPA guests after a short pause. "He said he was going to request this same commission to investigate racial conditions in Mississippi." Martin recorded the meeting's conclusion:

> We never really had a chance to get our views across for he literally drowned out the points we sought to spell out in detail.... We left the White House walking on air with no one quite sure what grievance the president had promised to act upon. Yet there was no doubt in any of our minds, certainly none in mine, that FDR was on our side, understood our complaints, and in due time would try to do something about them.[17]

❧ ❧ ❧

Before Martin could accept Bill Dawson's invitation and move to New York for the 1944 campaign, he had to clear his absence with his boss, John Sengstacke. The copublisher and editor of the *Chronicle* pointed out that his position in the campaign would inevitably give him an inside track on the allocation of campaign advertising funds for black newspapers, including theirs. Most black publications were eager for campaign advertising, because their sources of paid copy were severely limited. As Martin later explained, "Advertising revenues were necessary for growth, and almost any kind of paid copy, including ads for spiritualists, faith healers, and good luck items, represented business." Martin reminded his boss that his wife, Gertrude, was a Phi Beta Kappa from Ohio State and perfectly capable of taking over the *Chronicle* while he was in New York with the campaign. Sengstacke raised no objections. Taking a three-month leave from the *Chronicle,* Martin signed on as an assistant publicity director of the Democratic National Committee.[18]

When he arrived in New York, he found himself in a town where he had few political contacts. The connections he did have with black leaders there, however, were valuable. The NAACP was based in New York, so Martin knew he could talk to Roy Wilkins and Thurgood Marshall, and perhaps most valuable politically was his friendship of several years' standing with Adam Clayton Powell, Jr. Powell formed a perfect contrast to Bill Dawson. If Dawson was a machine politician, Powell was a brazen iconoclast, at war with New York's Democratic leadership in Tammany Hall. If Dawson took pride in his low-profile, behind-the-scenes tactics in Congress, Powell took pride in trumpeting his views from the church steps and in the press. After Martin arrived in the city, the first thing Powell asked him was what he thought he was doing working for "that Uncle Tom, Bill Dawson."[19]

Dawson knew what Powell thought of him and his brand of politics, and for his part he considered Powell a loud-mouthed radical. An elegant as well as eloquent preacher who was idolized by the 3,000 members of Harlem's Abyssinian Baptist Church, Powell had proved to be a very successful politician on the local level, and his views were heard around the country. He condemned the country's lily-whitism with open scorn. Although Dawson was accustomed to working with preachers, he felt as Michigan State Senator Charles Diggs did about their becoming professional politicians: uneasy. In Chicago, Dawson had run into quite a few black ministers who, he told Martin, looked upon politics as a sinful occupation and "warned their flocks to have no traffic with the political devils." [20]

Looking back at these two men two decades later, Martin noted: "In 1944, I did not realize that these two formidable figures in the Democratic party would for almost a quarter of a century symbolize the dichotomy in black political life about how best to advance the cause of the race.... Adam was militant and confrontational, ever ready to march and demonstrate, and Dawson favored skillful use of the rules of the political game, working within the power structure, collecting along the way IOUs for future use." [21]

The famed Theresa Hotel in Harlem had reserved its finest suite of rooms for Congressman Dawson, who expected Martin to stay there as well. But Martin quickly found that his room at the Theresa was tiny, and the toilet would not flush. He announced to Dawson that he would not be staying there and booked a room at the Commodore, which was close to the DNC headquarters at the Biltmore and housed many of the white staffers. During bad weather, Martin could walk from the Commodore at the east end of Grand Central Station through the station to the west end and into the Biltmore without braving the elements. At the time, even in New York, major hotels like the Commodore did not welcome black guests. Despite claims that they did not discriminate, these hotels often restricted black guests to rooms on the lower floors so that white guests would not have to share elevators with them. This is precisely what the Commodore did with Martin, who complained until he received a better-situated room. He stayed for the next two months, although the hotel charged him the daily rate for his entire stay. [22]

Martin worked under the direction of DNC publicity director Paul Porter, a young Kentucky lawyer. He calculated that considerable money and other resources would be required to win over the black press, which had grown to more than 200 papers and was more powerful than ever. His carefully designed advertising and publicity program carried a price tag of

$750,000.[23] DNC officials, however, informed Martin that very little money would be spent with black newspapers. Having promised several black publishers that he would fight for a big budget, he was severely disappointed. Most black newspapers had found it difficult, if not impossible, to secure contracts from national advertisers other than liquor and cigarette companies. Large department stores in most cities refused to advertise in the black press because their owners felt they already had enough black customers. If they attracted more, they explained, the influx might drive whites away.

Martin was resourceful. Until he was able to get substantial budget commitments from the DNC for advertising, he had to bypass publishers who refused to carry the campaign's official news releases. He began to write stories and features under assumed names and send them out on nonpolitical stationery. "Many political points I sought to make got through and appeared in the periodicals that sought to stick us up," he recalled. "I discovered that many publishers don't read their own newspapers. Indeed some of them were in other businesses, and their periodicals were used for promoting these other interests." The major black newspapers, nevertheless, maintained professional standards. Through his extensive contacts, Martin was able to get many of the top black editors to extend their valuable cooperation free of charge. They gave him editorial support, broad photo coverage, and prominent placement of his political news stories. During the last four weeks of the presidential campaign, he bought four full-page advertisements in every black paper of consequence in the United States.

Another key function of Dawson's campaign office was to find speakers for black political rallies. Invitations were screened to determine their importance and to decide which speaker was best qualified for each affair. One of the most effective orators was Marshall Shepard of Philadelphia, a black clergyman who had won a seat in the Pennsylvania legislature in 1934. A favorite of Eleanor Roosevelt's—she had visited his church—Shepard had also served a stint as recorder of deeds of the District of Columbia, at that time the top black patronage post in the nation.[24]

After the first few weeks, Dawson brought into their office an experienced black leader whom Martin had known since 1936, John P. Davis. Martin had met Davis at the National Negro Congress, which Davis had helped organize. "Davis helped bridge the gap between the new group of labor-conscious blacks, whom Dawson regarded as stooges of white left-wingers, and the party regulars whom he looked upon as true Democrats," Martin remembered. Although Dawson cared little for organized labor, he recognized Davis's talent for what it was and valued his work. Davis's key responsibilities involved financing rallies and fund raising. "Davis had developed all the mannerisms that we associate with the Napoleonic complex, including a finger-pointing, dictatorial manner of speech," Martin recalled, and yet, "he was a delightful raconteur and his great sense of humor helped take the edge off his sometimes abrupt and abrasive disposition."

During the campaign's last month, Dawson returned to Chicago to campaign in his South Side district, so Davis and Dawson's personal assistant handled most of the visitors. "The suite was always full of black party workers and salesmen of every description, including the music men who were always trying to sell us a new campaign song," Martin recalled. Before Dawson left, he and Davis often entertained those in the office with stories about their political experiences. Their tales of black political operators who were always on the fringes of the two major parties, Martin remembered, included many legendary hustlers "whose schemes for getting money strained the imagination."[25]

When Martin joined the Roosevelt campaign, he was concerned about the black community's response to FDR's new running mate, Harry S. Truman. Roosevelt's vice president, the liberal Henry Wallace, had not been renominated, an outcome that brought protests from many blacks and others for whom Truman was an unknown quantity. Blacks found cause for complaint as well in the civil rights plank that FDR agreed to at the Democratic convention. The NAACP's Walter White, despite his close ties to the Roosevelts, openly ridiculed the weak, vague statement on civil rights as not a plank but a "splinter." But while White was unhappy with the civil rights plank, he continued to support FDR for reelection.[26]

Martin's fear of an attack by blacks on Truman proved justified. Black Republican strategists made use of an interview in which Truman, who had once been a haberdasher, suggested that a businessman should be able to refuse to serve a customer whom he didn't like. The influential *Pittsburgh Courier* ran a story on its front page blasting the candidate as a defender of discrimination. Martin brought the *Courier* story to the attention of Paul Porter, who agreed that it was important to get a swift response from Truman to the charges. But the DNC's operators were unable to locate the candidate, who was constantly on the road. Not one to waste time, Martin went to work on a simulated interview in which he had Truman talk about his fight against the Klan and vigorously deny any support for segregation.

Before it could be released, of course, that interview had to be cleared by the vice presidential candidate, who was now somewhere in Wyoming. The DNC's expert switchboard operators conducted another telephone chase. "Every time we called, we missed him," Martin remembered. "We called, and he had just left. We would call the next city, and he hadn't arrived. All day long this went on. Toward the end of it, I had to do something with the story." Martin's superiors gave him the green light to release the "interview" anyway, at least to the black weeklies, on the theory that Truman would certainly approve it once he was found. The story was carried in most of the black papers and Martin judged it a genuine, if minor, victory.

About two weeks later, Martin got a call from Porter, who said that Truman was there and asked if Martin would like to meet him. Martin readily accepted the invitation. "Both men were standing when I entered the office," Martin recalled, "and Truman seemed small standing beside Paul Porter. They were laughing, and I guessed that Porter was entertaining him with one of his many stories.... There was something puckish about [Truman's] face." Martin asked the candidate about the interview they had sent out. While Truman paused, as if trying to remember, Porter remarked that Martin had done a good job on it. "It was obvious that Truman didn't know what we were talking about," Martin recalled. Martin was shocked. Apparently no one had read the interview release over the phone to Truman when they had found him. "Truman then asked to see the release, and my discomfort was accentuated when he began reading it. He made little throat noises and stopped smiling." Most of the words were Truman's own, taken from different contexts. The candidate finally said he could live with it, though he showed little enthusiasm. As Martin returned to his office, the thought hit him: suppose a reporter had asked him some questions based on the fake interview? Truman had a great reputation for "telling it like it is."

But Martin also knew that questions were not likely under the circumstances: the interview had come out only in the black papers, and most reporters covering the campaign were white and would have no idea what the black press was publishing. "I took some comfort," Martin said, "in the rationalization that Truman was a political pro, and that had he been cornered by reporters he would say nothing that he thought would alienate black voters." Fortunately for Martin, as well as for Truman, the questions never came.[27]

# DRAWING A LARGER CIRCLE

Less than a month remained before the election, yet Roosevelt had still not traveled outside Washington to campaign personally. With rumors circulating about his ill health, the president decided it was time to hit the hustings despite the crushing responsibilities of the war effort. In New York, DNC chairman Bob Hannegan called an urgent meeting, explaining that the president would be touring the city shortly and needed a big turnout. "I was shocked when Chairman Hannegan singled me out and said he wanted me to make certain that blacks were twelve deep on the sidewalks of Harlem when FDR's cavalcade came down from the Bronx," Martin recalled.

Although he knew Congressman Powell, he did not know most of Harlem's local leaders. Moreover, his friend Earl Brown of *Life* magazine had warned him that the Harlem Democratic machine was not to be relied on in an emergency unless there was good money at hand to keep it oiled. Hannegan had made it clear that there was no money for Martin's assignment and added that in any case the effort should go beyond the party apparatus. This, after all, was everyone's president, the man leading the country to victory in Europe and the Pacific, and they were no longer to think of this as a campaign event but as a tribute.[28]

Martin turned for help to Walter White. White laughed at his nervousness, telling him, "I'll show you how to work this out." At the appointed time the next morning, White pulled up in a taxi and took Martin to City Hall. Martin had never met New York's liberal Republican mayor Fiorello La Guardia, the "Little Flower," who had an almost mythic reputation as the defender of the downtrodden. When they entered his office, La Guardia jumped out of his high seat and rushed forward to pump Walter's hand. "I remember thinking that Walter was indeed a good friend of the mayor," Martin recalled. The mayor and the NAACP chief were both nonstop talkers, and their effusive greetings went on for several minutes before White got around to introducing Martin.

"I brought a friend of mine," White told the mayor, "a young man from the Midwest who's up there with the Committee working for Roosevelt. Louis, you tell the mayor what you want." Martin explained his problem, and before he finished talking La Guardia began pushing buttons on his desk. Several aides appeared instantly through doors Martin had not noticed. The mayor then picked up two phones and began giving orders, letting his guests see how efficiently he could get things done for his friends. He instructed his people to mobilize every payroller on the city's books, including their families. "He wanted them all out in the streets to let President Roosevelt know how much New York loved him," Martin recalled. "I knew immediately that our mission had been successful." The turnout at the parade, despite bad weather, was heavy and brought the campaign to a fine climax.[29]

Through the entire campaign, Martin had not seen or talked with Roosevelt himself. This was corrected after the election when all the campaign workers were invited to the White House for a reception. Martin remembered the scene:

> Roosevelt was in a wheelchair with a colorful blanket covering his knees, grinning, shaking his massive head and shaking hands as we filed past into the big room. After many of us had gotten our drinks and joined the little knots of close associates and friends scattered around the room, I noticed that FDR was in a corner talking and laughing with an aged, brown-skinned man whom I had never seen before.... Eventually he was identified as an old friend of FDR and the father of the famous Howard University civil rights lawyer Charles Houston. The last picture I retain of those years is of two old men laughing and chatting away in the White House, two old men who lived in separate worlds but who seemed to enjoy an unusual fellowship.[30]

᪾ ᪾ ᪾

Martin's first experience at the DNC expanded his already extensive national network of contacts to include senior operatives in the Democratic party. Having plunged into politics in Michigan, his brief sampling of national politics quickened his interest. However, with the *Michigan Chronicle* still prospering after the 1944 election, Martin was anxious to get back to Detroit and the newspaper business. Looking back on the ten years from 1936 to 1946, he summed up, "My challenge was how the hell to make a paper successful, promote the welfare and best interests of the community, and make money."

In 1945, Martin and his wife launched a news magazine, *Headlines and Pictures*, with the financial backing of the *Chicago Defender*, which provided the paper stock and printing. The following year they moved to New York, where much of the news about nationally prominent blacks originated. At that time, the city was the hub of black life, as well as the nation's power capital. Martin continued to direct the *Chronicle* from New York, with frequent trips to Detroit. Louis and Gertrude Martin liked the city's social climate, which they considered more racially liberal than the climate in Detroit or anywhere else. The Martin family enterprise in journalism flourished. Gertrude Martin became the managing editor of *Headlines*, and Lillian Scott, her sister, who had worked on the *Chronicle* in Detroit after graduating from Ohio State University, became a roving reporter for the new magazine.[31]

But during the war and for several years afterward, newsprint was very scarce. Eventually, paper stock was rationed according to the quantity each publication had used before the shortage. Despite John Sengstacke's generosity with newsprint, the situation became impossible for the new magazine, and the Martins were forced to suspend *Headlines and Pictures* after only two years, at a peak circulation of 20,000. Scott became head of the New York bureau of the *Chicago Defender*, and Sengstacke persuaded Martin to return to Chicago as editor-in-chief of the *Defender*. Thus, in 1947, began another period of frequent separation for Martin and his family, as he began commuting between Chicago and New York. Three years later, his family joined him in Chicago, where the Martins' three youngest daughters—Toni, Linda, and Lisa—were all born. In Detroit, meanwhile, the *Chronicle*'s business manager, Longworth Quinn, had succeeded Martin as publisher. Back in 1943, Martin had had to argue with both Sengstacke and Quinn to bring Quinn over to the *Chronicle* from the *Defender*. "Getting Quinn to work on the *Chronicle* proved to be the wisest move we could have made," he later said. "He turned out to be one of the ablest administrators of a black enterprise in the nation." [32]

⁂

Martin first saw with his own eyes the devastation the war had brought, particularly in Germany and France, in the summer of 1948, when the U.S. War Department invited him and half a dozen other leading members of the black press to tour the occupied territories. By coincidence, the group entered Berlin the very day the Soviets began blockading the city, adding an element of uncertainty and requiring that they be accompanied by a military escort. Visiting Alpine hamlets as well as the cities, Martin and the others were able to speak freely with German citizens, including academics and public officials. He was struck by how reasonable, civil, and well educated the Germans he met were. Covering the Nazi war crimes trials in Nuremberg in the course of his tour, Martin found it impossible mentally to bridge the gulf between the humanity he saw and the immense evil that had taken place.

Years later, he attempted to make sense out of what he had seen and heard in Germany: "The more I listened, the more incredible it seemed to me that it had been possible for a leader like Hitler, given his intellect and philosophy, to mesmerize the German people. Listening to some of the testimony at the Nuremberg trials only deepened this mystery. Recognizing the scientific, cultural, and educational level of the majority of the German people, the rise and rule of a character like Adolf Hitler seemed unreal, beyond imagination." How such a civilized society could "lose its collective mind, trample on its religious and social values, and succumb to the barbaric philosophy of a mountebank," as Martin put it, could not be explained simply as an inevitable end product of Germany's history. Fascism and the Holocaust did not seem to him inevitable. On the contrary, he had seen how segments of the American public, such as the Klan, had tried to pull his own countrymen toward the same extremism but had been thwarted by courageous individuals. "I was convinced that the role of leadership is supremely important," he reflected, "and that good and evil hang loosely on the whims and views of individuals who wield great power. In most societies, too often men seem to move like sheep." [33]

≈ ≈ ≈

The 1950s opened with the Korean war and President Truman's decision not to seek reelection. Martin believed Truman's failure to run again opened the White House door to Republicans, who had not held the presidency since 1933. After Dwight D. Eisenhower took office, Martin feared that the government was entering a do-nothing decade on civil rights.

When Rosa Parks challenged segregation and triggered the Montgomery bus boycott in late 1955, Martin and his family were following the developments from their home in Hyde Park, near the University of Chicago. Martin Luther King, Jr., was advocating Mohandas Gandhi's philosophy, accepting unjust imprisonment as the price for creating justice. King's strategy of nonviolent resistance was new to the nation, Martin believed, and was not at all universally accepted among blacks. "This philosophy was revolutionary to many of us who took pride in avoiding the consequences of militant protest and the violation of unjust laws," he recalled.

Gertrude and Louis Martin attended an address King gave at the University of Chicago's Rockefeller Memorial Chapel, not long after the Montgomery bus boycott. It was King's first major speech in Chicago. Before a packed audience, Martin remembered, King "demonstrated his oratorical skill, combining the colorful rhetoric of the Baptist preacher with the logic of a lawyer, to set forth his view of what our times required to effect social change. When Dr. King concluded, we realized that we were witnessing the rise of a new movement that would shake the society, black and white." [34]

# DRAWING A LARGER CIRCLE

During the closing years of that decade, the Martins participated in an informal, integrated discussion group that met in the homes of friends in their tree-lined neighborhood. At one gathering, the young political scientist James Q. Wilson argued that the new civil rights movement could not achieve what blacks sought because social changes in America could not be accomplished unless all of society was moved to action. The black minority and liberal whites like himself, he argued, constituted too small and limited a unit. Martin was not inclined to agree. "Professor Wilson, I remember thinking, did not reckon with Dr. Martin Luther King," Martin recalled, "and he underestimated the capacity of a black personality to arouse the total society." [35]

≈ ≈ ≈

Martin had become increasingly vocal about the common thread running through the political, economic, and cultural struggles of both African Americans and blacks in Africa. White hegemony was a common obstacle for both. With great interest he watched from afar as nationalist leaders redrew the map of Africa. Ghana gained independence from Britain in 1957. French Africa and British Africa were in ferment, and to the surprise of some African leaders, Belgium announced that it would grant independence to the Belgian Congo. Thus, within fifteen years of the close of World War II, colonial rule ended in most of west and east Africa.

At least, that was the perception. The reality was that neocolonialism still subjugated Africans. They had yet to regain control of their resources, and their economies remained at the mercy of Europe's giant cartels. Thus, the price of cocoa was set by a British-Dutch combine, and West Africa's farmers were powerless to do anything about it. This was also true for palm oil, basic to the manufacture of soap, and for many other products. Furthermore, white shipping tycoons set the rates for moving produce from West Africa to the rest of the world. Clearly, political changes alone would not overcome the continent's economic servitude. [36]

Nevertheless, the drama of what was taking place in Africa at this moment could not be overstated. No less than ten nations would become independent in the summer and fall of 1960. In October of 1960, Nigeria would gain its independence from Great Britain, and local parties and tribal factions were gearing up for the nation's first elections. Nigerian media were preparing as well. *Time* magazine asked Earl Brown to find an American journalist willing to spend a year as editorial advisor to Amalgamated Press of Nigeria, Ltd., a chain of newspapers. Brown sought Martin's help. Chief Obafemi Awolowo, head of the Action Group Party that controlled the western regional government based in Yorubaland, had hired a London public relations firm, Patrick Dolan and Associates (PDA), to develop his region's media. He expected the firm to oversee the establishment of a television station (the first in Africa) and to advise the West African Press, which published a number of newspapers, most in English, under the direction of Chief S. O. Shonibare, general manager. The business's major paper was the *Daily Service.*

For weeks, Martin canvassed friends and members of the National Newspaper Publishers Association (formerly named the Negro Newspaper Publishers Association). He found that while many black leaders were prone to romanticize African customs and most had never been on the continent, only a few were even interested, and none would commit himself to a year there. Anxious to see what African life was like and perhaps glean some insight into the future of the continent and, indirectly, of black America, Martin accepted the position himself.

The firm agreed to match his *Defender* salary and gave him an air-conditioned apartment, chauffeured car, and other perks. After a visa snafu that stranded him in London for three weeks, he flew to Rome, where he changed to another plane that landed about eight hours later at Ikeja's airport. The airport was about a half-hour drive from downtown Lagos, Nigeria's capital. Awaiting his arrival was Chief Shonibare.

Lagos's climate reminded Martin of Savannah's. Yet the two cities were starkly different. He was continually startled by the tiny, black-tailed, orange-backed lizards that darted in and out of the doors and occasionally slithered over the walls of his appointed residence. Cars, trucks, and bicycles came and went in massed, life-threatening waves; street merchants bartered with customers; and pedestrians hurried to and fro. He decided that those who pictured Africans as languid, lazy creatures, forever sitting under the shade of tropical trees, would be astonished by the frenetic pace Lagos kept despite oppressive heat. Generally, most Nigerians returned Martin's smiles, although a few seemed ill at ease in his presence. When he talked with them about his African ancestry and about blacks in the United States, some did not seem to understand that he considered himself a blood brother to them, despite his lighter skin. Martin hoped not to be regarded as the Europeans and other expatriates were.

Martin's new, two-bedroom apartment was in a building owned by Chief Shonibare and came with a resident houseboy named John. When Martin left his apartment to go to work for the first time in Lagos, he had a book in his hand. His driver literally snatched it from him and refused to let him carry it upstairs when he arrived at his office. Martin quickly learned that as an important person, he would not be allowed to carry anything himself. In Nigeria, this was the way the young and those lower in social status showed respect.

Predictably, Martin encountered the tribal friction and mutual mistrust that would become a contributing factor to the 1967–1970 Nigerian Civil War. When he arrived, leaders of Nigeria's four largest tribes—the Yoruba in the west, the Ibo in the east, and the Hausa and the Fulani in the Muslim north— were competing for power after gaining independence from Great Britain. The first independent elections were scheduled for the end of 1959. To Martin, the Ibo people seemed more Westernized in their thinking than the Yoruba. One of the most celebrated Ibos was Nnamdi Azikiwe, editor of the *West African Pilot* and head of the Ibo political party that controlled the government of the eastern region of Nigeria. In 1950, when Martin was president of the National Newspaper Publishers Association, he had invited Zik, as he was called, to make the major speech at the association's Detroit convention during his visit to the United States. Now, as editorial advisor to the *Daily Service,* he found himself in Nigeria working against Zik. The *Daily Service* was the voice of the Yoruba Action Group Party, Zik's principal rival.

Martin had not expected to find a cadre of English men and women filling most of the mechanical and press jobs at the Amalgamated Press. On the other hand, all of the editorial and policy-making positions were in the hands of Africans, several of whom had been trained in England. As an outsider, he found the Yoruba language, which was spoken very fast, difficult to learn. Fortunately, the Nigerians he worked with spoke English so well that he did not need to master the language.

As editorial advisor, Martin was given considerable authority, but he found that whenever one of the Action Group Party officials had something urgent to say, his attempt to balance editorial propaganda with hard news went out the window. "My hope was that by stepping up the hard news and subordinating the propaganda, we could win readers across the board and get a larger audience," he recalled. He believed that this would not only yield a better newspaper but also make the *Daily Service* a more effective instrument for its owners' political agenda. Nevertheless, while Martin won some editorial battles, the top management viewed the paper's function differently. "To confine political propaganda to the editorial page often seemed hopeless," Martin recalled. "It is fair to say that my young colleagues, who took journalism seriously, were always on my side, but they did not make the policy decisions." [37]

Awolowo himself soon announced that he would be the Action Group Party's candidate for prime minister in the upcoming national elections, and Martin occasionally found himself being asked for editorial advice that was essentially political. He soon discovered that one of the sharpest minds in the paper's hierarchy belonged to the London-trained managing editor, Lateef Jacande, who wrote long political articles supporting Chief Awolowo's Action Group Party. Initially Martin had not realized that Jacande, whose articles he had read in London under a "John West" byline, was also an active member of the Action Group brain trust.

Martin had more consistent success improving the paper's style and look and expanding its audience with special promotions. To prick the British colonials, he launched a contest in which readers voted on printed ballots for the "most courteous expatriate" in Nigeria. The contest upset some of the British, who looked down on the Nigerians with whom they were doing business. A second contest, a "Talent Hunt," urged readers of all tribal backgrounds to nominate persons who could sing, dance, or otherwise entertain. Nominees attended elimination tryouts, and a panel of judges picked the finalists. Tribal frictions, not only among the nominees but also among the judges, turned it into a mostly all-Yoruba contest.

To broaden their communications network and as supporters of Awolowo, Martin's Yoruba hosts also built the first television station on the continent with transmitters in Ibadan and Lagos. It went on the air in mid-November, 1959, and not long afterward the fledgling station was transmitting two hours of educational material at midday and two hours of entertainment in the evening. At the end of his year in Nigeria, Martin was also able to point with some pride to the *Sunday Express*, a new national newspaper he had helped launch for Amalgamated, which, at the time of his departure, showed promise of exceeding the *Daily Service* in circulation.

Awo, as the chief was called by his followers, used a helicopter to fly to rallies in rural areas of Nigeria that had never seen such a vehicle. However, the Hausa and Fulani elite, who controlled the feudal, predominantly Muslim northern region of Nigeria, barred Awo from campaigning in person. Hence, a skywriter pilot from England wrote the name *AWO* in cloudless skies over the northern region, where the Hausa and Fulani had threatened violence against Action Group Party members. In Nigeria's riverine areas, the candidate moved about in specially outfitted speedboats. Even so, Martin doubted that Awolowo's appeal could cut across the strong ethnic divisions.

With an estimated population of forty million at that time, Nigeria had only nine million registered voters on election day. Equipped with Amalgamated Press credentials, Martin visited the polls to observe the voting process. After casting a ballot, each voter had his or her thumb stamped with green indelible ink that could not be rubbed off within twenty-four hours; thus no one would be able to vote more than once. As Martin had expected, Chief Awolowo was defeated by Abubakar Balewa, a Hausa from the North.

However, Awolowo's party, which controlled one of the country's three federal regions, won seats in the new Independence Parliament. The only foreigner in the balcony press box, Martin had an excellent view of the proceedings of the parliament's first assembly. Tall, slender Hausas and Fulanis in white robes towered over everyone, while Ibos in colorful gowns rivaled the dress of the Yorubas. Martin was surprised that the Speaker was a white man who seemed to be fully at home with his African colleagues. Martin had discovered during the year that political corruption and greed were as common in west Africa as in his own country, but the sight of cooperative, reasoned discourse in the new legislature's proceedings gave him a strong measure of confidence.

It had been a lonely year: although he had made good friends among both the Nigerians and the expatriate community, apart from a two-week tour with his wife and his third daughter, Toni, he had lived without his family. He was anxious to return home. As his plane flew toward London, he reflected on the changing continent he was leaving behind. One fact that impressed him more and more was the miracle of human survival. The tough odds posed by the climate and by disease and poverty, he thought, were often overlooked in the glib judgments made on the capacity of Africans to meet the challenges of this century.[38]

⁂

Soon after returning to the United States in the summer of 1960, Martin escorted Chief Ayo Rosiji, a prominent Nigerian official, on a grand tour of the United States. Rosiji wanted to meet important business and political leaders, especially those with presidential aspirations. Accordingly, the tour included Martin's first meeting with the man who would later play a crucial role in his life, Senate Majority Leader Lyndon B. Johnson of Texas.

Johnson's top aide, George Reedy, had arranged to have Rosiji meet with the majority leader in the latter's Senate chambers. Martin had never met the Texas senator and was taken aback by his size when he burst into the reception room with a gracious greeting. Grasping Martin's hand, Senator Johnson spoke to him like an old friend. Rosiji was charmed by the warm joviality with which the senator pumped his hand and told him how happy he was to meet a royal Nigerian. Meanwhile, the senator's photographers were busy shooting, and Martin surmised that Reedy was going to get as much publicity capital out of the meeting as he could.

Johnson gave Rosiji and Martin cuff links and other souvenirs and talked at length about his interest in Africa and in black Americans. When the visitors returned to their hotel after an hour with the senator, the chief said he wanted to call a press conference and endorse Johnson for president. Patiently, Martin explained to his visitor that it was not politic for a foreign dignitary to endorse an American candidate, especially during a primary campaign.

Martin and Rosiji flew from Washington to Knoxville, Tennessee, to tour the Tennessee Valley Authority. By the time they arrived in Los Angeles, the Democratic National Convention was in progress. During their one-day visit at Democratic party headquarters there, Martin introduced the Nigerian to some longtime political friends. While en route to a meeting with officials of the Bank of America in San Francisco, they would learn that John F. Kennedy had been nominated at the convention and had chosen Senator Lyndon Johnson as his running mate.

When he returned from Nigeria, Martin found himself at a career crossroads. Should he again enter national politics, or should he become a full-time insurance executive? He had been elected vice president of the board of directors of the Savannah-based Guaranty Life Insurance Company, whose president was Martin's aging father-in-law, Walter S. Scott. Scott wanted Martin to join the company as a working officer to deal with the problem that most small enterprises faced—the need to expand and grow steadily with limited capital and manpower. If Martin joined Scott, the family would have to move to Savannah. He and his wife decided that for the sake of their children's education such a move was not possible. After Walter Scott died in 1961, Martin assisted the Scott family in negotiating the sale of Guaranty Trust to Atlanta Life Insurance Company. With the sale of the company, Martin's last links with the city of his childhood were severed, making it unlikely that he would ever return to Savannah to live.

# .4.

## RALLYING THE TROOPS: THE JFK CAMPAIGN

*Do you know that three southern governors told us that if Jack supported Jimmy Hoffa, Nikita Khrushchev, or Martin Luther King, they would throw their states to Nixon? Do you know that this election may be razor-close and you have probably lost it for us?*

*—Robert Kennedy to Louis Martin and Harris Wofford, October 1960*

As of midsummer 1960, the closest Louis Martin had come to meeting Senator John F. Kennedy was seeing him from a distance, boarding and disembarking from planes. He was at Washington's National Airport one day when he saw the presidential candidate marching through the terminal, surrounded by reporters and aides. Instead of climbing into a limousine, Kennedy jumped into the driver's seat of a Pontiac sedan, beckoning the others to get in. "The senator gave the car the gun and drove out of the parking area into the Washington-bound turn-off at top speed," Martin recalled. "When he sped away I remember wondering what life would be like around the White House if this young gladiator got in." The contrast with the aged Eisenhower, who had just escaped a near-fatal illness, could hardly be more sharp.[1]

In July, just before the Democratic National Convention, Martin was still escorting Chief Rosiji around the country when his friend Frank Reeves urged him to get in touch with the young gladiator's campaign, if he still had a taste for the "political wars." A Washington attorney and professor at Howard University's law school, Reeves had worked with Martin in earlier election efforts. He was currently a member of the Democratic National Committee and had already been committed to attending the convention in Los Angeles as a Hubert Humphrey delegate, although Kennedy had won the primaries and was clearly going to be on the ballot in November. Within days, Kennedy's top press aide, Pierre Salinger, called Martin from Los Angeles to ask if he would help their campaign win over the black press.[2] Martin was flattered at the recommendation. "I'm interested, of course," he told Salinger, "but there is simply nothing I can do until August 1." By that time, he explained, he would be free from touring with the Nigerian dignitary. He expected to hear back from Salinger after the convention.[3]

છ છ છ

Martin had been working in Nigeria when the most recent civil rights confrontations splashed across the news. He was delighted and impressed by what he read about the newest generation of fighters. Three years later, speaking to a gathering of teachers in North Carolina, he would recall his reaction to the protests that had been sparked in the nearby town of Greensboro:

> I remember just a few years ago when the thought of thousands of Negroes going to jail and refusing bail in the struggle for civil rights would seem unbelievable. I was in Nigeria in the winter of 1960 when I first read about the sit-in movement of the students here. I thought at first the dispatches from Reuters, an English news service, might not have been wholly accurate. When I left America in the spring of 1959, there was no hint whatsoever that a mass movement of young Negroes was about to write a new chapter in American history.[4]

The Greensboro lunch counter sit-in had begun on February 1, 1960, when four students at North Carolina A&T College refused to leave the local F.W. Woolworth's store after being refused service. Within three weeks, and without direction from civil rights organizations, student-led sit-ins had spread to cities throughout the state and into Virginia, Tennessee, South Carolina, and Florida. By the summer of 1960, many thousands of young blacks throughout the South had participated in lunch counter sit-ins. The strategy of nonviolent resistance was winning adherents nationwide just as the presidential primaries were under way.[5]

On his return from Nigeria, Martin played catch-up with the rest of America, reading every article and editorial he could obtain to find out what kind of candidate Senator Kennedy was and what his leadership might mean for blacks. He learned that Eleanor Roosevelt and Adam Clayton Powell had publicly stated they did not think Senator Kennedy could win a large black vote. He did not know how seriously he should regard these statements—were they considered judgments or perhaps just preconvention doubletalk?

Although he was still busy with Rosiji, Martin followed the convention closely. Several prominent civil rights leaders had organized a parallel meeting in Los Angeles down the street from the convention, to which they invited all the major candidates. When Humphrey addressed this large gathering, he was cheered. Kennedy was booed when he began to speak, though by the end of his address he received polite applause.[6]

Back at the convention, Kennedy's campaign director, his younger brother Robert (whom friends and coworkers all called Bobby) was instructing his staffers to go "all the way" in promoting the civil rights plank that the team had drafted. The plank was a surprisingly aggressive and detailed commitment containing all the recommendations of the U.S. Commission on Civil Rights. How John Kennedy would be able to campaign in the segregated South with such a radical plank was unclear. Even those who drafted it wondered whether the Kennedy brothers had read it carefully. For the moment it was the candidate's official position, and it helped him win the support of nearly every black delegate on the convention floor.[7]

The announcement of Kennedy's last-minute choice of Lyndon Johnson as his running mate, however, ignited a firestorm of protest. Liberals, labor leaders, and civil rights supporters felt betrayed by the unexpected alliance with the powerful senator from Texas. Given that state's pivotal role in national elections, it was understood that Kennedy's choice was aimed at delivering the southern vote, but Johnson was automatically suspect in the eyes of many black delegates.

Johnson immediately moved to allay these fears, signing a written statement that he would support the civil rights platform and asking Frank Reeves to organize a special meeting with black delegates. As the convention was ending, the Texas senator talked to these delegates about his work on the passage of the 1957 Civil Rights Act, pointed out that he was not a signatory to the anti–school desegregation Southern Manifesto, which a hundred southern legislators and officials signed, and stressed that his record on the race issue was a good one. Johnson concluded with a prediction: "I will do more for you in four years than anybody else has done for the last 100 years."[8]

❧ ❧ ❧

Salinger never telephoned Martin back. Instead, shortly after the convention, Martin received a call at his Chicago home from Frank Reeves and Harris Wofford. Wofford, a white lawyer and former staff member of the U.S. Commission on Civil Rights, had left a position at Notre Dame University two months earlier to work for Kennedy's election. "We're in trouble with Negroes," Bobby Kennedy had told Wofford, "We really don't know much about this whole thing. We've been dealing outside the field of the main Negro leadership and have to start from scratch." Wofford was recruited to work full-time heading up the so-called Civil Rights Section of the campaign, whose main thrust was to deliver black votes in November. Reeves, who was in touch with NAACP people around the country, was brought on board to travel with the candidate to speaking engagements.

Kennedy had good reasons for scrambling to strengthen his campaign's black outreach. Early in the summer, a group of prominent civil rights leaders from Detroit, including Mildred Jeffrey, an influential DNC member and brilliant right-hand aide to Walter Reuther, met with the senator at his Georgetown home to hash out their concerns about his candidacy. Dissatisfied with his record on civil rights, and disheartened that their favorite primary candidate, Michigan governor G. Mennen Williams, had bowed out for Kennedy, they arrived an angry group. Kennedy listened to them, as one put it, "as peers," and the group quickly warmed to his candidacy. Jeffrey recalled: "But then we said to ourselves, 'We will go to the campaign office and not see one black.' " They were close to the truth.

Encouraged by the Detroiters, Kennedy sent his brother-in-law, R. Sargent Shriver, to the NAACP's convention in St. Paul soon thereafter. Shriver, who oversaw the campaign's special constituency divisions, spent long hours in his hotel suite caucusing with civil rights leadership. It was at one of these meetings that Mildred Jeffrey recommended Louis Martin to head up the black media outreach. "When I mentioned Louis's name, Sarge's eyes lit up," Jeffrey recalled. A Chicago businessman (he managed the lucrative Merchandise Mart building there), Shriver knew quite a lot about Martin's talents as editor of the *Defender.* Martin, too, had heard much about the man who was president of the Chicago School Board and had helped found the Catholic interracial movement.[9]

Now Reeves and Wofford were urging Martin to come to Washington for a one-day meeting of their new campaign section, which would be chaired by Shriver. They told Martin he would be most helpful in mapping out vote-getting strategies for a tight race in which every vote would be vital.

# RALLYING THE TROOPS

Martin met Shriver and the others three days later at Washington's LaSalle Hotel. He recognized many of the thirty-odd black leaders at the meeting, among whom was Marjorie McKenzie Lawson, a distinguished Washington attorney with ties to professional, religious, and women's organizations who had been appointed director of the new section.[10] Despite the host of important black participants at the meeting, Martin realized that the Civil Rights Section was part of a close-knit family operation and that Shriver and Wofford, both white, would be calling the shots. The situation reminded him of an old saying he heard growing up in the South, namely, that the surest route to success for a young black man was to find a "good white man" and follow him. "Personally," Martin later noted, "I had come to the conclusion that the axiom might come closer to reality if the white man being sought were not only good but good and smart. It goes without saying that in the quicksand of racial relations and politics, a stupid white man, however friendly and full of goodwill, becomes of questionable value on a serious project." Before the meeting was over, he would conclude that Shriver and Wofford were, decidedly, not stupid.[11]

Shriver made it clear that hardheaded political realism undergirded their campaign activities. As he would say later, the primary push was for votes: "In those days the appeal to civil rights was not the primary appeal when you went to get black or other minority votes. I'm sorry to say that a lot of it was based on just distributing money at election time or just having very good contacts with leaders of the black community. And a lot of it was a case of everybody scratching everybody's back."[12]

Shriver briefed the group on the importance of black voter support, and then called on Reeves and Lawson to lead a discussion about tactics. When it was Martin's turn, he raised an uncomfortable matter: before black newspapers could be expected to endorse the candidate, the Democratic National Committee would have to pay a debt of $40,000 to $50,000 owed to black newspapers, including his *Michigan Chronicle* and the *Chicago Defender*. The DNC owed the money for political advertisements run during the 1956 presidential campaign, and Martin thought that unless these debts were settled, the black press would start off with mixed enthusiasm.[13]

He also stressed the importance of soliciting support from all black leaders, regardless of their past associations and party affiliations, rather than playing one against the other. "Certain Negro leaders were under scrutiny," he recalled of the discussion. "This person was not trustworthy, or this person was a faker, or this person was so on and so forth. My view was, let's forget all the petty things, and let's move on a broad front and get everybody in the act. Let the chips fall where they may as the campaign proceeds." He added that given how tight the contest was likely to be, they had better work just as vigorously to enlist the old guard as to welcome the new.[14]

While he was aware that endorsements from prominent blacks would not guarantee support, Martin argued that their presence in the campaign would send a valuable message. Political leaders like Adam Clayton Powell were only part of the picture. If the campaign failed to appeal to civil rights leaders as well, he argued, it would be in trouble, so the Democrats should get as close to an endorsement as possible from Dr. Martin Luther King, Jr.

When Shriver asked Louis Martin to name the single most important thing the campaign could do to win black votes, he replied, "Well, as an old newspaperman I may be prejudiced, but I think you've got to go after the Negro newspapers."[15] He expressed concern about how the black press might treat Lyndon Johnson, remembering how it had attacked Senator John J. Sparkman, Adlai Stevenson's running mate in 1952. In that campaign, the *Pittsburgh Courier* printed a special supplement—Martin suspected it had been paid for by Republicans—in which "they verbally lynched Sparkman," as he put it. Other black papers followed the *Courier*, prompting public speakers, ministers, and others to oppose Sparkman's candidacy.[16]

Black newspapers might treat Johnson the same way if nothing was done to prevent it, Martin warned. Proposing that money was the key to securing fair coverage, he balked at a proposed budget of $200,000 to fund the national campaign in black communities. Since even the 1944 DNC budget for the black vote had exceeded that amount, he questioned the party's commitment and insisted that a really serious effort required at least one million dollars if they wanted the cooperation of black newspapers.[17]

Martin's knowledge of the inner workings of the black community impressed Shriver. The journalist's longtime position of leadership in the black press gave him access and knowledge beyond what was possible for any white staff member. Shriver listened as Martin argued that the way to keep editors from attacking Lyndon Johnson was by purchasing advertising space. Shriver told him not to worry about money and promised to take care of it.

Martin had to leave the meeting before all of this was resolved. He had full-time responsibilities back in Chicago, not only as a newspaper executive but by then also as a board member of two insurance companies and a savings and loan association. In good faith, however, he did promise to devote whatever time he could spare to the campaign.[18]

## RALLYING THE TROOPS

The LaSalle Hotel session had given him a sense of the kind of people Kennedy was working with. Both Wofford and Shriver struck him as smart operators, anxious to get things done. Both had Yale law degrees, and Wofford had made many black friends among the student leadership at Howard University Law School, where he had earned a second law degree. Wofford had spent his childhood in Tennessee, a fact that reminded Martin of the saying that the black man was better off with a reconstructed white Southerner than a liberal Yankee. "Harris had become 'reconstructed' in the sense that his liberalism developed out of new, strongly held convictions rather than some vague liberal sentiment," Martin later said, adding that he found Wofford earnest and "thoroughly imbued with what I call the 'Kennedy vigor.'" Both of them struck him as lively, "quick with a joke and without pretensions. Sarge especially had the capacity for giving the impression that he was not taking himself too seriously. It was clear to me after the first hour that it would be great fun working with them." [19]

A day after returning to Chicago, Martin received a phone call from Wofford and Reeves, who pleaded with him to take full charge of the campaign in the black media. "My mood was receptive, because I was not certain what I wanted to do since my return from Nigeria," he remembered. "Ever since my experience at the Democratic National Committee in the 1944 campaign I had become increasingly interested in the crazy, unpredictable interplay of forces that characterize the political process." [20] His first step was to seek the seasoned political advice of Bill Dawson, the man who had brought him into the Roosevelt campaign. Dawson expressed a low opinion of the Kennedys, though he had never met them. Martin himself had been startled at Dawson's absence from the planning meeting with Shriver a few days before. It occurred to him then that Dawson was probably smarting over the Kennedys' failure to recognize his stature in the party. It would be a huge tactical error for Kennedy to overlook the leverage that Democratic machine politicians like Dawson could offer, Martin believed. [21]

Despite this concern, Martin decided to accept the campaign's invitation and flew to Washington. At first he commuted to the capital as a consultant, working three days a week at one hundred dollars per day. But after two weeks it became a full-time, seven-days-a-week job. He never had a title but soon found that he did not need one. He worked most closely with Wofford, the two of them becoming a team with freedom to do "almost anything we thought helpful," Martin remembered. [22] They soon developed a strong mutual trust. "He knew a lot in many corners of American politics," Wofford would later say of Martin during that period. "The management of all Kennedy advertising in Negro newspapers and magazines, his first assignment, was only one of many contributions. He soon became our chief counselor, colleague, and co-conspirator." [23]

Martin spent most of his days during the campaign at the DNC. When Stephen Smith, another Kennedy brother-in-law and the campaign's treasurer, returned to New York, Bobby Kennedy arranged for Martin to move into Smith's office next door to his own, although for the first six weeks Martin never saw Bobby. The staff's work never ceased, and often it was nearly midnight before they ate dinner.

*ta ta ta*

Pressure for genuine progress on civil rights had steadily mounted after the landmark *Brown* v. *Board of Education* decision on school desegregation six years earlier. There were local victories, such as the desegregation of city buses in Montgomery, Alabama, in 1956 after the famous boycott. But each victory brought political retrenchment and sometimes brutal white reaction. Eisenhower had to send federal troops to enforce the *Brown* decision in Little Rock, Arkansas, where the safety of black high school students required military escorts. Bombings and assassinations targeting activists had quickened in frequency. In 1957, Congress passed the first federal Civil Rights Act since 1875, establishing the U.S. Commission on Civil Rights and creating a Civil Rights Division in the Justice Department. The act was widely considered to be more symbol than substance. Much of it was unenforceable, although the Justice Department did gain the power to file suits against discriminatory voting registrars. As of 1960, while black college students were clamoring for justice, Jim Crow was still alive and well throughout the South.

Kennedy's Republican opponent, Vice President Richard Nixon, had a passable record on civil rights legislation, but as the campaign proceeded he became strangely silent on the race issue. His strategy of appealing to southern white voters induced him to stay away from discussions of civil rights despite the earnest pleadings of his well-connected black advisor, E. Frederic Morrow. Kennedy was far more vocal, although Martin knew he had few civil rights achievements to boast of. His eloquent speeches during the campaign had drawn applause from black audiences, but his legislative record was weak at best. He had not followed the example of trailblazing liberals like Senator Humphrey, and he had voted for the damaging amendment to the 1957 civil rights bill that Lyndon Johnson had engineered as a compromise. Furthermore,

Kennedy reportedly had made deals with southern Democratic politicians who had declared themselves enemies of civil rights.[24]

Prominent among these southerners was Alabama Governor John Patterson, a segregationist who enthusiastically backed the candidate in the primaries and during the convention. One reason for his support was the Kennedy brothers' strong record in attacking organized crime, including corruption in the Teamsters union. Any activity perceived as anti-union played well in the "right-to-work" South. Finally, John Kennedy had said that he found the Supreme Court's "deliberate speed" desegregation formula, which allowed southern states to use delaying tactics to avoid school desegregation, "a satisfactory arrangement." [25]

Based on his record, Kennedy seemed at best disinterested in civil rights. But Martin's instincts told him that the principled statements his candidate was making about opportunity and freedom were not merely rhetoric. He thought that over the past year Kennedy had said all the right things about black problems in employment, housing, and public accommodations. Kennedy openly supported the lunch counter sit-ins as being soundly in the American tradition of free speech. Less publicly, he admired King, whom he met with privately to ascertain his views.

To offset Kennedy's weak reputation on the issue, Martin disseminated Kennedy's pro-civil rights statements, his support of the right to protest through sit-ins and other direct action, and his commitment to a "New Deal in Race Relations." The senator's public statements, Martin reminded everyone, were far more liberal than those of his opponent. Nixon had begun backtracking from his own marginally liberal record on race matters.[26]

Soon after joining the campaign, Martin suggested to Shriver that their candidate should put Nixon on the defensive by sending him a telegram demanding to know his position on racial integration. That same evening, Shriver placed a midnight call from his hotel suite to the Kennedy family estate in Hyannis Port, and then put Martin on the line. It was the first conversation he and Senator Kennedy ever had. Martin quickly outlined his plan to put Nixon on the spot.

"That idea might sound all right, but you just don't know that s.o.b.," Kennedy replied. "Instead of answering directly, he'll curve and come back with another question. I don't think we can pin the bastard down that way." Kennedy raised more objections. The journalist was not so much offended as impressed by the candidate's blunt reaction, including his salty language, which he found refreshingly honest. "Here was no stuffed shirt," he recalled thinking. Martin accepted the verdict and then hung up.

"Now you see why he's going to be president, don't you?" Shriver said.[27]

Until now, Martin had not known what he would think of Kennedy as an individual. "This first verbal exchange with the senator," he later recalled, "affected me like a couple of splashes of champagne. I wanted to call Gertrude, in Chicago, and tell her about the intimate little exchange with a guy who now I knew in my intuitive bones would be the next president of the United States. Only the lateness of the hour stopped me."[28]

≈≈ ≈≈ ≈≈

Early on, Marjorie Lawson had identified a serious problem with black voter registration and turnout. The regular party organization in some places had been denying blacks the opportunity to contribute to campaign administration and planning. Not surprisingly, this punctured blacks' enthusiasm for the Kennedy campaign and for the election. Members of the Civil Rights Section argued that increasing black registration was essential but thought it best to shift that activity away from the Democratic party. A voter drive that was nonpartisan would draw greater financial support, since contributions would be tax-deductible. Franklin Williams, a black former NAACP attorney and then assistant attorney general of California, was persuaded to take leave from his California post in order to organize a major registration drive under the auspices of black churches. The drive added thousands of additional voters to the rolls.[29]

Martin moved swiftly to enlist the black press, secured endorsements of Kennedy from locally and nationally known blacks, scheduled appearances of the candidate before black audiences, and presented Kennedy's story engagingly. He was determined to staunch the bleeding away of black support for the Democratic party, fully aware that Eisenhower, who had won only 24 percent of black votes in 1952, had won 39 percent in the last election.[30]

Although most black publishers were willing to give Kennedy fair coverage in their papers as long as the Democrats settled their advertising debts, many reserved their editorial endorsement. They were generally unfamiliar with Kennedy, and several reminded Martin of what Eleanor Roosevelt and Congressman Powell had said about the candidate's chances among black voters. In any case, Martin was not concerned about commitments, editorial or otherwise, but rather that news and information about the candidate get fair play in their news columns. In this regard his efforts were completely successful.[31]

Among the papers he lobbied was the *Norfolk Journal and Guide* in Virginia, then the largest and most influential black newspaper in the South. This paper had been among the first in the black press to drop its pro-Republican stance, a move it made in 1928 after the Republican party in the South replaced black delegates with whites at the Republican National Convention. In the years between 1928 and 1960, the *Journal and Guide* was either largely independent or slightly tilted toward the Democrats. In October 1960, after discussions with Martin, its publisher, P.B. Young, endorsed Kennedy as "dynamic and brilliant" and wrote that he spoke "forthrightly" on equal opportunity, fair housing, and civil rights. The *Pittsburgh Courier*, with distribution in ten cities, pledged to develop a strong editorial policy to promote the candidate.[32]

Martin also purchased advertisements in *Jet* and *Ebony* magazines and other national publications that had a policy of not editorializing on behalf of politicians. He wrote what was in effect a weekly *Jet* political column, though it was clearly labeled advertisement. As Martin put it, he and his colleagues "used every legitimate approach we could." The only money his DNC office gave to these publications was to pay for the space on a line-rate basis.[33]

Black newspapers figured prominently in another strategy—securing endorsements from blacks with local influence. These leaders were flattered to be getting attention from the campaign and only too happy to have their pictures published in local papers. Martin's technique was to run the individual's picture along with a positive statement about Kennedy, negotiating with the editors to give him the best placement. "In several of the major newspapers we ran sometimes four or five testimonials in the same paper," Martin recalled.[34]

Of the hundreds of prominent blacks he approached for endorsements, only baseball hero Jackie Robinson turned him down. Although he started out as a supporter of Hubert Humphrey, after the Kennedy nomination Robinson had switched to Richard Nixon. Sitting in the back of the auditorium at several of Robinson's public speeches, Martin tried to make sense of his reasons for opposing Kennedy. It seemed that when Robinson had dined at the senator's home, he had become disappointed with the candidate's limited grasp of the American race problem. Worse still from Robinson's perspective, Kennedy had not looked him in the eye. "He kept talking about Kennedy refusing to look him in the eye," Martin recalled. "In one speech, he said,

'My mother always told me that if they don't look you in the eye, they aren't really sincere.' He belabored that simple line, and to the unsophisticated maybe it had some appeal." [35]

Martin met Senator Kennedy in person for the first time on August 31, at a Washington meeting called by Shriver in a conference room just off the Senate floor. When Kennedy walked in, fresh from a Senate debate, Martin was surprised by his boyish looks and wondered to himself whether voters would entrust the presidency to such a young man. But he was also impressed by his intellect and sense of purpose. "Here was a cool, tough Irishman," he recalled thinking, "handsome to be sure, but no pampered rich boy full of nonchalance." [36]

Martin had been worried all along that Kennedy's views on civil rights were essentially cerebral, and he was still looking for some sign that his candidate harbored a visceral concern. The brief meeting Kennedy chaired that day gave Martin no insight into his psyche, however, and was too rushed to allow Martin a chance to speak with the man. [37] Instead he and the others listened to the senator discuss his plans for the campaign's first press conference on the civil rights issue, to take place the next day. Wofford's group had been considering how their candidate could best present his response to a last-minute Republican ploy. The Republicans had announced that they were going to present their own civil rights bill during the rump session of Congress over the next two months. Although their bill was weak and Washington insiders knew there would be no time to debate it and no hope of getting it passed, civil rights organizations had begun talking hopefully about it. Martin and the rest of the Kennedy team felt it was all a ploy to embarrass congressional Democrats before the election.

Kennedy had decided to avoid this trap by asking two liberal colleagues, Senator Joseph S. Clark of Pennsylvania and Congressman Emanuel Celler of New York, to draft a comprehensive civil rights bill that he could then introduce the following spring, after the election. When Martin left the rushed meeting, he immediately began working on the press announcement. The following day, Kennedy stepped before several hundred news reporters in his first campaign press appearance on the civil rights issue, and said:

> We have not tried to match the eleventh-hour Republican tactic of substituting staged political maneuvering for effective legislation. Rather than yield to their efforts to play politics with a great moral question, we will take this issue to the American people. [38]

# RALLYING THE TROOPS

Many activists in the movement were disappointed to hear that Kennedy was planning to wait until the following spring before pushing for legislation. But Martin, who felt the approach was honest and reasonable, was satisfied with the outcome, noting that "the scattered flak—criticism—even among civil rights professionals did not appear to be malicious." [39]

That same week Kennedy spoke with a delegation from the National Bar Association, a black lawyers group that sought his commitment to appoint blacks to the federal bench. Although William Hastie, who by now had served as governor of the Virgin Islands, had been promoted by President Truman to the Third Circuit Court of Appeals, in the ten years since that time not a single black had been named to the federal bench. Kennedy was late for the appointment, so Martin spoke to the lawyers, who included several old friends. The two spokesmen for the lawyers group promised Martin that if Kennedy made a genuine commitment to black judicial appointments, they would do their part to campaign for him. Because Martin had helped draft the statement Kennedy was about to make to these men, he was able to assure them of Kennedy's commitment. He admitted he had not known the senator before the campaign but felt he was a young, vigorous champion who could initiate a new era in race relations. [40]

As the senator walked in, searching his pockets for the speech Martin had helped draft, Martin handed him another copy. "I was a little concerned because I knew he hadn't read it at all," Martin recalled, "but he delivered it beautifully." He noted the emphasis and seriousness with which Kennedy told the group, "The fact that no Negro has ever been appointed a federal district judge shows how far we still have to go in making our judiciary representative of the best of all our people." In the lawyers' responses, Martin witnessed for the first time how Kennedy could connect with strangers, something he attributed to his "electric quality" and to his ability to make "the most prosaic pronouncements sound like poetry." [41]

❧ ❧ ❧

During the campaign, a *New York Times* reporter once asked Martin to outline his plans for capturing the black vote, and when Martin began reciting what he had in mind, the reporter stopped him cold with the confident assessment that Kennedy's Catholicism would make it impossible for him to win. The senator's religious denomination and the allegation that his father was a Nazi sympathizer while ambassador to Great Britain in the 1930s were both, in fact, serious liabilities among Jewish and conservative Protestant voters, the latter group including many black clergy and churchgoers.[42]

Having grown up in a Catholic home, Martin naturally did not share the concerns these blacks may have had, but he recognized the need to address them. As part of that effort, DNC representatives conferred with black clergymen and attended numerous interdenominational meetings. Nevertheless, just one month before the election, Martin received a copy of an ominous letter to Congressman Dawson from D. Arnett Murphy, advertising director of the Baltimore *Afro-American*. The letter stated in part:

> … a very prominent young man in a very high supervisory position in the Housing Authority, said to me that several friends of his had written to him from Atlanta stating that a number of ministers were taking up the Catholic issue from their pulpits and alerting their members to the dangers of electing a Catholic to the presidency.[43]

Murphy proposed that the DNC secure Kennedy endorsements from prominent black Protestants or, at the very least, statements from them urging that persons of different faiths and religions should not allow this matter to influence their voting. The most valuable help on this front came, ironically, from a prominent black Republican, Rev. Joseph H. Jackson, then president of the five-million-member National Baptist Convention, U.S.A. Jackson had already made several public statements warning against anti-Catholic prejudice, and Martin and his associates lost no time in producing a pamphlet featuring Jackson's views. In published statements, Jackson had challenged the claim that the election of a Catholic might pose problems for Protestants. Jackson had urged voters, above all, to rise above prejudice and "vote as Americans for an American to be president of Americans." [44]

ॐ ॐ ॐ

Six weeks after joining the campaign, Martin had still not met the campaign director, Bobby Kennedy. This oversight was now corrected at a Civil Rights Section meeting in mid-September. A wiry young man, Bobby Kennedy looked to Martin for all the world like a college freshman, smaller than he remembered seeing him in photos. His voice carried authority, though, and seemed to Martin stronger than his slight frame would have led one to expect. And like his fellow Kennedys, he had unflagging energy, what Martin called "the closest thing to human electricity."

## RALLYING THE TROOPS

By this time, Martin had heard plenty about the candidate's younger brother, who was known as a hard-nosed, strong-willed taskmaster. Everyone in the campaign feared him. Martin began to see why some of the staff had dreaded the meeting. Head lowered, leaning forward in his swivel chair, Bobby Kennedy began asking Shriver and others about the section's activities. "His manner was mocking and acid," he recalled. "He said in effect, 'It was mighty late in the day to find out that the Civil Rights Section had not gotten off the ground.' I was surprised to see how much deference Sarge seemed to show him." [45]

Martin became angry. When his turn came to report, he described what he was doing boldly. Explaining that his DNC operation did not have enough money, he wondered out loud whether the Kennedys really wanted the black vote. "If you want it, you can get it," he said, "but you're going to have to work for it, you're going to have to fight for it, and you're going to have to spend money." Both Shriver and Wofford interrupted Martin, excusing his aggressive manner with the statement, "You know, this man is from Chicago." Martin took some exception to Kennedy's way of running the meeting—and especially to his blanket charge that staff were sitting on their hands. "You're talking about what we haven't done," Martin shot back. "You haven't done what you were supposed to do. You haven't linked up with the guys who have been in this party for twenty years. You don't know the officers. You don't know anybody. You're supposed to open these doors, you know." [46]

Everyone was stunned. As the meeting broke up, John Seigenthaler, a distinguished white journalist and now a Kennedy aide, whispered to Martin: "Wait a minute, I wish you'd stay. Bobby wants to talk to you." During an hour-long talk, Martin bluntly told the younger Kennedy that he, Louis Martin, knew more about what he was doing than his listener did about what *he* was doing. He made it clear to Bobby that he did not care about his experience because, as he later put it, "I didn't think he had any."

Martin explained that machine politicians in black areas, including Congressman Dawson of Chicago, might not have the clout they were reputed to have because the old patronage system was dying out. Nevertheless, the campaign should not risk losing votes in the major cities by failing to touch every base. He also contended that white bosses in the cities could not be depended on to boost black voter registration and turnout. Still educating Bobby, Martin explained that campaign speeches and literature meant nothing to many voters in poor black areas. Some literally had to be taken by the hand for voter registration and later escorted to the voting booths. The candidate's brother asked Martin what he thought he should do. Remembering his earlier conversation with Bill Dawson and the congressman's sour attitude, Martin replied, "The first thing you ought to do is to get to know these people that you don't know, whether you use them or not. You ought to touch bases with Dawson. He's one of the biggest vote getters in Chicago. He can guarantee 200,000 votes, and that's power. Whether he's stupid or not, I don't give a damn about what you think of him." [47]

Martin was surprised that Bobby Kennedy accepted his frankness in good faith. As the meeting closed, Kennedy asked him to arrange for a private meeting with Dawson as soon as possible. The response to his insistent advice and the impressions he had gleaned of Kennedy and the others lifted Martin's mood. "What started out as a fiasco now was beginning to appear a giant step forward," he remembered thinking. "Instead of entertaining stray thoughts about packing my bags and getting out, I left the headquarters with a new determination to go all out in the campaign." [48]

Still puzzled by the Kennedys' indifference toward Dawson, Martin later learned that they felt that as long as Chicago mayor Richard Daley supported them, they should not have to deal with anyone else in the city's party hierarchy. Still, he hoped something beneficial would come of Bobby Kennedy's meeting with the congressman. He accompanied Dawson in a cab to Kennedy's office and left him there for the private visit, hoping Dawson would describe to the candidate's brother his national work with the Democratic party since 1944, the strategic importance of Chicago's votes in the upcoming election, and his political leadership of Chicago's blacks. When Martin accompanied Dawson on his return trip from the half-hour meeting, he asked, "How did it turn out?"

"Well now, he's a young man," Dawson replied. "We had a nice, uneventful little chat." [49]

Though unable to coax more information from Dawson, Martin was nevertheless concerned that he be respected as an important Democratic leader who could deliver substantial votes. He conceded that Dawson could not galvanize younger, more militant blacks, but he could at least motivate older, more traditional black Democrats, inspiring them to participate fully in the campaign. Because Dawson had been quietly wielding this sort of political power since 1944, Martin and others in the Civil Rights Section urged Shriver to honor him by making him vice chairman of the DNC. Shriver agreed. [50]

୨ଈ ୨ଈ ୨ଈ

## RALLYING THE TROOPS

With the arrival of October, Senator Kennedy stepped up his appearances before black audiences and, for the first time since the convention, began to address civil rights policy questions head-on. Speaking to a gathering of black citizens on Chicago's South Side, he cited some harsh statistics on racial disparities that Martin and Wofford had researched for him earlier.[51] He had cited them just the week before in his first televised debate with Richard Nixon, and he would repeat them often in the coming years, including the evening in 1963 when he would announce his civil rights bill. In Chicago, Kennedy said:

> If a white baby and a Negro baby are born in houses next to each other, the Negro baby has one-half as much chance of finishing high school, one-third as much chance of getting to college. There are four times as many chances that he will be out of a job. Why should it be so?

Answering his own question, Kennedy told the Chicagoans, "It is because they do not have a fair chance to develop their talents." These lines drew ringing applause.[52]

A week later the candidate stood before a throng of talented students at Howard University. The Civil Rights Section had persuaded the American Council on Human Rights to invite both candidates to a debate on the Howard campus. Here the senator could delineate his civil rights perspective to an audience of young high-achievers from the black middle class. Nixon chose not to come, leaving Kennedy and the Democrats with the Howard students to themselves. "I regret that the Republican member has not shown up," Kennedy told the audience. "I would like to present their case for them"— the audience laughed—"but I'd rather speak for our own case."[53]

Kennedy again presented his case for equal opportunity as one that made economic as well as moral sense:

> I think we cannot afford in 1960 to waste any talent which we have. It is a matter of our national survival, as well as a matter of national principle, and I believe that the president of the United States must take the leadership in setting the moral tone, the unfinished business... of realizing the talents, in an equal way, of every American.[54]

Kennedy's remarks generated much applause, and he and his wife Jacqueline were mobbed following the meeting. The candidate's appeal to conscience was beginning to appear in many of his public statements, and

Martin later noted that his emphasis on civil rights as a moral issue "ran like a thread through all the patchwork of his formal as well as off-the-cuff remarks." [55] Days after the Howard speech, the Washington *Afro-American* pictured the Kennedys shaking hands with Lorraine Williams, Howard's vice president for academic affairs. In a revealing letter to Martin, D. Arnett Murphy, of the Baltimore *Afro-American*, wrote:

> You will note in the letter I sent Congressman Dawson that I have offered to send mattes of this picture, together with the story, to the same list of papers we used earlier this week when we sent out the mattes and story on Mrs. Roosevelt. We are always happy to render this type of extra merchandising service to our advertisers and we want you to know that we are ready to continue this type of assistance throughout the campaign.[56]

ᏋᎯ ᏋᎯ ᏋᎯ

Of all the events orchestrated by the campaign, the one that Martin felt achieved the most in encouraging civil rights leaders to support his candidate was not a political rally but a nonpartisan conference that the campaign put together in New York City. Others advising Kennedy in the campaign were opposed to the project, worrying it might stir up more trouble than it was worth. Lyndon Johnson suggested that they avoid the term "civil rights," which was poison to many southern white voters, by calling it a conference on constitutional rights. That agreed, the event was planned as a full-scale gathering of intellectuals, community leaders, social workers, and civil rights activists from all over the country. To encourage wide participation, black and white liberal Republicans were also welcomed.

The National Conference for Constitutional Rights opened on October 11, 1960, with the stated objective of drafting a set of civil rights recommendations for the next president. Martin worked hard to see that it was well attended. The list of featured speakers and attendees included many influential political and activist figures, Eleanor Roosevelt and Congressman Celler among them. The NAACP was represented, though quietly so because the fact that the event was sponsored by the Kennedy campaign made NAACP leaders uneasy about endangering their own organization's nonpartisan status. In the end, more than 400 participants came from forty-two states.[57]

After Senator Humphrey opened the conference, the participants separated into workshops on legislative and executive action on education, voting, the administration of justice, housing, employment, and public facilities. Senator Kennedy came and listened to the recommendations. Martin was proud of the fact that they had given the conference a substantive base and encouraged proposals that made sense to a wide spectrum of black leaders.[58]

Kennedy drew cheers when he agreed with Eleanor Roosevelt's comment that President Eisenhower should have called such a conference after the *Brown* decision six years earlier. He called the conference a "welcome precedent of consultation between those who bear responsibility in the government and those who live as citizens and work in the field and know it and feel it." Kennedy also used the occasion to stress the distinction between legislative and executive action on civil rights. He knew that the promise he had made a month earlier to submit to Congress a comprehensive bill might take several years to fulfill.[59] For this occasion, he emphasized his commitment to swiftly issuing executive orders in every area of desegregation over which the White House had jurisdiction: "The Constitution is a wonderful document, and it gives great power to the president and great influence. It is, as Franklin Roosevelt said, above all a place for moral leadership."[60]

As if by plan, Kennedy's words were suddenly counterpointed by the behavior of candidate Nixon. The night the conference opened, Nixon's running mate, Massachusetts senator Henry Cabot Lodge, issued a statement declaring that a Nixon White House would appoint the first black American to a Cabinet post. "It hit like a bomb," Martin said of the reaction at the conference. "Of course, everybody said, 'That's just cheap politics.' " The next day, while the conference was in full swing, Nixon issued his own statement contradicting Lodge. The retraction, Martin remembered, came just at the right moment.[61]

Martin later had to admit that the whole conference endeavor was mixed in its purposes, nonpartisan yet partisan, academic yet devoted to influencing the White House. While the nonpartisan character of the conference was preserved in some of the speeches, he later noted, "this was one of the most unusual and successful political 'clambakes' ever promoted in the civil rights field for a national campaign." When the conference ended on the afternoon of October 12, many participants abandoned their nonpartisan posture and joined a huge Kennedy rally at Seventh Avenue and 125th Street in Harlem. Visiting this corner of black life had become a staple of Democratic presidential campaigns since Franklin Roosevelt. Republican candidates had stopped here as well, though Nixon, not surprisingly, failed to do so.[62]

Martin knew that the black political leadership in Harlem and New York generally was riven by factionalism. But on this occasion, thanks in part to the organizational genius of Raymond Jones, a top aide to Congressman Powell, the New York black politicos were united. Eleanor Roosevelt, still remembered as a champion of equal rights, drew thunderous applause when she stood up to say a few words. Powell introduced the candidate with his usual flair. Handsome and charismatic, Powell was a man of whom Martin would say, "when he walked in the room the lights went on." Here he was in his element. With one arm around Kennedy and the other around Mrs. Kennedy, Powell presented them to the applauding throng of 6,000 and then held the intimate pose for the cameras.[63]

Powell gave a long speech of his own in which he described Kennedy as an old friend and a fellow fighter for civil rights. The audience caught his high spirit. By the time the senator was called on to respond there was no time for a long address. Kennedy reiterated the promise he had made to the black lawyers' group a month earlier, pointing out that the federal district court system lacked a single black judge and that he intended to change that.[64]

Asked later about the impact of Kennedy's various appearances, Martin would say of those two events in New York City on October 11 and 12: "I think this [Harlem] speech was a turning point in the election in a sense. The constitutional meeting just about wrapped up the Negro leadership for us. This rally was, of course, the icing on the cake." The conference, Martin was convinced, had changed the views of many civil rights leaders who might have been uncertain days before.[65]

The overwhelming reception Kennedy received in Harlem, where the black rank and file stood rows deep on the sidewalk to hear him, prompted Martin to record his impression of the scene in his memoir years later:

Here was the elite of the land, in the middle of the ghetto, vowing their concern and friendship for those born and living in exile from the main body of American society. Here too promises were being made that this exile, with its overtones and undertones of humiliation and debasement, would come to an end if the Prince and Princess got into the White House. The magic wand was in the hands of the little people, and on the first Tuesday in November they could put a piece of paper in a box and change the course of history.[66]

# RALLYING THE TROOPS

*a *a *a

Magic sometimes required cash on the barrelhead. Earlier in the year, while cruising on a yacht in the Mediterranean, Powell had radiotelephoned instructions for an emissary to open negotiations with the Kennedy staff, as he had done years earlier with Eisenhower's staff. Ray Jones flew to Washington from New York to present a special campaign proposal to Shriver, who asked Martin to join him.

Jones presented a thick, well-organized, proposal, replete with statistics and demographics, for a comprehensive, nationwide campaign that Powell and his associates promised would deliver the black vote to Kennedy. At the end of the ambitious proposal was a requested budget of $300,000. Martin laughed out loud at the figure. He pointed out that the proposal was not clear about Powell's specific role and responsibilities in the campaign and that some of the ideas had not been fully developed. But he did not want Powell to sit out the election or declare for the Republicans, as he had done in the Eisenhower/Stevenson race. Could Jones speak for Adam Powell? When Jones insisted he could, Martin suggested to Shriver that they accept those parts of the proposal that would make maximum use of Powell's considerable speaking talents. They agreed on a payment of $40,000 for ten speeches, with payment to be made in installments through New York mayor Robert F. Wagner's office after each speech. In this way they had some guarantee that Powell would, in fact, make the speeches he had agreed upon. If he reneged, the DNC would refuse to pay. When the meeting ended, Jones observed that Martin and Shriver had driven a hard bargain.[67]

Later in the campaign, Bobby Kennedy came up with the idea of a "flying caravan" of black athletes and entertainment celebrities that would stop off at selected cities and conclude in a mass rally in Detroit. There had been no warning when Kennedy dropped this plan on Martin and asked him to carry it out. Martin was instructed not to mention it to anyone else on the campaign staff until it got off the ground. "I never understood it," he said, "but that was the strategy the Kennedys used. They had forty balls in the air and different people designated to catch them, and one not knowing what the other's doing."

Martin was aided by a friend in New York City, where the project was to get started, named Frank Montero. Difficulties arose over the issue of who would be invited to participate in—and who was willing to join—the caravan. Baseball star Willie Mays agreed for five minutes, then changed his mind.

Martin and Montero finally secured the presence of the player's wife, Mae Louise Mays. They also had to settle for the daughter of Lena Horne after the singer herself begged off. When they were ready to launch the event from New York with a press conference, they discovered another problem: if it were simply an all-black affair it would look like a "Jim Crow flying unit," as Martin put it. Dorothy Bowles, the wife of Congressman (and former Connecticut governor) Chester Bowles, solved this problem by agreeing to go to New York to help launch the caravan.

Although the plane was loaded with campaign buttons, literature, and other necessities, none of the passengers was experienced in politics. They all had to be briefed. One problem was Henry Armstrong, former boxing champion turned minister. In the middle of political rallies, he often abandoned electioneering and started preaching. After a frantic search, Martin replaced Armstrong with former heavyweight champion Jersey Joe Walcott. "It was one absolutely impossible junket," Martin remembered. "You had to mesh the meetings in with the weather and the time of arrival." Notwithstanding the chaos, the whole effort paid off, especially in Baltimore, Louisville, and Detroit, where the local political machine turned out big crowds. On balance, Martin concluded that it was a success, particularly the Detroit finale, which drew a large and enthusiastic crowd.[68]

Less than two weeks before the election, an arrest and sentencing took place in Atlanta that would have a major impact on the black vote and the election. On October 19, Martin Luther King, Jr., was arrested at a lunch counter sit-in. The mayor of Atlanta intervened and managed to have the students released from jail. But a local judge, Oscar Mitchell, creatively found a way to keep King in jail, charging that the lunch counter "trespassing" violated the probation terms of an earlier minor traffic violation. Unbelievably, Judge Mitchell sentenced King to four months of hard labor for driving with an expired license. Just as his friends were getting this news, King was abruptly transferred from the DeKalb County jail to a rural state prison in Reidsville.[69]

This second development, coming on top of the first, sent many of King's friends into a panic, not least his wife, Coretta, who was pregnant. Jail was one thing, but leaving King to the mercies of hardened white convicts in a rural prison camp was possibly putting his life in danger. The news swept through black Atlanta. Coretta King made a call to Harris Wofford, asking him to please use his influence to do something. Wofford was with Martin at the time and turned to him to say, with a hint of sarcasm, "If these beautiful, passionate Kennedys would do something to show their passion—if John Kennedy could just call Coretta on the phone—"and before he finished his thought Martin interjected, "That's a wonderful idea." [70]

The rest of the Kennedy civil rights team also heard right away about King's situation from Frank Reeves, who was in Atlanta. Meanwhile, King's lawyer had notified the rest of the world, and telegrams demanding federal intervention began pouring in to President Eisenhower. Eisenhower drafted a statement announcing that his attorney general would take proper steps to join with Dr. King in an appropriate application for his release. But the statement was never released, and the president took no action. [71]

Martin and Wofford knew that their candidate had no authority to effect a release, but they felt it would be wrong to let the issue pass in silence—at least some kind words to King's family might be encouraging. Moreover, if Kennedy spoke to the family, it would send the clearest possible signal to undecided black voters on where their candidate's sympathies stood. As to the effect such a call might have on the election itself, their political instincts were mixed. Certainly it could anger more white voters than the black voters it gained. "We weren't sure what was happening," Martin recalled, "whether it was going to be a wise call or not. At least, I wasn't." [72]

While walking to the DNC office to brief Bobby Kennedy on the King incident, Martin decided he had to find some way to shock him into action. When he arrived, Bobby was leaving to catch a plane. Martin stopped him and explained the situation. "Bobby's outrage at the arrest of King was immediate," Martin recalled. Kennedy's face clouded over and he kept repeating, "Four months on a traffic charge!" He told Martin he would do something, and Martin informed him that Wofford was getting Shriver to talk to his older brother. [73]

Martin also told Kennedy that Jackie Robinson was pressuring Nixon to call a press conference and blame Georgia's Democratic party officials for the harassment and jailing of King. The story was, in fact, just that—a story. Martin had no reason to believe it, though of course it was quite possible, and he and Wofford thought it might stir their campaign director to action. As Bobby hurried off to the airport, Martin had no idea what the man was going to do, although he was convinced "he was ready to go on the warpath." [74]

When Wofford reached Shriver, he was with Senator Kennedy at an airport motel in Chicago. Wofford suggested that the candidate phone Mrs. King, and Shriver agreed it was worth a try. Before bringing this up with Kennedy, however, he waited until everybody else had left the motel room. Most of the staff with them knew little about King, and Shriver feared that between them they would have postponed or cancelled the idea if they got into the discussion. Finally, when the senator was alone packing his suitcase, Shriver seized the moment. "Listen, I've got an idea for you," he said. "You know Martin Luther King is in jail. His wife is sitting there at home. Everybody is terrified because they don't know what the hell is going to happen. Mrs. King obviously is very much disturbed about what is happening to her husband. I think it would be a marvelous gesture on your part to just call her up and express your understanding of her situation, your sympathy, your respect for King, and your hope that things will work out all right, and if you can do something about it, you will try to cooperate."

Kennedy glanced at Shriver, walked around, and then replied, "That's a good idea. How do we get her? You have her number?"

"Yes," replied Shriver.

"Well, get her on the phone." Shriver dialed the number that Wofford, a longtime friend of the Kings, had given him. "Hi, Mrs. King. It's Sargent Shriver in Chicago. I'm with Senator Kennedy, and he would like to talk to you. Okay?"

"Sure," Coretta King agreed on the other end.

Shriver handed the phone to Senator Kennedy. "I know this must be very hard for you," the senator told Mrs. King. "I understand you are expecting a baby, and I just wanted you to know that I was thinking about you and Dr. King. If there is anything I can do to help, please feel free to call on me."

"I certainly appreciate your concern," she replied. "I would appreciate anything you could do to help."

Shortly afterward, Mrs. King called Wofford and told him how grateful she was that Kennedy had called her. Kennedy, too, was pleased about having made the call, but apart from confirming it once for a reporter, he never spoke about it publicly.[75]

Kennedy's campaign plane flew to Detroit and then to New York's LaGuardia Airport. The only topic the press wanted to discuss was Kennedy's call to Mrs. King. Meanwhile, Robert Kennedy chewed out Shriver in Chicago. "Who in the hell do you think you are, screwing up the whole campaign?" he yelled. "You've gotten Senator Kennedy exposed on this highly volatile issue and you should never have brought it up without clearing it. You've wrecked the campaign. Who the hell do you think you are?"

"I didn't think I was anybody except I thought it was a decent idea," Shriver replied. "Jack is a decent man, and people will read the call as an indication of the kind of character that he has."

The candidate's brother then tongue-lashed Martin and Wofford. "Do you know three southern governors told us that if Jack supported Jimmy Hoffa, Nikita Khrushchev, or Martin Luther King, they would throw their states to Nixon?" he asked. "Do you know that this election may be razor-close and you have probably lost it for us?" Kennedy added, "The Civil Rights Section is not going to do another damn thing in this campaign." He ordered them not to issue any more controversial press releases or literature.[76]

Later that day something caused Bobby Kennedy to change his outlook. At about one o'clock the next morning, he telephoned Martin, awakening him, and said in his usual abrupt manner, "Louis, I wanted you to know that I told that judge down in Georgia today to let King go. He said he would." Bobby Kennedy had telephoned Judge Mitchell and expressed his belief as a lawyer that all defendants had a right to release on bond while they appealed a case. Jolted out of bed as Bobby repeated himself, Martin laughed and told him, "We hereby make you an honorary brother." Thereafter the two greeted each other as "brother," with affection and humor.[77]

Although King's release on bail the next day was only briefly mentioned in the mainstream press, the episode of King's jailing had riveted readers of the black weeklies. "I knew that we had a good handle to crank up the get-out-the-vote machinery," Martin recalled. He and Wofford telephoned Mrs. King to find out exactly what Senator Kennedy had said. The entire Civil Rights Section moved like a platoon into battle to blanket black America with the Kennedy-King story. Martin's favorite refrain at the office was "Let's get all our horses on the track!" With the election only a week away, Martin signed a telegram explaining the episode and had it sent to most of the nation's black public officials. He telephoned ward and district leaders in key cities, and at his own expense informed black newspaper editors across the nation so that their papers would get the news fast enough to meet their deadlines. None of the information went to the general press, however; Martin felt it might prompt a Republican counterattack. He recalled an additional tactic he set in motion: "I made personal phone calls to a few party wheels urging them to put 'messengers' in the streets to tell how the Kennedys sprang King from a Georgia jail and offered help to Mrs. King." In

New York City, Martin's party wheel of choice was Ray Jones, who had already proven his ability to get things done for the campaign.

Martin and Wofford proposed to Shriver that they be allowed to print a small pamphlet to be distributed throughout the black community. Assured that it would tell only the bare facts of the dialogue without editorial embellishment that could embarrass the campaign, Shriver approved the project.[78]

*The Case of Martin Luther King* was the name they gave to the slight but powerful leaflet. To maintain a certain nonpartisan distance, it was officially published not by the DNC but by the Freedom Crusade Committee, headed by two Philadelphia ministers. The Civil Rights Section broke its own non-editorializing rule with the bold heading:

" 'No Comment' Nixon versus a Candidate with a Heart, Senator Kennedy"

The leaflet told the story of the phone call through statements by King, his wife, and his father, as well as comments by Ralph Abernathy of the Southern Christian Leadership Conference (SCLC) and Gardner Taylor, president of the Protestant Council of New York. Quotes from the New York *Post* story on the episode rounded out the pamphlet's text.

The first 50,000 copies of what they dubbed "the blue bomb" rolled off a Washington press on light blue paper the weekend of October 29 and were dispatched all over the country. By the middle of the week, Shriver notified them that another 500,000 copies were being printed for release in the Midwest. They hoped to use church networks to get them distributed at every black church in Chicago and the region's other major cities the following Sunday, two days before the election. During his years helping the UAW in Detroit, Martin had found black churches to be the most effective way to reach black voters. The work went on continuously until the day before the election. On Sunday, November 6, they loaded the last large shipments of the blue bomb on Greyhound buses bound for churches in the South. When all was done, the campaign team had printed and shipped out more than two million leaflets.[79]

After King's release, the Kennedy campaign tried to arrange a public meeting between Senator Kennedy and Dr. King, but they could not come to an agreement with King on where the meeting should be or on what he would say afterward. They wanted an endorsement, but he would agree only to a nonpartisan statement. In a prepared message, Dr. King explained that as president of the SCLC, he was unable to endorse a political party or a candidate. Indeed, he said that his role in the South's emerging social order dictated that he remain nonpartisan. Then King made it clear that he was deeply grateful to Senator Kennedy for the genuine concern he expressed regarding his arrest. "[He] exhibited moral courage of a high order," King concluded.[80]

King's father was not hampered by institutional restraints. "Daddy" King, a lifelong Republican, had been planning to vote for Nixon. But after the Kennedys' telephone calls, he endorsed the senator from Massachusetts. "It took courage to call my daughter-in-law at a time like this," he said. "Kennedy has the moral courage to stand up for what he knows is right. I've got a suitcase of votes, and I'm going to take them to Mr. Kennedy and dump them in his lap."[81]

The massive publicity effort paid off. Martin later received a letter from a black woman in Texas who had been on his list of telegram recipients. She thanked him for the wire about Kennedy's phone call and explained that she had read it aloud at a meeting just before the election. Martin and his colleagues also received word from Ray Jones, who had sent messengers with the King story into the bars of Harlem, that blacks in New York were going over to the Kennedy side. There were widespread reports of entire congregations of black Baptists and Methodists pledging to vote for Kennedy. They sensed that the tide was turning for the senator in practically every black community. Even Richard Nixon's black chauffeur would later tell Nixon how sorry he was that after learning of Robert Kennedy's phone call, blacks who had been planning to vote for his employer all turned to the Kennedy ticket. Clearly, the dual Kennedy "interventions" in the King case came at the right moment—the campaign's eleventh hour.[82]

ta ta ta

In the popular vote, the 1960 presidential election was one of the closest in American history. Kennedy edged out Nixon by just 112,881 votes of the 67 million cast, a margin of two-thirds of one percent. Crucial to that victory were the Kennedys' phone calls to Coretta King and Judge Mitchell, together with the two million "blue bombs." Not only did the number of Democratic black voters increase well beyond the campaign's early expectations, but Kennedy's share of the black vote was 68 percent, seven percentage points better than Stevenson's results against Eisenhower in 1956.

Embarrassed by the Republican defeat, which he considered a repudiation of his administration, Eisenhower initially blamed Henry Cabot Lodge for losing white votes by promising to appoint a black to the Cabinet. Later, when the evidence accumulated on the critical role of the black vote in determining the election, Eisenhower credited the Kennedys' phone calls and admitted that the Nixon campaign had not paid sufficient attention to this crucial voting bloc. Nixon complained that Kennedy's civil rights gestures were just grandstanding and that if he himself had called the judge, he might have won. It turned out that Nixon's black campaign aide, E. Frederic Morrow, had indeed advised him to make a statement about King's imprisonment, but Nixon had rejected the advice.[83]

In his memoirs, Martin later jotted down his sense of the last days of the campaign:

> In our view, the calls were the icing on the cake. JFK, in our view, had won the endorsement of the black leadership and the rank and file. I repeat: the big question mark was the size of the black turnout. The King calls helped ensure a good turnout in an election that was so close that had we been short one vote per precinct in Illinois, Nixon would have won the election.[84]

# .5.

## A VOICE FOR CIVIL RIGHTS: THE KENNEDY YEARS

*I'm telling you, that public accommodations provision has got to get in that bill, or we're going to have one hell of a war in this country.*

*—Louis Martin to Bobby Kennedy*

When Kennedy took office, he did not have enough support in Congress "to pass a Mother's Day Resolution," as Martin put it. Given Kennedy's razor-thin victory and his party's loss of twenty-one seats in the House of Representatives, the incoming president lacked the support to pass any controversial legislation, including any serious civil rights measures. Yet in the winter of 1960, as the Kennedy team prepared to occupy the White House, the burning issue of civil rights could not be ignored, and the Kennedy brothers knew they would have to respond swiftly, even if only symbolically at first.[1]

For all their idealism and campaign promises, the civil rights arena was for them foreign ground. Bobby Kennedy later frankly admitted to Burke Marshall, his appointee to head up civil rights in the Justice Department, that he didn't know much about the issue. His older brother seemed to know even less. One day in August, John Kennedy had told Harris Wofford, as the two were hurrying downtown in Kennedy's convertible: "Now, in ten minutes, tick off the ten things that a president ought to do to clean up this goddamn civil rights mess." The regular reappearance in the press of black American students demanding simple freedoms was an international embarrassment that put new pressure on the incoming administration. Moreover, Kennedy found the new civil disobedience tactics alien to his way of thinking. Wofford knew this, but he felt as well that the president-elect showed he was willing to learn.[2]

In December, during the transition just before the inauguration, Roy Wilkins, then executive secretary of the NAACP, publicly complained about reports that the incoming administration was not going to push for legislation ending segregation after all, contrary to what was promised during the campaign. Martin and Wofford urged the president-elect to meet right away with Wilkins, who had remained a friend of Martin's since their early acquaintance in the 1930s. Before the month was out, the president-elect sat down with Wilkins at a New York hotel and explained that while he was not ready to risk offending a hostile Congress by proposing serious civil rights legislation in the immediate future, he would keep his promises on the issuing of strong executive orders.[3]

ঌ ঌ ঌ

Two days after the election, Sargent Shriver, assigned to supervise research on potential Cabinet and sub-Cabinet appointees, persuaded Martin to share that task with Wofford and attorneys Adam Yarmolinsky and Thomas L. Farmer. Martin was surprised to discover that Kennedy campaigners had been so focused on the election they had done little planning to staff key administration posts. He thought his role in the upcoming "talent hunt" could be an important contribution in launching the Kennedy administration.[4]

The Kennedy people recognized that racial integration at the higher levels of government was woefully inadequate. At the end of the Eisenhower years, one had to look very hard to detect any blacks at all not only in the White House but among the upper levels of any federal department. In both the Agriculture and Defense Departments, for example, the portion of black employees amounted to less than one percent of the many thousands of employees in the higher civil service grades. At the very highest pay level, only two black employees could be found. Even the civil rights branch of the Justice Department was run by white men.[5]

Appalled to find that, as he put it, "there were barely enough black staffers in many government agencies for a decent poker game," Martin began to compile a list of potential minority appointees. Working with his friend Judge Irvin Mollison, then one of the very few black judges in the federal system (President Truman had appointed him to the Customs Court in New York City in 1945), Martin collected resumes of what amounted to a *Who's Who* of African Americans in academia, law, and politics. When the new administration took office, the list already ran to some 750 names. "I had a candidate for almost every job in the federal government," Martin later said. "I turned out to be an inside agitator. I don't give a darn what the job was, I came up with a Negro. It got to be a joke in a way." [6]

Shriver's recruitment committee met almost daily for nearly six months to consider candidates for more than three thousand appointments in the federal bureaucracy. Tackling the problem agency by agency, they were nearly overwhelmed by the enormity of the task. Focusing on the institutional racism that had admitted only a few blacks to significant positions, Martin used the two-hour morning meetings with the Shriver committee to advance the principle of equal opportunity and to propose black candidates for a wide spectrum of jobs.

Occasionally an agency administrator would respond to Martin's recommendation of a black candidate by saying the appointment was impossible. "I'm so sorry," Martin would reply, "I'll have to tell the president that you couldn't do it." Often the administrator would squirm and then explain that he did not mean that he could not do it. "Well, what the hell did you say?" was Martin's standard reply.[7]

Martin had to consider the importance of loyalty and cooperation as he tapped black prospects, especially for the higher posts. Top civil servants in the federal bureaucracy, he learned, were often in a position to thwart policy changes and eviscerate a new president's programs. He became more aware of the enormous power of bureaucrats in the Bureau of the Budget Office (now called Office of Management and Budget), who screened items in the budget requests of each government department and often proposed cuts and changes. If not properly monitored, such alterations could subvert policy objectives and cause a new administration serious political problems.

Martin knew that members of Congress, particularly committee chairmen in the Senate and the House, also influenced appointments. A recommendation of a candidate for a job from a powerful chairman always carried great weight with the administration's department heads, even though they were the president's appointees. Chairmen therefore had to be handled with great care.

Before the election, Martin had told Senator Kennedy that he never wanted to join another campaign in which the question of appointing a black to the Cabinet or the Supreme Court was still an issue. What he wanted was a commitment by the administration to move toward making precisely such top-level appointments. Although his colleagues agreed that such a policy would be desirable, he never received a firm commitment. Nevertheless, Martin, Mollison, and others were determined to find blacks for policy-making positions, and in the end many of their candidates were appointed.

Martin also researched the backgrounds of nonminority candidates. Shriver assigned him to compile information on Robert S. McNamara, then president of the Ford Motor Company, who was being considered for Secretary of Defense. With his long-time contacts in Detroit and experience with auto industry management and labor, Martin was able to gather considerable material on McNamara for Shriver to take to his first meeting with the candidate in Detroit. Martin was surprised to discover that McNamara had already put together an enormous and meticulously researched list of potential appointees for the positions under his charge.[8]

The names of potential black appointees were sometimes advanced by others, subject to Martin's review. Postmaster General J. Edward Day told Shriver's recruitment committee he was willing to appoint a black to a top position and suggested Christopher Scott, a high-ranking Los Angeles postal official. The proposal cleared, and Scott was soon appointed the first black deputy postmaster general. Similarly, White House press secretary Pierre Salinger informed Martin that a black spokesman for the U.S. State Department was a possibility and asked whether he had heard of Minneapolis newsman and author Carl Rowan.

For a decade, Carl Rowan had been traveling to every part of the country and around the world as one of the Minneapolis *Tribune*'s star reporters. He had covered the United Nations and traveled throughout Southeast Asia, where during the mid-1950s he had made speeches defending American democracy against pro-Soviet critics. At home, he had been covering the civil rights revolution as well, in the course of which he, too, had gotten to know most of the leading figures. In the preceding few years, he had interviewed several of the rising new leaders of Africa, and during the 1960 campaign he had grilled both Nixon and Kennedy on their civil rights positions. Of course Rowan was on Martin's list.[9]

When he called Minneapolis, Martin learned that Rowan was in Pasadena, California, covering the Rose Bowl game. Martin tracked him down at his hotel. Awakened from a nap, Rowan heard a voice at the other end of the line say, "Hey Carl, Louis Martin here. President Kennedy wants you to join his administration." Martin explained that Kennedy wanted Rowan to consider becoming the State Department's spokesman.

Rowan was not immediately enthusiastic. He was making very good money as a lecturer in addition to what he earned from his *Tribune* assignments, and he figured that taking the job in Washington would cut his income in half. He went to his friend, Senator Hubert Humphrey, for advice.

Humphrey told him to take nothing less than the job of deputy assistant secretary of state but also added this: "There's never been a black at that level in State. Those stuffy sonsabitches haven't recognized that black Americans exist. If you aren't willing to come in and help change things, nothing is ever going to change."

Rowan called Martin back to say he'd take it if it meant the second position directly under the assistant secretary of state for public affairs. Martin called him back an hour later: the job was his.[10]

ख ख ख

As he continued to fill administration positions, Martin began to wonder what specific post he would call his own. Immediately after the election, all of the Kennedy campaign apparatus and operations were brought under the umbrella of the Democratic National Committee. The president chose John Bailey of Connecticut as DNC chairman. Bailey had been the first state chairman to support Kennedy's nomination and had assisted the campaign in its early efforts to win support from other state chairmen. But while Bailey was made the titular head of the DNC, the person really in charge was Robert Kennedy, according to Martin. "I had learned early that the Kennedy family was like a closed corporation, and they ran everything. Bobby was the uncrowned king of politics and either made the decisions or ratified those made by others."[11]

As if his influence over the DNC's political operations was not enough, Bobby Kennedy was also appointed, somewhat against his wishes, to the post of attorney general. Heading up the Justice Department's activities meant that on touchy civil rights matters, the younger brother would be able to deflect blame and controversy away from the president. Martin would soon find himself working closely with Bobby in this area as well.

In the DNC office, Bailey struck Martin as a man who cherished his rank-and-file acceptance as a smart political operator with no interest in high society or academia. This put him in sharp contrast with some of the so-called Camelot crowd that surrounded JFK. "Sometimes it seemed that Bailey sought to appear more of a cigar-chomping, smoke-filled-room character than he really was," Martin remembered. "He drank brandy and could stay up all night telling funny stories about politicians, mostly his Irish friends."[12]

Bailey decided that Martin and Charles Roche, a Boston-Irish roommate of Robert Kennedy's at Harvard, should have titles. After deliberating for two days, Martin and Roche decided on the title of deputy chairman. Bailey agreed that both men should be called "deputy" to distinguish them from vice chairmen, who were not salaried. Martin and Roche became good friends and worked well together. Neither took himself too seriously, and both were effective at working with people from all walks of life. Since the president and his aides considered the DNC to be an extension of their own staff, Martin and Roche received permanent White House passes and spent some part of every day in the West Wing of the White House or in the Executive Office Building a few yards away. When Martin faced surgery in 1963, soon after President Kennedy's assassination, it was Roche who gave blood for the transfusion. After that, Roche liked to tease Martin about the black man's "Irish blood." [13]

The theme of black and white cooperation had long marked Martin's thinking, at least as far back as his work with the Detroit labor movement. It was therefore a natural fit when he was asked to assume responsibility for the DNC Nationalities Division after Michel Cieplinski, who had established the division during the 1948 campaign at the request of President Truman, was appointed to the State Department in 1961. A former newspaper publisher in Poland, Cieplinski had fled to the United States when Hitler invaded and built a new career in American politics. In his new position at the State Department, Cieplinski continued to recruit ethnic minorities, this time for appointments to State. In this role he would encounter one of the few black foreign service officers in the department, a young man named Eddie Williams. A few years later, as head of the State Department's equal opportunity office during the Johnson administration, Williams would assist Martin in his ongoing search for black appointments. In 1972, Martin would ask Williams to run an enterprising new political research and training institution he helped to found, the Joint Center for Political Studies. [14]

Feeling that his work with ethnic whites should not be a one-man operation, Martin urged New York mayor Robert Wagner to serve as the honorary chairperson of the nationalities division. Wagner could utilize his contacts among ethnic groups on the East Coast and provide something of a buffer for Martin. Wagner promised to accept the post if the request came from President Kennedy. Martin took matters into his own hands and drafted a press release stating Wagner's acceptance of the post at Kennedy's request. He even included a statement by Kennedy praising Wagner and stressing the importance of the Nationalities Division. When he took the draft to the

White House, Kenny O'Donnell, the president's appointments secretary, read it carefully and then said, "Let it go."

"Doesn't the president have to clear words put in his mouth?" Martin wanted to know.

"Hell no. Put it out," O'Donnell replied. The following Sunday the story was front-page news in the *New York Times*.[15]

The DNC receptionists received a new instruction: "Look, if anybody comes in here with a funny name, give him to Louis." In addition to focusing on his regular constituency, Martin collected the names of Italians, Poles, Lithuanians, and people of other ethnic groups to be considered for appointments. He had not known till then how sensitive Italians were about Hollywood stereotypes of them as gangsters or how sensitive Poles were to so-called Polish jokes. Roman Pucinski, a Polish-American congressman from Chicago, promised Martin that he would be available for help if ethnic whites objected to having him as their DNC spokesman. In turn, Martin helped process the names of ethnic whites submitted by Cieplinski as candidates for appointment to the State Department.[16]

After the inauguration, JFK decided he wanted a permanent advisor in the White House to handle civil rights issues. Wofford thought Martin should get the position and sent a memo to the president recommending him, "since the Negro community is a particularly complex, isolated, and politically important one, and since a sensitive Negro is able to hear and sense the mood of his community better than a white man." But Kennedy rejected the advice because he considered Martin more valuable to him working from the DNC. The only black staffer Kennedy did bring into the official White House circle was Andrew Hatcher, appointed associate press secretary. In this capacity, Hatcher worked directly under Pierre Salinger, and on a few occasions it was Hatcher whom the public saw as the White House spokesperson. For its time, this was a bold gesture, even though Hatcher's role was essentially symbolic.[17]

Working out of the DNC offices, Martin could safely function as the White House's unofficial black civil rights liaison and advisor, an off-the-record position that he immediately made use of. His first White House assignment in this area came from Ted Sorensen. Apparently Roy Wilkins's early meeting with Kennedy had led Wilkins to submit detailed civil rights proposals to the White House. "Ted asked me to study the proposals and meet later to discuss them prior to his meeting with Wilkins," Martin recalled. "This was a piece of cake, and I entered into an analysis of the proposals and their political implications with great interest and enthusiasm." He did not know it then, but this task would become an integral part of his duties for the next eight years.[18] Martin was entering what would often be a difficult balancing act. As he later recalled, "The most difficult aspect of this situation was to advance the civil rights agenda and provide a response for the White House that would not promote promises that could not be made good. JFK was insistent on the latter point.... There were many times, of course, when I felt he carried that principle too far."[19]

Before he entered the White House, Kennedy was already being pressured on civil rights not only by the NAACP but also by all the major groups in the movement. King, like Wilkins, had become worried that the campaign promises might have been only that, and he issued public warnings that blacks would have to hold the president-elect's feet to the fire.[20]

In December, Wofford gave the president-elect a comprehensive proposal on civil rights strategy, tempering his and Martin's convictions about the need for change with political realism. Given congressional intransigence, Wofford suggested a series of executive orders to end discrimination in federal housing and federal hiring, combined with new and aggressive Justice Department action to enforce school desegregation and voting rights. He did not suggest serious new legislation for precisely the reasons JFK had mentioned to Roy Wilkins. Martin considered the proposal reasonable. As Wofford remembered it, Martin "didn't press for the president to go forth and ask for legislation the first year, when he would have been defeated, and the defeat would draw down the capital of Kennedy and the civil rights movement."[21]

The Senate's leadership included James Eastland, a Mississippian who did not muffle his segregationist views or refrain from making demeaning racial slurs while serving as chairman of the Senate Judiciary Committee. When Bobby Kennedy approached him about the committee's upcoming review of Burke Marshall, the nominee for assistant attorney general for civil rights, the senator replied, "I'd vote against Jesus Christ if he was nominated to that position."[22]

The Senate's parliamentary rules at the time allowed legislation that was sufficiently unsavory to any determined member to be buried by a nearly unbreakable filibuster—a two-thirds vote was required for cloture. Southern senators had generously employed the filibuster over the years, often to kill civil rights proposals. Early on, civil rights leaders were disappointed with the Kennedy administration's failure to push for a change in this procedure during its first year in office. The leadership of the House Rules Committee, which controlled the movement of House legislation, was also hostile toward civil rights issues and would likely kill any bill that was proposed.[23]

≈ ≈ ≈

Three months into the new administration, Wofford convened the first meeting of a new interagency group, formally titled the Subcabinet Group on Civil Rights, which he would later describe as "an open conspiracy (though never much publicized) to invoke the full power of the Executive Branch against racial discrimination in all parts of American life." Martin was an integral part of the group, which consisted of roughly a dozen representatives from all the major agencies and departments. It began meeting monthly to recommend actions that federal agencies could take to carry out the broad mandate of equal opportunity, bringing criticisms and warnings directly to the president. Some of the civil rights mavens who had been working ad hoc with Wofford saw in this new group a bureaucratic threat to their influence, but Martin was optimistic. "If it gets more horses on the track," he said, "it'll be good."

At the instigation of Wofford's group and others in the administration, the federal government quickly introduced a slew of new policies. It carefully scrutinized segregation practices in the U.S. Employment Service and the Bureau of Apprenticeship and Training, directed that all advertisements for bids to construct postal facilities contain anti-discrimination clauses, forbade racial discrimination in national parks, started extensive programs to recruit qualified blacks for federal employment at all levels through the Civil Service Commission, and required nondiscrimination in university programs funded with federal dollars. The changes came with a speed uncharacteristic of the ponderous federal bureaucracy.[24]

≈ ≈ ≈

As the Kennedy administration took shape, the distinctive personalities of the Kennedy brothers became clear to Martin. He was struck by JFK's charm, a quality that disarmed everyone from bright-eyed college students to frustrated civil rights spokespersons intent on a confrontation. The younger brother was far rougher, at least on the outside. In his political work many considered Bobby ruthless. He could explode at the drop of a hat. During the campaign, Martin had seen his brutal side. "The story was told of a young man seated in the outer office of Bobby's suite, working out a diagram on a big chart," Martin recalled. "When Bobby came in he asked the guy what he was doing. The guy said he was making a campaign organization chart to help clarify the roles and responsibilities of the staffers. Bobby didn't say anything at first, but he called Seigenthaler into his office and told him, 'As soon as that guy finishes that chart, bring it to me and fire him.' "[25]

Within a year of their stormy first meeting, Martin and Bobby Kennedy had developed a trusting relationship. As the challenges of the administration began to test the young attorney general, Martin felt, he grew in understanding and feeling both for the civil rights movement and for people in general. Martin watched him grow in this direction throughout what were to be the last eight years of his life. Seeing him with his children at Hickory Hill, his home in McLean, Virginia, was a revelation for Martin, who came to believe that much of Bobby's gruffness and arrogance was a cover-up for his sensitivity. "I think Bobby was sort of a visceral type," Martin later said. "He was a very strong Catholic. I always took the position that if you could get whatever your issue was inside his little moral framework, you got it. But if you did not, you were stuck." [26]

In spite of their differences, Martin was struck by the closeness between Bobby and his older brother. No member of the White House staff could come between them. After major Cabinet Room meetings, the president and his brother would go off by themselves to talk privately. Martin remarked that during the many special meetings he arranged so that the president could speak with black organizations, "It didn't matter what went on in the meeting. What you had to do when the meeting was over was go into the Oval Office, where JFK and Bobby were, to find out what was really important." [27]

Martin marveled at John Kennedy's nearly photographic memory. In the limousine on their way to a Delta Sigma Theta convention in Washington, D.C., in 1963, Martin gave the president a briefing paper on the history and membership of what was perhaps the most influential black sorority and philanthropic organization in the country. Kennedy had time only to skim the pages before handing them back. Somewhat apprehensive at what the president might say to a group of middle-class black women, Martin was astonished when the president moved smoothly through his speech, reeling off every one of the background paper's statistics and hard facts.[28]

Early in the administration's first year Martin impressed upon the president that it would be important for him to get to know the Urban League's new head, Whitney Young. The resulting encounter between John Kennedy and

Young, a vibrant young social worker who had just been appointed a few months earlier, reflected something of the character of both men. After Young arrived, Kennedy decided to give him what Martin called "the full-dress treatment"—inviting him and Martin and a few others over to the first family's living quarters for tea and a more relaxed discussion. Young filled Kennedy in on the Urban League and its purpose, and Kennedy, exuding charm, asked the visitor for his help in getting liberal measures through Congress. Martin recalled the moment in his memoirs: "Flashing through my mind as Whitney talked was the thought that he was as much of a politician as JFK. Here were two young, intellectually sharp, handsome, and personable Americans who lived in two different worlds, but shared a life mission, a noble idealism about the future of their native land. I wondered how far Whitney would have gone if he had been born white." He added, "This meeting between Whitney and JFK was the start of a great friendship." [29]

What happened on the way out of that meeting was, for Martin, equally illuminating about Kennedy's outlook and personal style. Walking down a corridor, the group, including the president, saw McGeorge Bundy of the National Security Council standing near the elevator. The president whispered to Martin, "When we get in the elevator, ask McGeorge Bundy if he resigned from the Metropolitan Club." Bobby Kennedy had resigned from the club because of its policy of racial discrimination, and pressure had been exerted on other administration members to follow suit. Such practices at Washington's major clubs led fifty members of the administration to contribute $1,000 each to organize a new club—the Federal City Club. As they descended in the elevator, Martin asked Bundy about his club. "Everyone laughed," he recalled, "and Bundy turned red as a beet." [30]

≈ ≈ ≈

On March 6, 1961, Kennedy issued Executive Order 10925, establishing the Committee on Equal Employment Opportunity, with Vice President Johnson as chairman. The committee's charge was "to permanently remove from government employment and work performed for the government every trace of discrimination." In this forum Lyndon Johnson began to win over black critics who had been skeptical about him for years. The potential impact of this committee was enormous—more than 20 million workers were employed by government contractors at that time. [31]

Johnson's appointment to chair this committee pleased Wofford, who had realized more than others in the inner circle how valuable the Texan's political clout on the Hill could be to their larger aim of getting sensitive legislation passed. Nevertheless, Johnson's relationship with the president's brother, which had gotten off to a rocky start at the Democratic convention, never smoothed out. Considerably older and more experienced than Bobby Kennedy, Johnson did not like the Kennedy family arrangement, which gave Bobby a say in nearly every White House decision.

Martin recalled a high-level meeting on civil rights that the attorney general and vice president as well as the president were attending. Realizing he needed to catch a plane, the president turned the meeting over to Johnson. Not long afterward, Bobby Kennedy, who was standing by the door to the Oval Office, beckoned to Martin. He wanted to leave early and had become impatient with the vice president's long talk.

"Tell him to shut up," Bobby whispered to Martin.

Stunned, Martin did nothing at first.

Bobby repeated, "Tell him to shut up." How could he, Louis Martin, silence the vice president of the United States to end his meeting? Between a rock and a hard place, he walked over to Johnson, received an odd stare from him, and then sat down. To his relief, the meeting soon closed.[32]

≈ ≈ ≈

As his unofficial civil rights portfolio took shape, Martin put to good use the many friendships he had formed with leading civil rights figures over the years. He had not yet met Martin Luther King, Jr., face to face, although he had begun speaking to King on the phone, especially to discuss federal strategies that he and others in Wofford's group felt could dovetail with the goals of the movement. In keeping with the White House's emphasis on voting rights, during the administration's first few months he spoke with King and others about the necessity for blacks to take greater advantage of the political process. "Blacks have no capital with which to produce great economic power," he remembered telling several of them, "but we have a lot of warm bodies, and each one has a vote."[33]

The new administration had not made clear, however, what it was going to do legislatively. Even Wofford, who remained dedicated to every aspect of the cause, concluded early on that if Kennedy had asked Congress for things he had called for in the campaign, he would have been stopped cold by the House Rules Committee or a Senate filibuster.[34]

Few leaders in the civil rights movement had sympathy for the White House's political problems. Although King remained optimistic about the new crowd in the White House, he had already made public his view that the administration must not wait before taking legislative action on every area of civil rights and that he and the black community generally would hold it to a very high standard. Bobby Kennedy and his aides were meeting, of course, with a number of civil rights leaders, if only to tell them that they would have to wait before any legislative action was possible. King had not been invited to these meetings, one of which was an important gathering held at the Justice Department in early March. Frustrated, King tried to obtain a private meeting with the president himself, only to be turned down. Preparing for the ill-fated Bay of Pigs invasion and facing other foreign crises, the president pleaded that his time could not be spared.[35]

Martin and his colleagues in the interagency civil rights group understood the White House's dilemma, but they also knew they couldn't keep the renowned leader waiting forever. Moreover, the Justice Department wanted to know what King thought of its plans for pursuing voting rights suits and other actions. They all wanted at least to send him a positive signal. King's high profile was a major sticking point. Any official White House visit, any agreement or demand made before a government official, would be sure to receive media attention, putting the administration in a vulnerable position. Accepting this reality, Martin came up with a solution: bring King and the attorney general together at a quiet, off-the-record encounter on neutral ground. This would give the White House a chance to assess King and the prospects for a productive relationship with him before making any public gestures. Martin knew from his early experiences in Detroit, especially during the explosive labor strikes, that confidential meetings could go a long way toward building coalitions among factional leaders without the destructive nuisance of public posturing and rhetoric. And a good meal went even further toward relieving tension. He argued that if informal political meetings with King were not going to work out for the Kennedy team, it would be better to find out right away.[36]

The Mayflower Hotel, an elegant place in downtown Washington, was popular with the Kennedy crowd. Martin made arrangements for a luncheon meeting there in April, to be paid for out of his DNC funds. Present from the administration were Martin, the attorney general, Burke Marshall, and a handful of other Justice Department officials. According to Martin, King brought along only Stanley Levison, a white attorney and frequent advisor to King, so that King and Martin were the only two black people at the meeting. Levison's presence further justified Martin's decision to keep the meeting secret.

In time, J. Edgar Hoover would apparently convince the president that Levison was an active communist. In a period marked by the building of the Berlin Wall and the Cuban missile crisis, this gave the White House one more reason to treat any direct contact with King as a sensitive matter.[37]

Marshall explained to King the Justice Department's immediate plans: because the federal government had little latitude in enforcing school desegregation, the *Brown* decision notwithstanding, the White House felt its best chance of success in securing equal rights in a variety of areas was to focus on voting rights. Marshall's attorneys were filing suits in southern counties already and had begun sending federal agents to collect evidence in person of discriminatory registration tactics. King agreed that this kind of work was necessary and important. Also raised at the meeting for King's consideration was a proposal for a substantial new voter registration effort that would both increase the number of black voters and provide the Justice Department with further instances of discriminatory violations. "There was a need now to mobilize blacks to register and to put all the community, state, and national pressure that could be mustered to force changes," Martin recalled. "We felt a massive educational and propaganda job was required."[38]

Martin and Wofford knew this would require a lot of money, which, for many reasons, could not come from the government, so Wofford and Marshall had already begun feeling out the major nonprofit foundations for support. They had heard back that the project would be supported as long as it was not tied to either political party. King was receptive to the idea of the project. As the meeting broke up, King smiled on seeing that the bill for the luncheon was being paid by the sole black Kennedy insider in the group.[39]

Throughout the Mayflower meeting, King had listened quietly to everything Marshall and the others had to say, without making any demands. Martin was impressed by King's uncanny combination of intellect, eloquence, and moral passion. Looking back at this and other meetings with him, Martin would recall King years later with these thoughts: "He could walk into a crowded room and remain unnoticed until he opened his mouth. He had a natural eloquence and the words seem to roll off his tongue in private conversation as well as in formal speech with benign authority." Martin would comment later that in a movement filled with strong personalities and powerful leaders, King's integrity as an activist was perhaps his most valuable quality: "It was not King telling anybody what to do, but to do as I do," he said, adding, "He was an intellectual, and he did these things he did not have to do—his legitimacy was beyond question."[40]

# A VOICE FOR CIVIL RIGHTS

Within a few weeks of that meeting, as Martin put it, "the wheels were rolling" to get the voter registration effort organized. Throughout the summer, King's SCLC and the young students of the recently formed Student Nonviolent Coordinating Committee (SNCC) discussed the voter registration effort, hoping to put together the most coordinated approach possible. At first a few student leaders suggested that collaborating in a plan that came out of the White House meant selling out—the men in Washington, for all they knew, wanted to undermine their direct-action campaign. But by August, SNCC and the rest decided to participate fully in the voter registration project while continuing their protest action for desegregation. As they all later discovered, the voter drive, particularly in rural counties, was no sell-out and in fact required a good deal of physical courage in the face of hostile attacks.[41]

By the end of that summer, the five major civil rights groups—SCLC, SNCC, the NAACP, the National Urban League, and the Congress of Racial Equality (CORE)—had agreed to work together on what was now called the Voter Education Project. Funding had been offered by several foundations, notably the Taconic Foundation in New York, and for tax purposes it would be handled through the Southern Regional Council, an interracial, nonpartisan group dedicated to advancing equal rights.

It had been agreed earlier that whoever was chosen to head up the voter effort would have to be acceptable to King, Wilkins, and Whitney Young. Not long after the Mayflower meeting, Martin got a call from Wilkins, asking what he knew about a young man named Wiley Branton. Martin soon learned that Branton was an NAACP attorney active in Arkansas and had a fine reputation among fellow civil rights lawyers. By the following spring, Branton was officially inaugurated as director of the Voter Education Project, which was headquartered in Atlanta. In Martin's view this was ideal, since most of the black political leaders in Atlanta had Republican backgrounds, giving the project a bipartisan neutrality. The White House thereafter kept the project at arm's length.[42]

*ᘔ ᘔ ᘔ*

Martin's work on appointments continued throughout the three years of the Kennedy administration. He targeted the government's Housing and Home Finance Agency, which he knew Kennedy was hoping to convert into a bona fide Cabinet-level department, for a possible breakthrough. His candidate for administrator of the agency was Robert Weaver. Weaver's resume was impeccable. In addition to his Harvard Ph.D. in economics and his varied and important roles in Roosevelt's Black Cabinet, he had acquired a reputation as a leading housing expert. Martin had worked extensively with Weaver during the discrimination investigations of job transfers to war industries during World War II. Two months before the election, John Kennedy had met privately with Weaver (who by 1960 was also chair of the NAACP's board) and Roy Wilkins at his Georgetown home.[43]

When Martin phoned Weaver to ask if he was open to the possibility of being tapped for the federal agency spot, Weaver at first did not understand that Martin was, indeed, talking about the job as head of the entire agency. When this was clarified, Weaver accepted. He was approved swiftly as administrator of the Housing and Home Finance Agency in 1961, becoming the first black person to head a federal agency in the nation's history. For Martin, the appointment confirmed his hope that at long last the American presidency would have not just black advisors but black decision makers.

Persistent rumors about the housing agency's elevation to Cabinet status led political observers to ask President Kennedy if he would name Weaver to head the future Cabinet department. His affirmative response at a press conference aroused angry opposition from southern, anti-civil-rights forces that were poised to block just such a development. Moreover, they warned Kennedy that if he signed the executive order banning housing discrimination, which he had campaigned on, they would block the creation of the new department. Kennedy was not about to give up on both Weaver and the housing order simply to save the new department. Weaver stayed, but both the new department and the housing order were delayed.[44]

Martin also was absorbed in helping the president make good on his campaign promise—so enthusiastically received at the Harlem rally—to bring blacks into the federal judiciary. He asked Andrew Bradley, a Pennsylvania Democratic party official, to recommend a candidate for a federal judgeship in his state. "There's a guy out here who headed the NAACP, a lawyer from Yale, smart as hell," Bradley replied a week later. "I think this is a guy you might take a look at." The man was A. Leon Higginbotham, Jr., a distinguished Philadelphia lawyer. As an undergraduate at Purdue University, like dozens of other black students on campus, he had been forced to live in a dormitory attic without heat. When Higginbotham had finally summoned the nerve to confront the university president directly, he was told that the law did not require the university either to have "coloreds" or to give them heat.

Martin telephoned Higginbotham, secured his resume, and asked him to come to Washington. Finding him to be a very attractive judicial candidate with great presence and verbal skills, he introduced him to the attorney general, who was equally impressed. "We thought we had it all set," Martin recalled, "but we forgot to check Higginbotham's age. You have to be 35. He was only 34." All was not lost, however. Martin remembered that at one meeting of Shriver's recruitment committee a southern representative of the Federal Trade Commission had promised: "I'll take one of your boys, too, if he's qualified." Accordingly, Higginbotham served as a federal trade commissioner before his appointment as a federal judge, beginning what would turn out to be a long, distinguished judicial career. In 1995, he would receive the Presidential Medal of Freedom, the highest award the government gives to civilians.[45]

ን‌ል ን‌ል ን‌ል

The White House executive orders, laudable as they were, did little to restrain the escalating civil rights confrontations under way in both the South and the North. Faced with implacable political forces, the Kennedy administration publicly affirmed its support for the decisions of the U.S. courts. Speaking at the University of Georgia on May 8, 1961, two days after the admission of two black students (Charlayne Hunter and Hamilton Holmes) after months of turmoil, the attorney general reiterated the administration's position. He maintained that his personal belief was not the issue and that the Supreme Court's decision was the law.[46] He urged "amicable voluntary solutions" but declared that if court orders were circumvented, the Department of Justice would act. Bobby Kennedy made this message more palatable to his southern audience by criticizing northerners who opposed discrimination in the South but overlooked it in their own lives. The students applauded.[47] A day later, Martin wrote to him:

> Dear Honorary Brother:
>
> Your speech in Georgia was a peach. Congratulations are pouring in from brothers everywhere, here and abroad. If you keep this up, one of these days I might be able to go back home. Seriously, you showed great statesmanship, and I am honored to call you "honorary brother."
>
> Louis Martin[48]

The administration's commitment to enforcing court orders would have remained hollow if individual blacks had allowed local laws and local officials to intimidate them into silence on the matter. In May, the first of a series of activist bus rides, dubbed "Freedom Rides," was initiated in Washington, D.C., to trace a course through the South all the way to New Orleans. The aim of the project, headed by CORE director James Farmer, was to call the administration's bluff and force federal intervention. The sixteen-year-old federal court decision banning segregation in interstate travel had been openly ignored throughout the South. Many of the young Freedom Riders, both black and white, were members of SNCC. Farmer, who had been fighting discrimination as a CORE leader and student of Gandhian tactics since 1942, prepared the riders as if for an exam. Before they embarked, social scientists told them about southern customs, lawyers told them their legal standing, and several NAACP activists told them, "You're going to get yourselves killed." They rehearsed mob scenarios and practiced ways to take a beating without getting killed.

When the first two Freedom Ride buses reached the Alabama border, they were attacked by angry white mobs. One was stoned and then firebombed just outside of Anniston. The occupants of the other bus were savagely beaten by a white mob at the Birmingham bus station; one Freedom Rider, William Barbee, was paralyzed for life. The Birmingham police, under the direction of Commissioner Bull Connor, an avowed racist with a reputation for brutal tactics, were conspicuously absent during the melee. Alabama governor John Patterson publicly blamed the Freedom Riders, suggesting that they had brought the trouble on themselves. At the White House, the president called an emergency meeting with Justice Department officials to deal with the first serious racial violence he had to confront head-on. Bobby Kennedy tried to persuade Farmer to stop the rides for a cooling-off period. But the Freedom Riders were determined to continue.

Alarmed at the possibility of more widespread disorder and possible deaths, the attorney general sent John Seigenthaler, his administrative assistant, to Governor Patterson to secure protection for the riders. Patterson, who had been a Kennedy supporter in the 1960 campaign, made a hedged promise to guard the riders' safety during the trip from Birmingham to Montgomery, and Floyd Mann, head of the Alabama Highway Patrol, promised to guard the single remaining bus until it reached the jurisdiction of the Montgomery police.

On May 20, when the bus reached the Montgomery city limits, all police protection disappeared, and a white mob attacked the riders. Seigenthaler, who had been following the bus in a car, tried to rescue a young woman who was being brutalized, but he was knocked unconscious and left on the ground for some time before being hospitalized. Mann, who had also been following the bus, tried to stop the mob and belatedly called for state troopers. The Montgomery police never showed up. Realizing that Patterson had not kept his word, the administration ordered federal troops to Alabama immediately to protect the lives of the riders and to demonstrate the federal government's commitment to enforcing court rulings. In his public statements, Patterson continued his resistance to federal authority. Relations between Washington and the government of Alabama reached a state of open hostility.

Meanwhile, the administration quietly advised SNCC leaders to abandon direct action for a season and focus on voter registration. The advice was rejected, and Freedom Rides continued throughout the summer. On May 29, at the suggestion of King, the attorney general asked the Interstate Commerce Commission to issue regulations banning segregation in transportation and in all interstate facilities. Under intense pressure from the Justice Department and after an entire summer of violent confrontations, the Interstate Commerce Commission complied on September 22, 1961.[49]

≈ ≈ ≈

The fall of that year found Martin busy considering black candidates for federal judicial appointments. One name that naturally came to mind was that of his friend Thurgood Marshall, who by this point in his career as the director-counsel of the NAACP Legal Defense and Educational Fund was so well known that the media had dubbed him "Mr. Civil Rights." Marshall had successfully argued the landmark *Brown* case, as well as 30 other cases, before the U.S. Supreme Court.

Martin had openly stated during the campaign that he wanted to see a black sitting on the Supreme Court. But although Marshall would one day break the High Court's color barrier, Martin recalled that in 1961, as a candidate for appointment, "Thurgood Marshall was not, at that moment in the early days, the number-one guy in the thoughts of most people." Simply put, Marshall was viewed as a leader among the civil rights forces and therefore the last man on earth likely to be confirmed by the southerners in the U.S. Senate. Martin had also heard through Marshall's friends that he was not interested in a federal judgeship. But the idea of seating "Mr. Civil Rights" on a federal court was too appealing to abandon, so regardless of the obstacles, Martin circulated the idea persistently among the White House's inner circle.[50]

Eventually the attorney general invited Marshall to meet with him, having decided that he could offer him, at best, a judgeship on the federal district court in New York. When Marshall declined the offer, the attorney general wanted to know why. Marshall explained that anything less than a circuit court position, one of which he knew was vacant, was of no interest to him. Kennedy told him that seat was no longer available. The rather unpleasant conversation ended abruptly, with Kennedy startled and offended.[51]

By a fortunate coincidence, Martin was at New York's Idlewild Airport two days later and ran into Marshall at a snack bar there. "What can you say about the language you used with my attorney general?" Martin asked him.

"As far as I can remember," Marshall answered, "all I said was, 'Go to hell,' and believe it or not, I can do better than that."

"Thurgood, I want to know now, what does it take to move you? What about this judgeship?"

"I'm not going to do it. I've got to be a circuit judge, or I don't take anything."[52] Marshall emphasized that he considered a seat on a circuit court of appeals "a hell of a job," adding that he'd take it "any way I can get it."

Martin remembered that Marshall's former colleague William Hastie, beside whom he had fought many NAACP battles, had already been appointed by President Truman to a circuit court judgeship. He wondered if Marshall was showing a "sensitivity" about coming in at a lower level than Hastie did. Regardless, Martin felt reassured about Marshall's interest in the higher position. "I felt I had pinned Thurgood down," he recalled, "and I could get to work on the project with no misgivings."[53]

Martin went back to Washington and plied the attorney general. As he later recalled, "A day or so later when I mentioned Thurgood as an excellent candidate for the circuit court whose appointment would strengthen our ties with blacks, Bobby shocked me by his response. He said that I was out of my mind and had no idea of the political realities in the Senate, which had to consent to such a presidential appointment. He also noted that Thurgood's legal experience had been limited to civil rights cases. This issue came up several years later when I discussed with LBJ the possibility of Thurgood going to the Supreme Court." Martin recognized that the attorney general was probably on target—the NAACP, in Martin's experience, "was no more popular among some senators than the Communist Party."[54]

Nevertheless, Martin was unwilling to rest his case. Referring to Bobby Kennedy, he remembered, "I just stayed on him. You know how you do it, you start talking to everybody that's close to him. I had a campaign on to get it straight."[55]

Two weeks later Bobby Kennedy telephoned him. "Well, I think I might go for the court," he announced. The vague reference momentarily baffled Martin. "You remember—Thurgood?" Kennedy asked him.

"Oh my gosh," Martin responded, "You don't mean—"

"Yes, I think I might," Kennedy answered, and then gave Martin the go-ahead to telephone Marshall with the good news. Reaching him at his vacation spot in New England, Martin filled him in, adding "The last thing you had better do is tell anybody else about it." Marshall soon heard from the president.

"Did you call my brother the things it is reported you said to him?" the president asked.

"And more than that," Marshall replied.

"Well, he probably brought it on himself," the president said, and then offered Marshall the circuit court position.[56]

To secure Marshall's confirmation, President Kennedy struck a deal with Senator Eastland, who desired that his former college roommate and fellow Mississippian, William Harold Cox, be honored with a district judgeship as one of Kennedy's first judicial appointments. Roy Wilkins and others warned Kennedy that Cox, despite his high rating by the American Bar Association, would be bad news for integration. The attorney general interviewed Cox before the nomination and would later say that he was misled by the nominee's private promise of loyalty to the U.S. Supreme Court and all its rulings. The next few years would show how much damage Cox and a few other Dixie appointees would wreak on the administration's civil rights efforts.[57]

Although Eastland stalled the confirmation for almost a year, as Martin recalled, "Most of our fears about the tough time in store for the appointment of Thurgood Marshall never really materialized. A deal is respected on the Hill, and Senator Eastland went through his angry role according to the script." After long, wrangling hearings, Eastland's Judiciary Committee approved Marshall. On September 11, 1962, the Senate confirmed the appointment by a vote of 54 to 16, placing the most famous black civil rights lawyer in America on the Second Circuit Court of Appeals.[58]

Martin's lobbying for appointments was not always successful. For six months he sought a district judgeship for Marjorie Lawson to reward her for the two years she had spent introducing Kennedy to black leaders and for her assistance during his campaign. Lawson was a well-respected lawyer as well, but Bobby Kennedy was unwilling to find her a district judgeship.

"Either she takes this juvenile court job or else," Robert Kennedy warned Martin. "You handle it, and don't bring it up to me. Get her okay on it."

Martin believed the district judgeship Lawson wanted was not available to her mainly because she was a woman. He felt that the "typical Irish attitude" at the time was to view women as properly dedicated to domestic duties, leaving the political domain to men. "The Irish political machine," he later noted, "was an all-male operation." When Martin conveyed the message to Lawson that the juvenile court was the best he could do, she accepted it.[59]

Because of Martin's persistence, dozens of blacks were appointed to positions that had previously been held only by whites—ambassadorships, judgeships, sub-Cabinet-level positions. Martin sought prominent coverage of these appointments in the black press. Nevertheless, appointments did not mitigate the disappointment many black leaders felt about the administration. Kennedy's failure to come through with the promised civil rights bill was not offset, most felt, by even groundbreaking black appointments, which some dismissed as just a political ploy. Civil rights leaders were not the only ones who knew that executive orders would not be enough and that legislation alone had the power to bring equal opportunity in employment, education, housing, and voting participation. Martin knew it, too.

In the spring of 1962, Wofford left the White House to work with Shriver in the Peace Corps. He urged Kennedy to appoint Martin as his replacement, but the president chose instead to appoint Lee White, an attorney and aide to Ted Sorensen.

ɜ℮ ɜ℮ ɜ℮

In the fall of 1962, the Kennedy White House was again drawn into a violent confrontation in the South. This one would convince the president that his political trade-offs with southern politicians had achieved little for party unity but had caused a costly delay in making civil rights progress.

James H. Meredith, a student at black Jackson State College and an Air Force veteran, had sought to enroll at the University of Mississippi in January 1961 but had been repeatedly denied admission. More than a year of legal battles and appeals elapsed before the U.S. Supreme Court upheld Meredith's right to be admitted to the all-white state university in Oxford. Publicly, Mississippi governor Ross Barnett vowed he would never allow integration of the school. Privately, Barnett knew he would have to accept the High Court's ruling, and he negotiated with Kennedy over how to minimize the political fallout from his racist constituents when the black student was admitted. Barnett asked the president to send in federal troops to escort

Meredith, so that it would appear that Barnett had no choice but to comply. When Kennedy refused, Barnett offered to allow federal marshals to smuggle Meredith onto the 'Ole Miss campus on the evening of September 30. He promised that once Meredith was safely there, he would announce on television Mississippi's compliance with the court order.[60]

On the evening of September 30, unaware that Meredith was already in one of the dormitories, a white mob gathered to harass the federal marshals at the administration building. Eventually numbering more than two thousand, the mob attacked the marshals with guns, bricks, bottles, Molotov cocktails, and a bulldozer. The marshals fought back with tear gas. The Mississippi state police abandoned the scene and, despite Barnett's continued assurances to federal authorities, never returned. In the view of many, the situation resembled a state of civil war.

In the midst of the rioting, the governor made his televised speech. Instead of announcing compliance with the law, he claimed he had just been *told* that federal marshals had placed Meredith on the campus, and he reiterated his position of defiance. The rioting continued for more than nine hours. The federal troops, sent in from Memphis, arrived much too late. By the time it was all over, two people had been killed, and more than 160 federal marshals had been injured.[61]

After the violence subsided, Martin began receiving calls from friends in Mississippi informing him that black troops in the federal contingent assigned to Oxford had been inexplicably removed. "I couldn't find out where these orders were coming from until someone told me that [Mississippi senator John] Stennis, I think, had gotten hold of McNamara or Cy Vance or somebody and told them to get those Negro troops out of there," Martin later said. "I recall getting hold of [Adam] Yarmolinsky and was screaming mad. I raised so much hell Yarmolinsky tried to cool me off." After twenty-four hours had passed, the black troops were restored.[62]

&a. &a. &a.

In early 1963, the White House was hoping to celebrate the 100th anniversary of the Emancipation Proclamation. The official Civil War Centennial Commission had rejected requests to honor the Emancipation with a ceremony as part of its own schedule. At the same time, civil rights leaders were pressuring the White House to use the anniversary to issue a statement, however symbolic, on the need to emancipate Americans from segregation. Toward this end, King was communicating frequently with Martin,

Arthur Schlesinger, Jr., and Lee White, as well as Berl Bernhard of the Civil Rights Commission. All of them advised the president that a public statement was necessary, yet Kennedy was hesitant to step out before the public with what might sound like the promise of major legislation. He had none in the offing.[63]

Martin had an idea and broached it with Lee White. "Hey chief," he said, "how would you like to steal Lincoln's birthday from the Republicans?" It occurred to Martin that a formal reception for eminent black citizens at the White House would be a fitting and newsworthy event. White thought it was a great idea. Martin reasoned that while Kennedy did not have an outstanding record on civil rights, his social strengths in this area were excellent and set him in great contrast to his predecessor, Eisenhower. The Kennedys were gracious hosts and, unlike almost every first couple before them, they made black guests feel welcome in their home. Martin ran the idea past Schlesinger, Bernhard, and other top Kennedy advisors, and all of them supported it. Martin compiled a list of the most sparkling and diverse black guests he could think of, including poet Langston Hughes and singer Sammy Davis, Jr. There would be a secondary political payoff as well: many Republicans would have to celebrate Lincoln's birthday without the most popular black speakers. The Democrats had cornered the market on black celebrities and had co-opted the Republicans' patron saint.[64]

The planning ran into one snag. As always for a White House activity, the guest list had to be cleared for security by the Secret Service, which also meant it was examined by the FBI. The list came back to Martin and Lee White with many of the names rejected—people who had apparently been arrested for civil disobedience actions in the past or were connected with groups that J. Edgar Hoover's office found objectionable. This was hardly surprising, since the list included the names of civil rights leaders and even celebrities who had joined in protests. The Secret Service queried Martin about Langston Hughes's alleged links with communists. The fact that Sammy Davis, Jr., was married to a white woman, Mae Britt, raised sensitive issues as well. In the end, Martin and the others were able to deflect the concerns, and the White House insisted that everyone on the list be invited.[65]

Few blacks had ever been invited to any White House social function, yet here was a whole galaxy of eminent black Americans with the president in one place at one time, raising wine glasses. In all, more than eight hundred attended. Martin had been sure to invite many members of the black press, with the result that the event received very broad coverage in the black community. The president and the first lady threaded their way through the crowd, exchanging greetings. Although Mrs. Kennedy retired early, the president stayed to talk and make friends. Martin felt that the event sent a symbolic message: "The point was made that if the president and first lady could entertain black guests in their home, who were the whites who felt blacks were socially unacceptable in *their* homes?" [66]

❧ ❧ ❧

Despite the highly successful Lincoln reception, as of early 1963 Martin felt that in political terms, the president was more concerned about the condition of Germany than the condition of blacks. A few weeks before the reception he had warned the president that whatever his white advisors were telling him, blacks around the country were on the edge of revolt. It was time, Martin argued, for strong civil rights legislation.[67] Martin had begun his own crusade to push the White House on the issue of desegregating public accommodations—hotels, restaurants, and the like. In a memo to Ted Sorensen, referring to the Interstate Commerce Commission's order a year earlier mandating the desegtgtregation of interstate travel, Martin wrote: "The fact that progress has been made by this administration in integrating air, bus, and railroad terminals and other areas tends to focus more attention on hotels, motels, and other public facilities which have a color bar." [68]

Although Martin's voice on this was a rare one inside the White House, the president was certainly hearing similar warnings from authoritative outsiders. In February, the U.S. Civil Rights Commission, which by now Kennedy had come to view as a group possessing little sense of political realism, submitted a report documenting the fact that civil rights in the South remained in a terrible condition. Several states had actually passed tougher new laws to prevent blacks from voting, the commissioners reported, and police violence was not the exception but the rule. They recommended that the president completely cut all federal funds to Mississippi—more than half a billion dollars—until the state began complying with federal court orders. The president was unwilling to release such a frank report, feeling it would not only worsen matters by raising a public firestorm but also threaten his reelection. In fact, he did his best to downplay its conclusions.[69]

At the same time, however, Kennedy took his first step toward serious civil rights legislation, submitting on February 28 a narrowly tailored voting rights bill aimed at ending the widespread southern practice of so-called literacy tests for voter registrants. These tests, which sometimes amounted to graduate-level exams that the registrars themselves could not have passed, were selectively used to screen out blacks. Kennedy's bill required that literacy tests be limited to proof of sixth-grade reading ability. Expecting much more far-reaching legislation, civil rights advocates were so disappointed that they began to talk about abandoning Kennedy in the next election and throwing their support behind liberal Republican candidates.[70] In any event, the bill was soon killed in Congress. Martin could be pleased, however, that in his lengthy written message introducing the bill, the president had made an unusual appeal to moral principle:

> Therefore, let it be clear... that it is not merely because of the Cold War, and not merely because of the economic waste of discrimination, that we are committed to achieving true equality of opportunity. The basic reason is because it is right.[71]

The last four words of that statement were included at Martin's urging.[72]

≥▲ ≥▲ ≥▲

By 1963, Birmingham, Alabama, a hard-bitten steel-mill town, had already earned a reputation as the most violently racist city in the South. In the previous fifteen years, white extremists had set off bombs at black churches and homes on more than fifty occasions. In January 1963, Rev. Fred Shuttlesworth, King, and others in the movement drafted plans for a major boycott and demonstration that, they hoped, would paralyze the city and draw the whole nation's attention to the problem.[73]

On April 12—Good Friday—King, his aide Ralph Abernathy, and others marched and were promptly arrested. King was put into solitary confinement and kept there for three days. After he was released on bail, he and the protest organizers opened phase two of their plan: 2,000 young black volunteers, ranging in age from six to sixteen, marched in waves toward downtown Birmingham in defiance of the city's ban on black marches. By the time 959 of them had been arrested and thrown in jail like King before them, Bull Connor's police force had run out of paddy wagons.[74]

Over the next several days, as more young people continued to march into town, Connor commanded his police and "irregular" recruits to beat back the children with truncheons, high-pressure fire hoses, and attack dogs. The pressure of the water hoses was calibrated to tear the bark off trees. The police chief publicly expressed his disappointment that Rev. Shuttlesworth had survived a water-hose assault. Photographs and televised images of the mayhem were shown around the world.[75]

Meanwhile, King and others were meeting with the city's officials and leading businessmen, to negotiate the movement's demands. The attorney general sent Burke Marshall down to participate in the talks. After about a week, an agreement was finally reached, including the promise of changes in Birmingham's segregation codes.[76]

Two days later, A.G. Gaston's motel, the unofficial headquarters of Birmingham's civil rights leaders, was bombed, as was the home of King's brother. A small riot ensued. Young blacks who were not attached to the nonviolent movement had had enough. In response Governor George Wallace sent in state troopers, who put down the riot in the style of Bull Connor.[77] The day after the bombings, Martin warned Robert Kennedy in an urgent note: "The accelerated tempo of Negro restiveness, and the rivalry of some leaders for top billing, coupled with the resistance of segregationists, may soon create the most critical state of race relations since the Civil War."[78]

During the weeks that followed, protesters in one southern town after another held mass events and were beaten, jailed, even tortured. On May 31, King sent a telegram to the president requesting a personal audience and immediate actions "to avert a national tragedy." A new sense of urgency had taken hold in the White House.[79]

The next day, Martin received an unexpected call asking him to come to the White House. The president was bringing together a Cabinet-level group to orient him on what the administration ought to do next in response to the latest dispatches from the Negro revolution, as it was then called. When Martin entered the Cabinet Room, he found not only the vice president and attorney general but also Health, Education and Welfare (HEW) Secretary Anthony Celebrezze, Labor Secretary Willard Wirtz, and Lee White, as well as O'Donnell, Sorensen, and several Justice and HEW aides.[80]

After the president took his seat, Bobby motioned to Martin to sit next to him and his brother. Tense and unhappy about the heavily publicized disorders in Birmingham and elsewhere, the president asked officials around the table to interpret what was happening and to suggest how he might respond. After an exchange with Celebrezze, the president turned to Martin.[81]

"We need dramatic action," Martin told the president, "action that will be understood by Negroes as clearly as the picture from Birmingham of Negroes being attacked by police dogs." The mood among blacks, he went on to say, was bad and getting worse by the moment. "It's infuriating Negroes who have local grievances," he pointed out, "and it is doubly infuriating when they find out about these bombings." He went on to warn of potential explosions in New York, Detroit, Chicago, and other northern cities.[82]

As far as he was concerned, Martin told the group, the administration had not done very much to deal with segregation. Right in Washington, he said, several black employees in the administration were being kept out of white neighborhoods and couldn't find housing. "Apparently," Martin told the group, his anger rising, "we don't really want to get to the bottom of this and to demonstrate through action to the American Negro our real concern about all this. We have to do more than make speeches."[83]

Urban unemployment was among the problems on his mind when he said, "I know all you latter-day liberals don't think much of the WPA and the programs of Roosevelt, but I came up under Roosevelt, and I think that that prescription is needed right now for Negroes.... As far as I'm concerned, we ought to figure on putting one billion dollars, some way, into this business of economic relief."[84]

His little speech "caused quite a flurry," Martin recalled. "I kept repeating this 'billion dollars,' and Bobby was sitting next to me and punched me on the leg and whispered to me, 'Well, we might think about half a billion.' He tried to shut me up. But this was a high point of my fight because I was really upset."[85]

The president asked Martin one last time what he felt was needed to avert further violence. "Only action," Martin replied. Celebrezze pointed out that he'd just visited Cleveland and hadn't seen any racial unrest there, attributing this to an interracial committee that had been put together there to keep the peace. Martin interrupted him with this notice: "I've just toured ten cities, including Cleveland, and I want to assure you that Cleveland's going to blow just as quick as anyplace else."[86]

The president intervened to cool off the debate, asking the vice president to add his thoughts. "Louis is right," Johnson told the meeting. Martin was shocked to hear the vice president back him up so strongly. Then again, he thought, this Texan had come up under the New Deal, as he had, and knew what poverty and unemployment were all about. As the turbulent meeting ended, most of the participants agreed with Martin that something had to be done to address drastic economic needs. The president, however, did not indicate one way or the other what he thought of Martin's suggestions.[87]

Moments after the room emptied, Martin was asked into the Oval Office, where he found the president in a huddle with his brother and the vice president. Recording what transpired there in his office journal two weeks later, Martin wrote:

> Bobby and the president told me about the request from Martin Luther King for a private meeting. Both said they wanted to send the civil rights bill to Congress before they met with King. They did not want it to appear that King had told the president what to do.[88]

After two years of hesitating, the president had decided to go forward with the comprehensive civil rights bill he had promised. Martin attended many of the numerous meetings that followed to hammer out elements of the bill and work through the political maneuvering necessary to get it through Congress.[89]

One of the first meetings took place at the attorney general's office on a Saturday afternoon. Martin spoke out on the need to ban discrimination immediately in the nation's hotels, restaurants, and other public places. "I was taking the lead in being sure that we keep in this bill a provision on public accommodations," he later recounted. He insistently reminded those at the meeting that "blacks being turned down at these cafes and lunch counters and all was just so provocative that, in the end, it was going to cause more and more trouble."[90]

Martin plainly told the lawyers and others at the attorney general's office that this kind of discrimination had to be acted on by the federal government, that they could no longer leave it up to the states. He was also worried, he said, that the White House might send insufficiently strong legislation to Congress. "I was very much disturbed by these proposals that would stir up hopes of people and not get anywhere with it," he recalled.[91]

He told the group about an Italian restaurant in Silver Spring, Maryland, that barred blacks. "I live about three blocks from that place," he told them. Referring to the restaurant's owner, he went on: "If one of my daughters got turned down there, I'd shoot him. I'm an old man, and if *I* feel like shooting someone or throwing a rock, what do you think about Negroes who aren't educated?" He repeated, "That's exactly the way I feel about it, and I feel it every time I pass. I feel like throwing a rock at the damn place."[92]

When he finished, someone asked him what he could possibly mean. "Bobby looked at me," Martin recalled, "and I said, 'Listen, do you think I'm kidding? I'm telling you, that public accommodations bill has got to get in there, or we're going to have one hell of a war in this country.' "[93]

The civil rights bill that John Kennedy soon submitted to Congress did, after all, include strong measures mandating nondiscrimination in public accommodations, in what would become Title II of the bill. Five years later Ramsey Clark, who had been a Justice Department lawyer at the time and was later appointed attorney general, wrote Martin a long letter thanking him for the pressure he had applied toward making the bill a reality:

> Your contributions to equal justice these past eight years are immense. One of my most vivid memories is of your forceful argument on Saturday afternoon in the spring of 1963 when the first meeting to consider a civil rights bill was held in Bobby's office. Inclusion of Title II was never in doubt after that.[94]

≈ ≈ ≈

On June 11, after weeks of behind-the-scenes negotiations and with the lessons of Ole Miss well learned, Robert Kennedy sent Nicholas Katzenbach down to the University of Alabama to escort two black students onto the all-white campus, thus enforcing the Supreme Court's ruling. Knowing he could not finally prevent desegregation, Governor Wallace nevertheless wanted to show his white supporters that he had no choice in the matter. By prior agreement, he allowed the black students to enter the campus quietly under guard, while he arranged to make a show "at the schoolhouse door" of defying Katzenbach before the television cameras. While Alabama lawmen physically barred Katzenbach from entering the university building, Wallace managed to make the federal government look like an invading army. "We are God-fearing people," he declaimed before the cameras, "not government-fearing people." [95]

That same day, Kennedy received another telegram from King, this one pleading with the president to use the prestige of his office to speak openly before the nation about the moral imperative of racial justice.[96] Within a matter of hours, Kennedy decided to announce his civil rights legislation in a television address the same evening. None of his advisors was prepared for this. Sorensen pointed out that no speech had been drafted. Nor was there any complete bill to discuss, nor had Congress been consulted. Nevertheless, Kennedy had made up his mind, and he handed Sorensen a few ideas and some notes from Martin and others that he liked. With just minutes to go, the president was still unhappy with the speech draft before him, and when he looked into the news cameras at eight o'clock what he held in his hands was a smattering of notes. What he delivered, however, was soon hailed as one of the most passionate appeals he had made as president:

> We are confronted primarily with a moral issue. It is as old as the Scriptures and is as clear as the American Constitution…. We preach freedom around the world, and we mean it, and we cherish our freedom here at home; but are we to say to the world, and, much more importantly, to each other, that this is a land of the free except for the Negroes; that we have no second-class citizens, except Negroes; that we have no class or caste system, no ghettos, no master race, except with respect to Negroes?

Not since his election campaign had Kennedy spoken about civil rights in such bold terms, and never had he publicly invoked the power of the Scriptures and the authority of conscience this way. Until now, Kennedy had spoken of civil rights primarily as a matter of enforcing existing laws, reserving his bully pulpit for other issues. King was pleased at last and publicly said so. For his part, Louis Martin was especially glad to hear the president promise to submit strong legislation on desegregation:

> If an American, because his skin is dark, cannot eat lunch in a restaurant open to the public, if he cannot send his children to the best public schools available, if he cannot vote for the public officials who represent him… then who among us would be content to have the color of his skin changed and stand in his place? Who among us would then be content with the counsels of patience and delay? [97]

To mobilize support during the summer of 1963 for the pending bill, Martin solicited help from civil rights leaders and friends at more than one hundred newspapers and magazines. Martin continued as well to bring black groups to the White House and telephoned others to explain administration policies.

*≈ ≈ ≈*

Early in the year Martin had heard that A. Philip Randolph, still the nation's preeminent black labor leader and the elder statesman of black protest, was working with other civil rights leaders to bring a massive rally to the nation's capital. He reported the rumor at a monthly meeting called by Johnson.

"Oh, they tried that before," one of the participants said with a laugh. "You can forget that."

"I don't know whether you can forget it or not," Martin rejoined, "I just want to report that this is what I heard."

Martin remembered well how in June 1941, Randolph's threat of just such a march had forced President Roosevelt to establish the Fair Employment Practices Committee (FEPC), an important early step toward ameliorating job discrimination.[98]

As it turned out, since late 1962 Randolph had been quietly considering a new massive rally to highlight the need for jobs and economic justice. King had been simultaneously considering a nonviolent demonstration in Washington primarily to demand action on civil rights legislation. By the spring, the two leaders were working on a single event to accomplish both purposes and were negotiating with the more mainstream groups, including the NAACP and the Urban League, to give the event a unified voice. By May, King began speaking publicly about the march in connection with his complaint that Kennedy's action on civil rights was inadequate. After the president's June 11 televised speech, which King called "one of the most eloquent, profound, and unequivocal pleas for justice... ever made by any president," King changed his approach, deciding the march would do the most good by focusing on getting the president's civil rights bill passed.[99]

When Kennedy's inner circle realized a demonstration was likely to take place, nearly all of them viewed the prospect with alarm. The president, too, feared that a capital filled with a hostile crowd of black activists, however nonviolent, might cause Congress to dig in its heels even further on his civil rights bill. In late June, just after Randolph and King announced to the press that the March on Washington for Jobs and Freedom would be held on August 28, Kennedy met with them and tried to dissuade them. What if the rally led to rioting, he asked. But Randolph evenly replied, "Mr. President, the Negroes are already in the street. Isn't it better that they be led by organizations dedicated to civil rights and disciplined by struggle, rather than leave them to other leaders who care nothing about civil rights nor about nonviolence?"[100]

Martin had been making an additional argument for supporting the event, urging the administration to cooperate with it. "I argued that those who saw in the plan a political attack on the administration did not reckon with the possibility of guiding it along a constructive path," he recalled. Not everyone shared Martin's view. "Suddenly I found myself lobbying inside the White House to support the march and lobbying the leaders, most of whom were in New York, to strengthen the hand of the president rather than to discredit him politically." [101]

Gradually, Martin's view prevailed inside the White House, while most of the march leaders had begun to treat the demonstration as one aimed at pressuring the Congress to support Kennedy's bill. Martin persuaded Walter Reuther to pitch in with every resource at his disposal and help make the event more than an all-black protest. Reuther took up this challenge with gusto, joining as an official organizer. "The advice and counsel of Walter Reuther was that of a professional who knew all that one needed to know about mass rallies," Martin later observed, adding that most of the placards carried by march participants were printed by the UAW. Labor's involvement meant a lot from Martin's perspective. Believing that images of a united population would send the strongest message to the public and the politicians, he pressed the event's organizers to embrace as wide a cross section of Americans as possible: "I told them I didn't want just blacks in there. I told them I wanted blacks and whites coming out of the TVs.... One of my philosophical points of view was that we do this together." [102]

To stay abreast of the organizers' evolving plans in New York, Martin called on his friend Frank Montero, the man who had helped him carry out Bobby Kennedy's last-minute "Flying Caravan" during the 1960 campaign. Montero kept Martin posted and at one point reminded the White House that adequate sanitation was essential for a rally of this size, estimating that the portable toilets alone would cost $17,000. Martin got on the phone with some business acquaintances and obtained assurances of financial support.[103]

In the last weeks before the march, Martin got a call to meet a young man at the White House and accompany him to the office of the Washington, D.C., chief of police. The young man turned out to be Joseph Califano, then the legal counsel to the Department of the Army. Only later did Martin find out that Califano's superiors at the Pentagon had worked out strategic plans so that in the event of a crisis, enough federal troops could be deployed to take over the city. When Martin and Califano arrived at the police chief's office, they were joined by Bayard Rustin, who was coordinating the demonstration's every detail. Rustin, a long-time pacifist who had worked with both A. Philip Randolph and King, who was an original member of CORE and helped found the SCLC.

The police, Rustin argued, need not be concerned about rioting. Rumors among the city's white business owners to the contrary, the marchers would be peaceful, and he himself had worked out a system for self-policing. He had arranged for black off-duty police officers to be on hand among the participants, and then, of course, there would be numerous clergymen of all faiths and colors. Martin recalled the conversation: "It was fascinating to watch the reaction of the police officials to the language of Bayard, who spoke with all the precision and diction of a Harvard English professor. Several words he used were not familiar to the officers in the room." [104]

As the event approached, some blacks in the administration remained unsure what their position about the march should be. Should they step forward publicly at an event some would view as a protest against the government? Martin urged them to participate openly in the event. He obtained special tickets so that black White House appointees could be seated with him near the podium on the steps of the Lincoln Memorial.[105] He later recorded his impressions of the rally:

> As I sat on the stone steps looking out on the vast throng I was fully conscious that this was one of the great moments in the history of blacks in America. Never had so many black Americans come together from all sections of the country to strike a blow for first-class citizenship.... It was the speech of Dr. Martin Luther King, however, that seemed to wipe out all that had gone before. His magnificent voice rolled across the vast throng and the imagery of his words, the "mountains" and the "valleys," seemed to transport and lift the spirits of the multitude.[106]

"I have a dream," King called to the crowd of 200,000 and to the nation watching, "that one day on the red hills of Georgia the sons of former slaves and the sons of slave-owners will be able to sit down together at the table of brotherhood." [107]

After King's speech, Martin hurried from the Lincoln Memorial to a waiting car that sped him to the White House to welcome the march's leaders, who after careful negotiations had been invited to meet President Kennedy. As Martin escorted the guests into the Cabinet Room, his longtime friend Walter Reuther turned to him and said: "Louis, I want to see how much clout you have around here. How about some coffee?" Martin instructed an attendant, and coffee was served. Smiling broadly as he entered, President Kennedy, who had watched the march on TV, told King how moving it had been to listen to his eloquent speech and then pledged to fight for the pending civil rights legislation.[108]

The March on Washington was a stunning success. In the context of the times, Martin later recalled that the white establishment, especially in

Washington, D.C., had looked forward to the March with grave apprehension. Many were convinced that no matter what the event's leaders were saying, the whole thing would end in rioting and violence. But, Martin recalled, "Bayard Rustin and the leaders of the March were fully conscious of the fact that the 'whole world' would be watching the demonstration." In fact, the event proceeded like clockwork, and before nightfall every bus had quietly departed with the March participants.

Coverage by the media had been intense. Martin concluded that "the peaceful, soul-stirring demonstration made an impact upon the minds of Americans that no other single event possibly could.... When you consider the general indifference of the majority group to the concerns of the minorities, I believe that the March on Washington gave the struggle a new impetus and an expanded constituency." [109]

*❧ ❧ ❧*

On November 22, 1963, only three months after the March on Washington, Martin and Chuck Roche had just finished lunch with Michel Cieplinski at the Federal City Club when an employee rushed up and said, "I just heard the president's been killed."

"Are you kidding?" Martin asked with disbelief.

"I wouldn't kid about a thing like that," she replied, shaking her head.

Maybe the woman got it all wrong, Martin thought, it simply can't be. The two men were so distressed that they left Cieplinski behind—he had stopped to talk to a friend—and half-walked and half-ran the two blocks to their offices at the DNC. Martin noticed that traffic moved normally. Word about President Kennedy had not reached the streets. As soon as Martin and Roche left the elevator on the seventh floor of their office building, they crowded with the rest of the DNC staff in front of a television set in Chairman Bailey's office.

They were still hopeful, because television commentator Walter Cronkite kept saying that no official word on the president's condition had come from Parkland Hospital in Dallas. Periodically repeating descriptions of the shooting, he revealed new details every few seconds. DNC staff had been watching for about ten minutes when Cronkite gave the word that it was now official: the president was dead.

The room was hushed. Some staff members began to cry. With a hollowness in his stomach, Martin began pacing back and forth between the offices. Kennedy's advance man, Jerry Bruno, paced back and forth cursing, saying repeatedly, "I picked that route." Feeling sorry for him, Martin tried unsuccessfully to persuade him to stop accusing himself. Martin suggested to Roche that they go to the White House, since there was nothing to be done at the DNC.

When they arrived, they found Sargent Shriver in conference with military leaders. Martin, who was permitted to sit in on the meeting, was surprised to learn that the Pentagon was in charge of contingency plans for the funeral rites of a president. Shriver informed the Pentagon brass that Mrs. Kennedy had her own ideas about the funeral, which were at odds with the military plans.

Martin learned that the body would be arriving from Dallas in a few hours. Shriver, who was in touch with Jackie Kennedy, set everyone to work getting the East Room ready for the arrival of the body. In accordance with Mrs. Kennedy's wishes, history books were sent over from the library to determine the arrangements. Every detail was meticulously researched to conform with the treatment of previous presidents—from the construction of the catafalque, to the draping of the doorway and the number of guards stationed at the North Portico.

Shriver also put Martin and Roche to work drawing up a list of close friends and associates of the president. A telegram signed by Robert F. Kennedy would invite them to the White House between 2:30 and 5:00 p.m. the following day to view the bier. He and Roche had been working on the list for several hours when a helicopter approached the White House grounds. From the tall French doors in the Cabinet Room, Martin could see the floodlit landing space. As the noise of the blades grew louder, he walked across the Rose Garden and joined scores of reporters and photographers waiting behind a roped-off strip of lawn.

Stepping out of the helicopter, Lyndon Johnson managed a weary smile but said very little to anyone. He stopped to shake hands with officials and reporters. When he shook Martin's hand, the journalist sensed that the man who was now president of the United States was dazed, tired, and mentally elsewhere.

Shortly after midnight, the whole team was satisfied that everything had been done to ready the East Room for the arrival of the body of the slain president. Martin was among those awaiting Mrs. Kennedy's arrival with her husband's body, while Shriver maintained two-way radio contact with the funeral home. At about 3:00 a.m. word came that the motorcade was near. To Martin, it was an eternity before the first car slowly nosed its way up the North Portico drive. Shriver opened the limousine door and helped Mrs.

Kennedy, still wearing the same blood-stained suit, out of the vehicle and up the stairs. She walked into the East Room, and when the coffin was placed on the catafalque, she knelt before it alone.[110]

&.

# .6.

## MAKING HISTORY: THE WEAVER, BRIMMER, AND MARSHALL APPOINTMENTS

*I can remember clearly Lyndon Johnson in early 1965 stating in his most diplomatic profanity that Louis Martin was the most persistent person he had ever known and when he wanted something, you might as well give it to him right away or he would worry the hell out of you until you wished you had!*

*—John Cashin, Alabama civil rights activist*

The telephone rang in Louis Martin's hospital room, where he lay recovering from an operation to remove his spleen. Just two weeks had passed since the assassination of President Kennedy and a little more than that since Martin's fifty-first birthday.

The new president began abruptly: "What's this you told me about this attorney out in St. Louis that you wanted on the Civil Rights Commission—Frankie Freeman?" Martin had expected a polite inquiry about his health, not a business call.

"Yes sir, Mr. President. That's right," he answered.

"You recommend her?"

"Yes sir, she's excellent. She's a black woman and ought to get the job. She's smart," said Martin. He pointed out the political significance of his proposal, playing on Johnson's sensitivity to charges that blacks were denied equal job opportunity in the federal establishment.[1]

"Well, now, who else could I check with on this?" Johnson asked.

"You could talk to Bob Weaver or some of the guys. They know her."

To Martin's chagrin, Johnson rang off without any mention of his health. Flowers and letters had arrived from the White House bearing Johnson's signature, but Martin knew they came from Lee White, the president's legal counsel.

Martin had gone in the hospital for minor surgery. It was successful but immediately afterward became complicated by bleeding and a dangerously low platelet count. After attempts at treatment with medication failed, the doctors were forced to remove his spleen. They speculated that the stress of the assassination might have exacerbated his bleeding problem. When he required a transfusion, his friend Chuck Roche from the DNC came to his aid with a dose of "Irish blood." [2]

A second presidential call came that evening. "I've got your sidekick, Bob Weaver, over here," Johnson said. "Tell him about that Frankie Freeman and what you guys think about her." The president said nothing about Martin's health. Martin talked to Weaver briefly about the appointment. Two days later, Johnson phoned Freeman, in effect substantiating news leaks that he was considering her for the Civil Rights Commission. But while Johnson had sought Martin's advice, he had not consulted Missouri's two senators, Edward Long and Stuart Symington, an omission that violated the White House's usual recruitment procedures. Still in the hospital, Martin received angry calls from the two slighted legislators demanding to know, "Who told the president? Where did he get this name? Who's making these appointments, anyhow?" As Martin made clear, he simply produced names; he did not handle protocol between the White House and Congress.

By now Martin realized that Johnson had done something far more important than wish him a speedy recovery—he had given him a reason to get well quickly. The president had let him know that he was not forgotten and that he was expected to continue to play as important a role in the new administration as in the last. As he lay recuperating in the hospital, Martin was on the brink of the most momentous days of his career. On the horizon were the most important civil rights accomplishments since the freeing of the slaves a hundred years before.

After six frustrating weeks of recuperation, Martin returned to his position as deputy chairman of the Democratic National Committee. He retained the White House pass he had received in the Kennedy administration, with its unrestricted access. His role was the same, but the dynamics were as different as the two men he served. Martin had spoken with Kennedy frequently. His friendship with Kenny O'Donnell, John Kennedy's appointment secretary, had allowed him to stick his head in the Oval Office to see if the president had time to see him. With Johnson, he had to write memoranda. [3]

To ensure that he had the president's ear, Martin had to watch Johnson's aides closely. Two of LBJ's top aides were Harry McPherson, his speechwriter and advisor of many years' standing, and Joseph Califano, who left Robert McNamara's office to become his chief legislative aide. "Johnson would be very thick with Califano one week," he recalled, "or Harry McPherson one week, and he would play all the guys, and my job was to find out which one he was close to that week, and I'd send that guy the memorandum."[4] Despite the formal office procedures, Martin spoke frequently with Johnson, particularly on the phone late at night. During these calls the president peppered him with questions, allowing Martin to debate and argue with him, a privilege denied many of his other aides. "He was forthright and straight," Martin recalled. "I've never seen anybody like him—white or black."[5]

More than Kennedy had done, Johnson consulted with Martin often about people and issues outside the area of race and civil rights. He also took Martin into his confidence. On one tense occasion, Martin was left alone with the president in what moments before had been a roomful of people. Despondent, the president turned to him and asked, "Why do I want this goddamn job? What am I doing here?" Listening to Johnson unburden himself, Martin did not know what to say.[6]

Because Johnson had strengthened his ties with blacks while he was vice president, many people assumed that Martin was close to the president. At one DNC meeting, the new president boasted about his interest in party affairs and stated that he had met regularly with Martin. Martin was somewhat taken aback, since their meetings had rarely been about DNC affairs. But Johnson's unexpected statement worked to Martin's advantage: in dealing with agencies on personnel matters, he suddenly found himself with enhanced clout. It was easier for him to get any bureaucrat on the telephone or get his call returned the same day.[7]

Martin's responsibilities were never clearly defined, and in both the Kennedy and Johnson administrations he broadened their scope. In addition to his strictly political duties—attending meetings, making speeches across the country, constantly rallying the troops, overseeing registration drives, bringing as many blacks as possible into the White House, setting up meetings for various groups with one or more Cabinet officials—he had unofficial but substantive policy and legislative responsibilities. He met with the president as well as with sub-Cabinet officials when necessary to seek their help. He gave advice on legislation and helped to marshal votes for the president's programs. He helped draft and review speeches for the president and Cabinet members. In all his roles, he brought the views of black Americans into the discussion and took the administration's views to the black leadership. In the years of the Johnson administration, he would be extremely successful in achieving this goal, particularly in pushing forward the appointment of Thurgood Marshall, Robert Weaver, and Andrew Brimmer to the most senior positions of power in the federal government.

Both as vice president and as president, Johnson was receptive to Martin's campaign for top black appointments, viewing those who could fill these positions as role models who could inspire young black citizens. In 1964, Clifford Alexander, a Harvard graduate with a law degree from Yale and with good political connections to Harlem, was assigned as deputy special assistant to the president at Martin's suggestion, leaving his post as a National Security Council analyst. Increasingly, Alexander won Johnson's admiration. After two years on the White House staff, Johnson appointed him to serve as chair of the Equal Employment Opportunity Commission (EEOC), the successor to the Committee on Equal Employment Opportunity. He worked in this capacity while continuing as an active member of the White House staff. Years later, Alexander would serve even more visibly in the Carter administration.[8]

Martin continued to pursue his goal of having as many highly qualified blacks as possible appointed to important government positions that had never before been open to them. High on his list were economist Andrew Brimmer, appellate judge Thurgood Marshall, and housing administrator Robert Weaver, all names that had been bandied about for months. If Johnson desegregated the Federal Reserve Board, the Supreme Court, and his Cabinet (and if the housing agency became a Cabinet department), there would be no levels of federal authority that would remain all white.

Working with Johnson, however, was much different from dealing with Kennedy. Years later, writing in a 1987 *Chicago Defender* column, Martin compared the appointment styles of the three presidents he had served. He mentioned Kennedy's toughness, Johnson's thoroughness, and Jimmy Carter's reliance on staff. Martin recalled that when Kennedy considered a prospective appointee, he would ask simply: "Has this guy got any balls?" No president, however, dug deeper into a candidate's life than Lyndon Johnson. Once when Martin extolled the virtues of a candidate, describing his superior intelligence and flawless credentials, Johnson cut him off abruptly. "Yes, I know he's a genius." he said. "What I want to know is, can you trust the son of a bitch?"[9]

Appointments were often delayed as Johnson sought to investigate other candidates or to line up support. Sometimes it seemed the president was just toying with the individual, extracting every possible bit of suspense, political

The founding editor of the *Michigan Chronicle,* Martin (right) quickly became a leading figure among Detroit's labor and civil rights activists. When the federal government proposed to designate its Sojourner Truth housing project a whites-only residence in 1942, Martin led a coalition to pressure authorities to return the project to its original purpose, providing homes for blacks. Despite Klan-inspired mob violence, the effort succeeded. The *Chronicle* (below) highlighted Martin's role as a featured speaker when the coalition led a historic rally of 20,000 people in Cadillac Square.

THE CHRONICLE PRESENTS NEWS IN PICTURES

HIGHLIGHTS IN PICTURES OF SOJOURNER TRUTH PARADE AND RALLY

Martin achieved some notoriety after Detroit's deadly 1943 race riot (right) when local officials blamed him, the *Chronicle*, and the NAACP for instigating violence by speaking out against inequality.

After forbidding discrimination in federal employment, President Truman receives the 1948 Robert S. Abbott Memorial Award from the *Chicago Defender*. Among those presenting are (left to right) John Sengstacke, William Dawson, Martin, and Mary McLeod Bethune.

Martin spent a year in Nigeria training journalists as that country prepared for independence. In the photo above he meets with rising Kenyan leader Tom Mboya (left) and a West African reporter (right). Immediately on returning to the U.S. in 1960, Martin first meets Senator Lyndon Johnson as he escorts Chief Ayo Rosiji of Nigeria around the country (below).

The sidewalks are crowded with attentive listeners when Senator John F. Kennedy brings his presidential campaign to Harlem, New York, on October 12, 1960—an event Martin credited with gaining key black support. Top photo: seated directly behind the candidate are Jacqueline Kennedy, Adam Clayton Powell, and Eleanor Roosevelt.

A relaxed moment at daughter Trudy's graduation from the University of Chicago, 1960.

In January 1963, Martin accompanies JFK on a speaking engagement at the 50th anniversary of Delta Sigma Theta, the eminent black sorority, in Washington, D.C. The president greets a visitor as Martin and Beth Reeves look on.

Martin was delighted at the success of the White House's 1963 Lincoln Birthday reception, which he arranged. Here he makes introductions as JFK mills among 800 black celebrities, academics, and leaders (above).

Martin worked closely with Robert Kennedy, who was not only attorney general but his brother's chief political advisor (left).

Martin was behind the cameras when the leaders of the 1963 March on Washington posed for a White House portrait shortly after the massive rally. Robert Kennedy (center) is flanked by Martin Luther King, Jr., and A. Philip Randolph. UAW leader Walter Reuther stands to the right of Vice President Johnson.

Though recently returned from extended hospitalization, Martin braves bitter weather to escort the great contralto Marian Anderson to LBJ's 1965 inauguration.

Top: Martin accompanies LBJ in July 1967 to a reception at the DNC's new headquarters. Former DNC chairman John Bailey is behind Martin and LBJ. Above: Just a few months after becoming the first African American to join the Cabinet, Robert Weaver shares a moment with Martin, April 1966. Right: During a White House reception for DNC delegates the same month, Martin finds himself in a familiar position with the commander in chief.

This undated Oval Office photo accurately reflects Martin's five years with LBJ, who would routinely wake him in the middle of the night to discuss a proposal over the phone.

The White House holds a reception for Thurgood Marshall after his Senate confirmation as a U.S. Supreme Court justice in August 1967. LBJ is speaking with Gertrude Martin (far left); facing the camera, left to right, are Clifford Alexander and his wife Adele, Marshall and his wife Cissy, and Lady Bird Johnson. Marshall is speaking with federal district judge and former NAACP colleague Spottswood Robinson.

Above: Listening to Martin at an Oval Office huddle in February 1967 are (facing Martin) Ramsey Clark, Harry McPherson, and Vice President Humphrey; policy advisor Joseph Califano stands at the rear. Left: With Clifford Alexander and Thurgood Marshall on June 13, 1967, the day LBJ announced Marshall's Supreme Court nomination.

April 5, 1968: the day after Martin Luther King's assassination, as riots break out across the country, LBJ seeks the advice of top civil rights leaders. Thurgood Marshall and Clarence Mitchell, Jr., are seated; standing are (left to right) Roy Wilkins, Robert Weaver, Hubert Humphrey, Leon Higginbotham, Clarence Mitchell III, Dorothy Height, Walter Washington, Walter Fauntroy, (unidentified guest), Richard Hatcher, and Martin.

Above: Martin receives an honorary degree from Howard University with Ted Kennedy, Lena Horne, and Clarence Mitchell, among others, 1979. Below: Martin joined Harvard's president Nathan Pusey in 1970 after being similarly honored at Harvard University.

Above: Vice President Walter Mondale and Martin enjoy a mid-air lunch in the summer of 1978.
Middle: Carter holds a strategy session in October 1978 to get the Humphrey-Hawkins Full Employment bill passed; seated (left to right) are chief staff aide Hamilton Jordan, the president, Martin, League of United Latin Americans representative Ed Peña, and Senator Muriel Humphrey.
Bottom: As an aide to President Carter, Martin first worked out of a White House office rather than from the DNC.

Top: In his last month in office, Carter meets with (clockwise) Coretta Scott King, Benjamin Hooks, Rosalynn Carter, Jesse Jackson, Louis Martin, an unidentified guest, Vernon Jordan, and Dorothy Height. Above: Clarence Mitchell, the NAACP's Washington lobbyist during the fateful 1960s, visits Carter as Martin looks on, March 1979.

Above: Martin meets with Jesse Jackson and NAACP Executive Director Benjamin Hooks to devise a strategy for battling Congress's effort to end busing, December 1980.
Middle: Even after he resigned as ambassador to the U.N., Andrew Young, seen here with Martin and the president in late 1980, remained on warm terms with Carter.
Bottom: Martin, Hamilton Jordan, and Sol Linowitz relax with the president during a break in the July 1979 Camp David sessions, where Carter asked leaders and ordinary citizens to critique his administration.

At a Congressional Black Caucus Dinner, Martin joins a discussion with Caucus executive director Gus Adair (center) and Eddie Williams, president of the Joint Center for Political and Economic Studies. Martin (pictured in middle photo at a board meeting) remained active with the Joint Center after helping to found the organization in 1970.

Celebrating their 50th wedding anniversary in 1986, Louis and Gertrude Martin are surrounded by their five daughters Trudy Hatter, Linda Purkiss, Anita Martin, Lisa Martin, and Toni Martin, and extended family.

advantage, and (eventually) gratitude. Even the most distinguished candidates were seldom allowed the luxury of being certain of their appointment until it was announced. Among the top black candidates Martin was promoting, Johnson was especially impressed with Andrew Brimmer, particularly the fact that he, like Johnson himself, had come up the hard way. When Brimmer was a high school student in Newellton, Louisiana, his counselors advised him not to go to college. They judged that he was not college material and reminded him that professional opportunities were nearly nonexistent for blacks. Ignoring their advice, Brimmer graduated from Harvard and eventually became one of the nation's most respected economists. In May 1963, he was on leave from a professorship at the University of Pennsylvania's Wharton School of Business when President Kennedy appointed him deputy assistant secretary of commerce. Twenty months later, Johnson promoted him to assistant secretary of commerce for economic affairs.[10]

"Luther Hodges, the outgoing secretary of commerce, recommended my promotion," Brimmer later recalled. "Johnson said it was a good idea but thought the incoming secretary should have a chance to make a judgment. Meanwhile, word got out that the slot was going to be vacant. Louis [Martin] got word that there was competition for the slot and he stepped in and encouraged Johnson to go on and appoint me."[11]

About a year later, Johnson was considering Brimmer for a vacancy on the Federal Reserve Board. In addition to making a statement about racial equality, the appointment of Brimmer would tip the board to a liberal majority, something LBJ had been wanting to do—in open defiance of the board's conservative chairman. The president had Brimmer's resume in his desk drawer when Louisiana senator Russell Long came to push another candidate for the position. Johnson asked Long to read Brimmer's resume.

Reluctantly, Long agreed. Although the senator had voted to confirm Brimmer as assistant secretary of commerce, he had since forgotten about him. As Long prepared to leave, Johnson fished around in his desk for a photo of Brimmer and then handed it to Long. Shocked when he saw that Brimmer was black, the senator said, "What the hell am I going to tell the people in my state?"

"Tell them he's from Louisiana," Johnson answered.[12]

Johnson's appointment of Brimmer to a fourteen-year term on the Federal Reserve Board surpassed the expectations of civil rights leaders, who had not been aware that it was even a possibility. Martin, however, had been actively seeking the appointment for Brimmer, who had telephoned him several times in pursuit of this ambitious goal.[13] Brimmer knew that he owed his appointment to Martin's quiet persistence and to Johnson's confidence in Martin's advice. Martin chalked the Brimmer appointment up to Johnson's desire to have the best person for the job. "Johnson did it without prodding," Martin later said. "Nobody pressured Johnson. Nobody marched. Nobody did anything. Johnson saw the merits of this guy. Brimmer was super-qualified—better qualified than anybody on the board."[14]

❧ ❧ ❧

As LBJ's administration was getting under way, widespread urban rebellions across the country had begun to expose urban slum conditions to many whites who had not given much thought to them. Johnson was determined to launch a concentrated assault on urban poverty. As part of this effort, he persuaded Congress by September 1965 to create a Cabinet-level Department of Housing and Urban Development (HUD). Many observers expected him to appoint Robert Weaver, then administrator of the Housing and Home Finance Agency, as the first HUD secretary. However, Weaver was not regarded as a strong advocate for civil rights. Given the racial aspects of urban poverty, and at a time when many civil rights leaders were tackling urban conditions as their newest challenge, this view of Weaver could prove harmful. To moderate any antagonism, Martin spoke to the leaders of the major organizations, telling them to put aside whatever they thought of Weaver's lack of militancy. "Let's make some history," he told them.[15]

Weaver's appointment to head the newly created department had been rumored for months before HUD was even in existence, and he was deluged with advice from a variety of sources—much of it anti-Johnson. Some blacks suggested that since Weaver had not been appointed immediately after HUD was created, he should resign from his housing administration post. According to this reasoning, the president was not going to appoint a black to his Cabinet, and Weaver was being humiliated by media stories that Johnson was talking to other candidates for the HUD post.

Martin knew that Johnson enjoyed toying with prospective appointees, dragging out the process, seeing how they reacted to the pressure. He and the president had discussed Weaver on twenty or so occasions, some of the calls initiated by Johnson himself. Some nights he would call up Martin at home simply to talk about Weaver. Johnson instructed Califano (now the White House legal counsel), Lee White, and Martin each to give Weaver a different message. When Martin told the president that Weaver was becoming impatient with the slow pace of the appointment, Johnson became angry and threatened: "I can accept that resignation [from his current housing position] just as quickly as he can give it to me. You just tell him that you're working on it, and he's not ruled out. I'm after the best man." [16]

For months, Johnson continued to play with Weaver. Martin learned from some labor leaders who had just spoken with Johnson that they were not going to push for Weaver. Indeed, one of them told Martin, "You're doing a disservice. You should tell Bob to quit."

"I'm not going to tell him to quit," Martin shot back. "I'm going to tell him to stick, and I'm going to fight to the end to get this job."

Conferring with Weaver, Martin urged: "Don't listen to these people. I think I know this man. He puts whites through the wringer; he puts everybody through a wringer. Don't let that disturb you." But Weaver remained anxious. [17]

Nearly two months after Congress created HUD, Califano alerted Johnson to a law requiring him to appoint a secretary or acting secretary by November 9, 1965. Not only did Johnson object to making such a decision while Congress was adjourned, but he also revealed that he had not yet settled on Weaver for two reasons: First, his votes on Capitol Hill were not lined up. Second, the appointment did not have enough backing from the public or from interest groups to make it politically attractive.

Nevertheless, in late October, Weaver brought documents to Califano that he claimed Johnson had to sign within two weeks to establish HUD and pick its secretary. The president did not operate under any such deadline, Califano told him. According to Califano, Weaver was thunderstruck. Johnson instructed Califano to secure an opinion from Nicholas Katzenbach, who was now attorney general, on whether he was required to act by the early November deadline. Katzenbach affirmed Weaver's claim. As this was not the answer Johnson wanted, he secured a contrary opinion from another lawyer. He then postponed action on HUD and instructed Califano and Katzenbach to reconsider their opinions. Weaver still wanted his papers signed, but Johnson was wary of the difficulties he might face in gaining Senate confirmation of Weaver as the nation's first black Cabinet secretary. The candidate was unpopular on the Hill and was disliked by Senate Majority Leader Mike Mansfield of Montana.

When Califano informed Weaver that the attorney general had revised his opinion, the man was distraught. He felt that if he were not named either secretary or acting secretary by November 9, the deteriorating situation would be, in his words, "embarrassing, downright humiliating," and he would have to resign. Califano urged Weaver not to do so. Told about Weaver's response, Johnson reacted angrily, "Let him resign. If he's that arrogant, the hell with him. You just tell him to resign. Call him tonight and tell him." Califano argued with Johnson to no avail. That evening, Califano avoided contacting Weaver. The next morning Johnson called about Weaver's resignation. "Did you get it?" he asked. "Did you get it?" Califano admitted he had not. "Goddamn it. Get it," the president snapped. "Have him deliver it to you this afternoon." [18]

By the next day, Johnson had changed his mind. Unaware of that fact, Califano persuaded Weaver to write a letter of resignation and informed the president that the housing official was en route with his letter.

"What the hell is he doing that for?" Johnson asked, completely reversing his previous position. "I don't want him to resign."

Califano reminded the president that he had instructed him to persuade Weaver of the opposite, but Johnson was adamant.

"My God—what am I supposed to do?" Califano asked in exasperation.

"You tell him not to resign," Johnson ordered. "That's what you do. What the hell is he resigning for? Tell him I have a list of names, he's on it, and I'm going to make a selection in January when Congress comes back."

"Mr. President, after what he's been through, he may just hand me his resignation and walk out."

"You have no authority to accept his resignation. You tell him, if he wants to resign, he can't resign to you. He's got to resign to the president. Tell him he has to give it to me." [19]

Early one morning not long after, Johnson telephoned Martin. "I'm going with him," he said. "I'm going with Bob Weaver."

"Mr. President, that's wonderful," said Martin.

"Yes, I know. That's what you say, but if I didn't appoint him you'd call me a Confederate son of a bitch."

"You said it. I didn't say it."

Martin assumed that the announcement would come the next day and said nothing about it to anyone, not even his wife, but he saw Weaver the next day, looking depressed as he walked down K Street. "Bob, why the hell are you frowning?" he asked. "You should be smiling!" Weaver merely glanced at Martin. "Now, didn't I tell you to keep your courage up?" Martin asked, adding, "Smile."

"You sound like you know something," Weaver said.

"No. I don't know a thing." But Martin was smiling, and Weaver perked up. [20]

# MAKING HISTORY

Martin went to the White House, thinking an announcement was imminent. But there was nothing. He scanned press briefings. Still nothing. He chitchatted with insiders, listening for a hint of something big. The next day, and the next, and the day after—nothing. Martin was at a complete loss. Then one morning about ten o'clock a call came from the White House. "I was sitting on the toilet here, and I got to thinking about you," the president said matter-of-factly. "Why don't you come over here for a while? And when you come over, hang around Watson's office."

Following Johnson's cryptic instructions, Martin showed up at Marvin Watson's White House office. Watson smiled knowingly. Then Cabinet members started arriving, and Bob Weaver and his wife came down an inside corridor. When Martin saw Weaver, he knew the wait was over. A press conference was called, cameras were rolled in, and another historical barrier had been broken.[21]

*&. &. &.*

In July 1965, Judge Thurgood Marshall was having lunch in New York City when his law clerk unexpectedly walked in. "I told you, don't bother me when I'm eating," the judge snapped.

"But it's the president," the clerk explained.

"President of what?"

"President of the United States."

"That's a little different," Marshall answered, though he took his time to finish eating before telephoning back the White House. President Johnson immediately offered to appoint him solicitor general of the United States.

"No way," Marshall declared. "I'm not going *down* the ladder. I'm going *up* the ladder."

"You don't seem to understand—"

"No."

"Well, you come down and talk to me about it. I'll call you in a day or so," the president promised. "Take your time." [22]

Driving home that evening, Marshall pondered Johnson's offer. As solicitor general, he would leave the judicial bench and go back to arguing cases, but this time he would be the lead attorney for the United States, not a one-issue lawyer concerned only with civil rights. Now he was considering yet another change, as he discussed Johnson's offer with his wife and two sons. They assured him that whatever was good for him was good for them. The next morning, the president was on the phone. Marshall protested that he had been promised a day or two to consider. Johnson was firm: "I said you could take as much time as you want, and you've had as much time as you want. What are you going to do?"

"Well, I don't know. I'll take it. You know I'll take a hell of a cut in salary."

"Yes, I know that," Johnson replied.

"You know I'll be giving up a lifetime job."

"Yes, I know that."

"I don't see what's so good about it."

"Yes, I know that." [23]

The next morning, Marshall boarded a shuttle flight from New York. As the plane flew into cloudy conditions over Washington, the pilot announced over the intercom that due to the weather they would be circling for another twenty minutes. A few minutes later, however, he announced: "Ladies and gentlemen—Let me contradict what I just said. I just got a call, and the orders have been changed. Who's on this plane that's important? We have orders to come straight in."

Peering out the window of the airplane, Marshall saw a gray White House limousine wheeling around nearby. Within minutes of landing, he was rushed to the White House, where the president's wife, Lady Bird Johnson, greeted him and kept him occupied during a presidential press conference. At the appropriate time, both were ushered into the press conference room.

The president announced his appointment of Marshall as the solicitor general of the United States, the federal government's chief lawyer. Afterward, Johnson told Marshall that he had absolute authority, that if Attorney General Katzenbach gave him any trouble, he, the president, "would kick his pants." "Yes sir, I understand," Marshall replied, "but I'm sure we can get along."

Johnson also warned Marshall that he was not grooming him for the Supreme Court. "Don't take your solicitor general appointment as a step to any place," the president told him.

"What do I get after this?"

"The street." [24]

&agrave; &agrave; &agrave;

One evening in June 1967, Marshall was at a private party for Justice Tom Clark, who was retiring from the U.S. Supreme Court. The president pulled Marshall aside and said, "Thurgood, you know there's no future in this for you. I want to continue to emphasize that." But the next morning, Johnson paced the floor in his inner office, ready to call key senators to share a most important announcement. Unable to find Martin, who had pressed for Marshall's appointment as the first black justice, the president would not begin the historic formalities without him. Searching frantically, the White House switchboard finally located Martin—at his DNC office, according to Martin's recollection, although others said he was at the golf course where he sometimes went for his lunch hour, following his doctor's advice.

"How do you come into the White House when you come to the White House?" the president asked.

"Normally, I come in the Executive Office Building at the 17th Street side, and then go through the EOB, and then go through the basement," Martin replied. He took the circuitous route to avoid being waylaid by news reporters in the White House foyer.

"Come on over here," Johnson ordered. "Make sure nobody sees you." [25]

Around ten that same morning, Ramsey Clark, who had since become attorney general, phoned Thurgood Marshall's secretary to find out if he was in.

"Yes," she replied.

"Is anybody in there with him?"

"No."

"Put security down," Clark instructed, "and don't allow anybody to go in there. I'm on my way."

As Marshall later recalled it, the attorney general entered his office from a back hallway and started talking about the weather, a football game, and other trivia.

"I was wondering where you're going this morning," Clark finally said.

"I have an appointment at the White House," Marshall told him.

Clark then asked Marshall to change his plans and arrive fifteen minutes early, at eleven-thirty. He told him as well not to take his usual route coming in, which would bring him past the White House reporters, but to make an unusual detour. "Go up to Fifteenth Street," Clark said, "where the big line of tourists goes into the White House." [26]

Marshall followed the odd instructions. Once at the White House, he broke away from the public group and walked unimpeded down a corridor leading to the Oval Office. After ten minutes, Lady Bird Johnson came to tell him that the president would see him. Marshall entered the Oval Office and, finding Johnson hunched over a ticker tape machine, he coughed. "Oh—Thurgood!"

"Yes sir. What's up?" asked Marshall.

"Sit down," the president ordered gently. "I might tell you." After about five minutes of keeping Marshall in suspense, he said, "I'm going to put you on the Supreme Court."

"Well, that's new," Marshall replied.

"What do you mean by that?" Johnson asked.

"Last night, you said no. Now you're saying yes."

"That's the way I wanted it. Now I have to ask you, will you accept it?"

"That you don't have to ask. You know damn well I will."

The president gave Marshall these instructions: "The press is all lined up out there. We're going out there. I'll make a statement, and you can say something or not."

"I will not answer any press questions," Marshall said.

When they reached the Cabinet Room, Marshall turned to Johnson and said, "Mr. President, I'd like one more favor. Would you mind me telling my wife about this?"

"You mean you haven't told her?"

"I just found out."

Johnson promptly instructed an operator to dial Mrs. Marshall at home. "Take a deep breath and sit down slowly," Marshall told his wife, and then handed the phone to the president. "Cissy!" Johnson greeted her.

"Yes, Mr. President," Cissy Marshall answered at the other end.

"Cissy, I'm going to put Thurgood on the Supreme Court."

"I'm sure glad I'm sitting down," she replied.

Later, turning to Marshall, Johnson said, "This is about the end of the road for us. We won't be getting together, I don't guess."

"No sir," Marshall agreed. "You stay in your bailiwick and I'll stay in mine. You know Tom Clark was Harry Truman's best friend. When Truman went wrong on the steel case, it was Tom Clark who wrote the opinion that kicked him in the ass. If you get out of line, I'll do the same thing for you."

"That is as it should be." [27]

In high spirits, Johnson phoned around the country, speaking to Chief Justice Earl Warren and to key members of Congress, explaining: "Now, I'm about to do this, and I want you to go with me." The president phoned Illinois' Republican senator Everett Dirksen. After some warm-up flattery and a general discussion of how terrific Marshall was, he offered Dirksen his choice of a candidate for another position. "Incidentally, I want you to give me a candidate," the president told Dirksen, in his best political blarney tones. "I've got a vacancy. So if you will give me a candidate, I would really appreciate it." Johnson knew he would need the powerful Republican senator to swing Republican votes for Marshall's Senate confirmation.[28]

Marshall's appointment to the Supreme Court was generally well received around the country. "We had moved beyond the question of any black appointment being a colossal production," Martin later recalled. "By the time of the Marshall appointment, we had put several hundred blacks in various positions of importance. And I think the feeling in black America was that sooner or later Marshall's turn would come. We were moving beyond this business of appointments being the thing that black America was keenest about."

.7.

## WALKING THROUGH NEW DOORS: THE JOHNSON YEARS

*The guy who is on the inside, not compromising, but understanding how the game is played, is the one that lifts the level of life for Black America. That's what Louis Martin did.*

*—Carl Rowan*

When President Johnson delivered a long speech that devoted only forty-five words to the civil rights crisis, Louis Martin complained to Harry McPherson, Johnson's senior aide and speechwriter: "If you are going to write speeches for the man, at least you can give him a few more words." When the president spotted Martin a few days later in a White House corridor, he grabbed him by the lapels and said: "I know you've been around here arguing about my speeches. Now, what the hell do you want, rhetoric or action? I'm giving you action."

"My business is publicity," Martin replied. "I want the action." [1]

Action came quickly and abundantly. Five days after Kennedy's assassination, Johnson made it clear that he would pursue the slain president's goal of demolishing institutionalized racism, telling a joint session of Congress:

No memorial oration or eulogy could more eloquently honor President Kennedy's memory than the earliest possible passage of the civil rights bill for which he fought so long.... We have talked long enough in this country about equal rights. It is time now to write the next chapter—and to write it in books of law. [2]

For Martin, the first challenge was to persuade the black community that this new president would be sympathetic to the cause of civil rights and, as a southerner, bend over backward to prove he was not a racist. [3] Martin was by now fully confident that Johnson had meant what he said to black delegates at the 1960 convention—"I will do more for you in four years than anyone else has done in a hundred years"—words that had been repeated throughout the 1960 campaign to allay fears about his views.[4]

Directly after taking office as vice president, Johnson had begun meeting regularly with Martin, Robert Weaver, and other high-ranking blacks in the administration, to ask questions and brainstorm about the civil rights problem generally.

After President Kennedy established the Committee on Equal Employment Opportunity (EEO) in 1961 and made Johnson the chair, Johnson named Martin to the committee's advisory group, and in this role Martin and a dozen other top blacks in the administration worked closely with LBJ each month. Of Johnson's approach, Martin later said, "I thought he showed exceptional realism in dealing with the problem. He was a good listener, and everyone was free to say everything they had on their minds. I was very much attracted to him personally."[5]

Martin found that Johnson, like himself, had a political outlook strongly molded by the New Deal. "One of the reasons I think I was sold on him," Martin said, "is that he talked so much like Roosevelt. My view was that whether he liked you as a black or not was secondary to the greater interest he seemed to have in humanity in terms of poverty and these other things which were my overriding concern."[6] Johnson's philosophy, Martin believed, was heavily influenced by his experiences in Texas, where he witnessed the devastating combination of racism and poverty.[7] Martin's own experiences in Detroit and Chicago, going back thirty years, had brought him face to face with parallel problems in the urban ghettos.[8]

Given the friction between Johnson and Bobby Kennedy during those years, it was ironic that Martin found himself getting along famously with both men. "Lyndon Johnson was charismatic. He was bigger than life itself." Martin meant this literally as well as metaphorically. "Everybody was startled, the first time seeing LBJ. The pictures and stories never gave you an idea of how big that man was. He was a mountain."[9] While Johnson seemed able and willing to frighten some of his aides, Martin's response was to enjoy the man's game as an exercise in shadowboxing. "There was nobody in power I could have ever hoped to be able to talk to, to argue with, like Johnson. We had a big fight once on the [congressional] black caucus. I'll never forget it. I used to be able to debate and argue with him, and none of the others would do it. He would bother me a little bit, but I was persistent."[10]

Johnson had used his EEO committee assignment under Kennedy to try out an idea for something he had long advocated, a voluntary equal opportunity program. Called Plans for Progress, it brought major businesses to the table to sign pledges that they would promote fair employment practices. Although many black leaders were skeptical, Martin believed that with persuasive and able leaders, the program could make a real difference. The approach was similar to the one FDR had used to gain jobs for blacks under the FEPC during World War II.[11]

Johnson placed Hobart Taylor, Jr., in charge. Taylor asked Martin about getting a public relations assistant to work with him. Ofield Dukes, who was then managing editor of the *Michigan Chronicle*, was the person Taylor preferred. Martin called Longworth Quinn, the paper's general manager, and told him to tell Dukes that he was fired so he could take the position in Washington. The new team, according to Martin, worked well together and garnered considerable support among businesspeople.

During the Kennedy years, Martin had had the chance to learn what Johnson's views were away from the glare of publicity and apart from campaign postures. He saw that Johnson put great stock in the power of grassroots politics, believing it could be used to force broader social changes. "He felt that once you got in there and became politically active, part of the mainstream of the political apparatus, the white attitudes and the black attitudes would both change, and they would both be more practical and pragmatic about things, and less ideological or racist," Martin recalled. "He was not, I don't think, particularly emotionally in love with any one race. He just felt that the way you get social justice, the way you get all these other things you want in society, is through the political process."[12]

ɞ ɞ ɞ

Johnson's legislative record on civil rights had been as mixed as John Kennedy's before 1960. As a senator he had consistently voted against anti-lynching and anti-poll-tax legislation and opposed many amendments that would have denied federal funds in education and housing to those who practiced discrimination. In speeches to Texas voters, he avoided talking about the Supreme Court's *Brown* v. *Board of Education* decision, and he also ducked congressional debate on the ruling. As Senate majority leader, he engineered the compromise amendment that made possible the passage of the 1957 Civil Rights Act—but unfortunately, this compromise harmed the bill's provision for voting rights enforcement, allowing southern officials to be tried by all-white juries. One notable and courageous stand Johnson did take concerned what was called "The Southern Manifesto," a declaration signed by 101 southern state officials defiantly denouncing the *Brown* decision as an attack on the southern way of life and promising massive resistance to integration. Johnson refused to sign it.[13]

Martin had watched Johnson turn his earlier record inside out during his three years as vice president. After Kennedy was assassinated, LBJ seemed to take on his predecessor's unfinished civil rights agenda as a personal crusade. In the months following his unexpected accession to the presidency, he often told Martin that they did not have much time, that the mood of the country would change, that they must press hard for quick passage of the Civil Rights Act. The new president employed all the legislative techniques and tricks he had learned during twenty years in the Senate. The advantage of Johnson's friendships with recalcitrant southern politicians now became apparent. He knew what they wanted, how to talk to them, and how to embarrass them into cooperating.

President Johnson's skillful prodding was reinforced by shifts in public opinion. In the year since Kennedy had submitted the civil rights bill to Congress, much had happened. Television screens and newspaper front pages had depicted a nearly constant barrage of violence against black demonstrators who were merely asking for the rights that other Americans took for granted. The arguments of southern segregationists crumbled as the nation witnessed the ugliness of racial prejudice up close. The 1963 March on Washington helped solidify public opinion behind the bill, as people saw that the demonstrators on the Mall represented a broad cross section of America, that they were peaceful, and that they were committed. The bombing death of four black girls in a Birmingham church immediately after the march, followed three months later by the president's assassination, brought a sense of urgency to the problem. Throughout the period, letters, telegrams, and additional protests pressured Congress and the White House. One lobbyist who Martin felt merited far more public credit than he received was Clarence Mitchell, head of the NAACP's Washington office. Later dubbed the "101st senator" by Hubert Humphrey, Mitchell worked tirelessly to persuade undecided senators and representatives to support civil rights legislation.

Just three years earlier, serious legislative action on civil rights had been deemed impossible by nearly everyone. Now the bill that Kennedy had submitted to an uncertain Congress was supported by more than two-thirds of the House and Senate. The most comprehensive legislation addressing discrimination since Reconstruction, it mandated an end to segregation and discrimination in all facilities open to the general public, outlawed discrimination in employment, and prohibited bias in federally funded programs.

The new law, signed by President Johnson on July 2, 1964, had an immediate and profound impact on American life. Looking back on its application, Martin recalled: "Compliance was smoother than anybody had anticipated.... In my town, Savannah, it was a new world. When I was a kid, we couldn't go to any of the theaters. It was just off limits. None of the hotels.... Martin Luther King held a conference of his civil rights movement in the DeSoto Hotel. When I heard they were holding a conference in the DeSoto Hotel, I couldn't believe it. Because in my years, if you didn't have on one of those white coats or a mop in your hand, hell, you couldn't get in the place." [14]

Martin himself had fought hard with many of Kennedy's advisors to ensure that the bill contained the vital provisions integrating public places. He attributed the remarkably swift compliance in part to the careful groundwork laid by Ramsey Clark, who was deputy attorney general at the time. Clark told Martin about a survey that showed that the only way to get compliance with such a law in the South was to make sure no one was exempt. If there were any loopholes, the whole thing would fall apart. Before the bill passed, Clark met with major hotel operators to impress on them the importance of cooperating with the forthcoming law. [15]

≈ ≈ ≈

In early 1964, as deputy chair of the DNC, Martin turned his attention to the forthcoming Democratic National Convention in Atlantic City, New Jersey, and the election campaign to follow. DNC officials feared that the party would be split by efforts of the Mississippi Freedom Democratic Party (MFDP) to be seated in place of the official Mississippi delegation. The new group had been formed by members of several of the younger activist organizations as part of the voter registration drive in the South. Two representatives of the MFDP, Charles Evers and Aaron Henry, met with Martin to request that the DNC refuse to recognize the Mississippi Democratic party delegation, which was still all-white. Although he could not influence the DNC to honor their request, Martin was encouraged that blacks were seeking power through the political system. He urged Evers and Henry to go back to Mississippi and build up a political base at the local level, precinct by precinct. Only that would give them the political power they hoped for. While he feared that they would lose the convention battle, as they in fact did, he was heartened by the fact that they could do something the DNC had been unable to do: register black voters and motivate them to become politically active.

Other developments were not so promising. Many younger blacks were impatient with the gradual progress in civil rights and expressed contempt for the nonviolent principles of King and the SCLC. Martin worried about this upcoming generation and the potential for violence. Democratic party leaders were concerned about the possibility of racial confrontation at the convention and the effect this might have on the election. If violence did occur at the convention, Martin thought, he would be held responsible no matter what he might have done to contain it.

Up to this time, Martin had been handling his campaign work by himself, but now he thought he needed a hand from another black professional who was at ease working closely with whites and blacks alike. Clifford Alexander was his choice for the job. Alexander was interested in helping Martin, but in his current position he was covered by the Hatch Act and was therefore ineligible to participate in campaign activity. To solve this, Martin decided to ask Walter Jenkins, Johnson's most influential aide, if Alexander could be transferred to the White House staff temporarily. Martin pointed out that there were no blacks among Johnson's senior staff. Jenkins resisted the idea at first, but Martin came back a week later with the same request, emphasizing that the position would only be temporary. Jenkins finally agreed. After the convention, Jenkins suddenly resigned in a sex scandal. Since no one else was aware that the appointment had been temporary, Alexander simply remained as special counsel to the president. Alexander's work at the convention had been first-rate, and Martin was thrilled to have him continue on the staff. Martin reasoned that he would have been asked to stay anyway because of the staff's great respect for his legal work. But fate had played a role in making Alexander the first black on the White House senior staff.[16]

One source of anxiety at the convention was the animosity between LBJ and Martin's old boss, Bobby Kennedy. Before the convention, speculation about Johnson's vice presidential selection had been the hottest topic around Washington. The Kennedy people had clearly wanted LBJ to offer the vice presidential slot to Bobby. Martin thought that Bobby probably wanted the chance to turn it down. After a meeting at which Johnson told Kennedy that he would not be the choice, their very different versions of what was said turned into a nasty, well-publicized spat. The hostility between the two men placed yet another barrier between those Kennedy staff members whom LBJ had asked to stay on and the new members of Johnson's staff. Martin tried to sell the idea of Sargent Shriver as a compromise choice for vice president that would pull the two camps together, but he soon concluded, "There was no way to make a bridge out of Sarge to connect LBJ and Bobby. The gap was miles wide." [17]

When Senator Hubert Humphrey's name came up as a vice presidential possibility, Martin was pleased. Humphrey was well respected by labor and by blacks who remembered how at the 1948 convention he had urged the southern element of the Democratic party to "come out of the shadow of states' rights and into the broad sunshine of human rights." As usual, Johnson kept everyone guessing until the last minute, when he arrived in Atlantic City with Humphrey beside him.

Another potential problem at the convention was Bobby Kennedy's speech. DNC chairman John Bailey had done his best to keep the Kennedy forces in check. The president, despite his complete domination of the convention, was apprehensive about Kennedy's appearance. To calm LBJ's fears, Kennedy's speech was scheduled for after the nominations. Martin assessed the speech as "eloquent... one of the great speeches of all time in the annals of the Democratic party." Seeing Kennedy on the platform and listening to his voice must have stirred memories for Martin. He recalled: "[Bobby] won the hearts and minds of the teary-eyed delegates whose memories of JFK and his cold-blooded assassination were strong and fresh." [18]

Before the convention, Kennedy had called Martin and asked him to stop by his office at the Justice Department for a private talk. The two men ended up walking up and down the Mall with Kennedy's dog Brumus for an hour or more while they discussed the attorney general's future. Martin had been urging him to run for the U.S. Senate. Referring to Johnson, Martin pounded home his point: "There's no use trying to make this thing work. The chemistry between the two of you is not going to work." Kennedy agreed. On August 22, 1964, just before the convention, he announced his candidacy for a New York Senate seat. Martin even went up to New York and helped with his campaign for a while, although he never mentioned it to Johnson. "I knew better than to bring it up. I never discussed Bobby with him," Martin explained.[19]

Since 1960, Martin's campaign job at the DNC was to focus on foreign-born, ethnic-minority, and black voters by working through the DNC's Nationalities Division, which Martin later renamed the All Americans Council. Martin worked with New York mayor Robert Wagner, whom he selected in

1960 to head this group. Together they created a strategy for reaching out in the 1964 campaign to the foreign-born and second-generation Americans who still were in close touch with their homeland, culture, and language. They picked Craig Raupe, a Texan and a Johnson man, to coordinate the efforts of the individual nationality groups. Martin hoped that by picking a Johnson ally he could get full funding for his operation.[20]

Martin also experimented with new ways of bringing black voters to the polls. Traditionally, in the major cities it was the party's ward and precinct leaders who supervised the distribution of campaign literature, though often they were not motivated to help state and national candidates. Volunteers were not plentiful in the ghetto, and Martin knew that unless precinct workers were paid, campaign literature might end up in the rear trunks of their automobiles. He came up with a more effective means of getting out campaign information. With the help of the National Beauty Culturists League, the United Beauty School Owners and Teachers Association, and a barbers' union in Chicago, he established a grassroots organization to distribute campaign literature through the members' shops. The idea was brilliant in its simplicity. The shops served an exclusively black clientele and had historically provided a place in the black community for the exchange of ideas and information. Nearly every black person in America could be counted on to visit such an establishment at least once during the campaign. After all, white shops did not do black hair.[21]

For the first time, Martin also broadened his media campaign to include radio. He tapped Howard Woods, a long-time friend of Lyndon Johnson's, who had good contacts with black radio stations. Under Martin's guidance, Woods convinced his friends to spend their public service time broadcasting nonpartisan get-out-the-vote appeals, which Martin had prerecorded and made readily available. Although the ads were nonpartisan, Martin knew that blacks could be counted on to vote for Lyndon Johnson if he could just get them to the polls; and, of course, public service ads cost his DNC operation almost nothing. He also used sound trucks to play taped endorsements by nationally known blacks. In Philadelphia, they even tried using helicopters outfitted with loudspeakers to play the tapes.[22]

The most troubling event of the campaign concerned a black Republican ploy to use Martin Luther King's name to syphon off votes that would otherwise go to Johnson. Martin received word that some black Republicans were plotting to flood Philadelphia with flyers urging blacks to vote for "one of their own" by writing in the name of Martin Luther King, Jr., on the presidential ballot. Millions of black voters could become confused and divided by the anonymous circulars, especially since they were printed in a telegram format that suggested the message was in some way official. Within hours of reading one of the leaflets, Martin was on a plane to Atlanta. He knew his first task was to convince King that he was not simply on a partisan mission. Ever since their first meeting at the Mayflower Hotel in 1961, they had had a good relationship. Martin met with King at the leader's Atlanta home situated in a quiet middle-class neighborhood. He later noted that King had the ability to make his visitors feel that they had his full attention, an ability that all the presidents Martin served also had. King's response was just what Martin had hoped. He was appalled at the attempt to use his name to negate the effect of black votes and readily agreed to repudiate the effort at a press conference. On his way to the airport, Martin heard on the radio that King had already called a press conference for noon the next day to clear up the matter.[23]

꒰ ꒰ ꒰

On the campaign trail, Lyndon Johnson was in his element. Eager to be liked, he loved campaigning. Unlike his opponent, Arizona senator Barry Goldwater, Johnson believed in drawing bigger and bigger circles, appealing to every voter. Martin was amazed at his unflagging energy, his capacity to shake every hand, and his ability to draw strength from the adoring crowds. Martin described him this way: "At the center of every stage stood the president with arms outstretched, shouting himself hoarse in an eloquent appeal for every patriot to rally behind him in his crusade for a more prosperous, a more just, and a more united America."[24]

But Johnson always remembered that he was a southerner, and he knew that his popularity with black voters could produce a backlash among southern white voters. Like southern writer Lillian Smith, he believed that racism had produced poverty and psychosis in both black and white southerners. In his campaign addresses to southern audiences, his message was essentially that of the adage generally attributed to Booker T. Washington: "You can't keep a man down in a ditch without staying down there with him." He urged southerners to "get on board the twentieth-century train bound for prosperity and the promised land now occupied by the Yankees." Johnson's forthright approach to the race issue placed his campaign on a high moral ground. Blacks particularly appreciated his willingness to preach the same message to every audience.[25]

In the end, Goldwater was no match for Johnson, who received the highest margin of victory ever in a presidential election. His winning percentage of the popular vote also broke an election record, even exceeding the 61 percent won by Roosevelt in the 1936 election. Goldwater carried only six states—Alabama, Arizona, Georgia, Louisiana, Mississippi, and South Carolina—while Johnson won the remaining forty-four.[26]

In just four years, the Democrats had increased their share of the black presidential vote from 68 percent (in 1960) to an amazing 94 percent.[27] While Martin recognized that the momentous civil rights legislation accounted for much of this change, he also felt that his campaign strategy of reaching out to every segment of the black community had proven effective. When he and Cliff Alexander told LBJ proudly that he had received 94 percent of the black vote, Johnson asked: "What happened to the other 6 percent?"[28]

One fact boded ill for the future of the party, however. Every state Goldwater won except for his home state of Arizona was located in the Deep South. Already the Democratic party was paying a price for its stand on civil rights.

❧ ❧ ❧

Not long after the 1964 election, Martin became interested in the upcoming British election and decided to combine business and pleasure with a trip to England. He convinced DNC chair John Bailey that it would be worthwhile to observe these elections to see how the British way compared to ours. Martin called his British friend Pat Dolan, who had recruited him to go to Nigeria in 1959, to tell him. Dolan invited him to stay at his home.

In England, Martin attended press conferences and rallies. While he found much of the politicking similar, he was surprised that the well-known heckling by British crowds, particularly students, was more civilized than he had imagined it would be. In fact, he found it much more like a question-and-answer session at an American town meeting. He was amused by the ridiculous hats students wore at these occasions, though frustrated by how difficult it was to understand some of the many regional accents and dialects. Unfortunately, the issues under debate were often so parochial that he was at a loss to judge their significance.[29]

All the while, an idea was percolating in his mind. King was to be awarded the Nobel Peace Prize in Oslo in a few days, and Martin thought it would be a wonderful thing to witness. Although he had not planned to make the trip, he felt he knew King well enough for his presence to be welcomed. When he arrived at the Grand Hotel in Oslo, he found Bayard Rustin, one of King's top advisors, at the desk. After a happy reunion, Rustin briefed him on who was there and what the schedule was. Along with King's extended family, many SCLC members had made the trip to witness the historic event. Too many, Rustin confided, because it was impossible to keep their behavior under control.

Martin communicated to King the personal greetings of the president of the United States, despite the fact that LBJ had no idea he was there. Martin later explained his exuberant gesture: "I was sure that the president would have wanted me to convey his greetings if he had known I was going." Although Martin had arrived too late to receive invitations to some of the social events, he was able to get his credentials squared away to attend the award ceremony. He found King's acceptance speech mesmerizing. Many in the audience may not have understood English well enough to know what King was saying, but their warm response showed Martin that the cadence and timbre of the man's voice—combined with his noble achievements—transcended language. Many times King was interrupted by applause. Martin could only compare it to the effect of poetry whose meaning may be abstract but whose beauty still comes through.

Following the ceremony, Martin went to the celebration at King's hotel suite. Andrew Young, Ralph Abernathy, the King family, and others from the movement were all there. After many, including Martin, had made speeches and offered toasts, members of the King family began to talk about the early days of the struggle, and their stories left everyone teary-eyed. Young and Abernathy gave eloquent speeches, each expressing his gratitude to King for his leadership and guidance to them personally. Moments later, Rustin and King began discussing a speech King was scheduled to make in Harlem. Martin was impressed at how easily they moved from emotions and high principles to practical reality—like politicians, he thought.[30] Less than a month later, in January 1965, King and the SCLC would launch their voting rights campaign in Selma, Alabama.

ᥡ ᥡ ᥡ

Martin had been touting the power of the vote for decades. Twenty-five years earlier, he had written:

> The Southern attempt to deny democratic rights to its colored citizens is an open violation of all that democracy stands for. Eventual Negro suffrage in

the South is as inevitable as was the abolition of slavery, and if the South wants to fight about it they will find themselves with just another lost cause.[31]

Martin had learned back in 1960 that LBJ's views on the franchise, despite his southern roots, were much the same as his. Johnson believed that in the long run the future of racial progress, in every area, depended on access to the ballot. "The only real way to get the kinds of treatment [blacks] want is through the ballot box," he told Martin. "Politicians will do what they have to do."[32] Although after the Civil War the U.S. Constitution had been amended to give blacks the right to vote, the black man's franchise in the South effectively ended when Reconstruction did. Violent attacks and threats of economic reprisal eventually kept most blacks in the South away from the polls. Their periodic attempts to register ran up against a white establishment that used a variety of legal and illegal ploys to deny this right. Legal ploys included so-called literacy and citizenship tests, impossibly inconvenient registration locations and hours, and poll taxes. Other ploys included harassment, intimidation, and even murder. Since 1955, at least nine people had been killed specifically for working to give black people the right to vote. Three of the most recent victims were James Chaney, Andrew Goodman, and Michael Schwerner, one black and two white civil rights volunteers abducted and slain in June 1964 in Philadelphia, Mississippi.

Kennedy's strategy had been to attack the problem through the courts rather than through the legislative process, where there was little chance of success. But that strategy had proved slow and uncertain and had been subverted as well by Kennedy's southern judicial appointees.[33] Starting in October 1963, a series of organized attempts by blacks to register in Selma, Alabama, had amply demonstrated the need for tough new voting rights laws: the registrants were met with police beatings and arrests. Yet despite tireless efforts by Clarence Mitchell and other civil rights figures, the 1964 Civil Rights Act did not include sufficiently strong measures to protect voting rights.[34]

King knew that a strong voting rights bill would pass in Congress only if the broader public's attention were sharply focused on the problem. Selma seemed just the spot to make that happen. On March 7, 1965, a day that came to be known as Bloody Sunday, 500 demonstrators, including members of both the SNCC and SCLC leadership, were confronted at the Edmund Pettus Bridge in Selma by a mass of state troopers and armed white citizens recruited by Dallas County sheriff Jim Clark. The ensuing unprovoked attack with tear gas, clubs, and electric cattle prods was captured by television cameras and photographers from across the nation. King, who was not present at the demonstration, called for a protest march from Selma to Montgomery the following Tuesday.[35]

At this point, Martin was receiving telephone updates and urgent requests on a regular basis from activists down in Alabama. One reason they made calls to him rather than to the Justice Department was security. John Cashin, one of the Alabama activists, phoned Martin more than twice a week throughout that period. "Sometimes we'd send messages up there to Washington," Cashin recalled, "and they'd just get into the wrong hands. The next thing we knew, the FBI would be sending someone down here." The assistance offered by J. Edgar Hoover's men at that time was not always friendly. Martin could pass the requests directly to the most senior person at the White House without getting the wrong people involved. To those working in the civil rights trenches, Martin's leverage was invaluable. "Louis was the ringleader," Cashin commented. "Whatever Louis wanted, we did it for him."[36]

King's aides called Martin to express their fears that an attempt might be made on King's life during the scheduled march. They hoped Martin would be able to help guarantee King's safety. Martin immediately got in touch with King, who told him that he feared a repeat of the police brutality that had characterized the first demonstration. King suggested that Johnson appoint a federal official of stature and credibility, such as Attorney General Katzenbach, to negotiate with Alabama governor George Wallace to end the crisis. Without significant federal action, King felt that he had no choice but to continue with the demonstration, in which case Johnson would have to use federal marshals to prevent another violent attack by the police.[37] Negotiations between the administration and King continued up to the moment of the march. In the end, King led the marchers on a limited endeavor, turning around after they crossed the bridge. The Alabama state troopers blocking the highway watched as the column of marchers returned to Selma.[38]

On March 15, 1965, a little more than a week after Bloody Sunday, Lyndon Johnson submitted a voting rights bill. The president addressed a special joint session of Congress to explain why he thought its passage was imperative:

> There is no constitutional issue here. The command of the Constitution is plain. There is no moral issue. It is wrong to deny any of your fellow

Americans the right to vote. There is no issue of states' rights or national rights. There is only the struggle for human rights.... Because it's not just Negroes, but really it's all of us, who must overcome the crippling legacy of bigotry and injustice. And we shall overcome![39]

The audience of legislators—liberal, moderate, and segregationist alike—was hushed for a moment. A thunderous ovation followed.

Meanwhile, events were still unfolding in Alabama. The following Sunday, 4,000 marchers set out from Selma to Montgomery, under heavy federal protection. As they walked the fifty miles to the Alabama capital, they were subjected to heckling from white bystanders, but there was no violence. More important, they were joined by supporters in ever-growing numbers. By the time the racially integrated group reached Montgomery on March 25, they numbered over 25,000. Carried live on network television, the peaceful march rallied support for the voting rights bill then before Congress. It was a momentous event. There in Montgomery, where ten years earlier Rosa Parks had initiated an era of pathbreaking change by refusing to move to the back of a city bus, the whole pantheon of civil rights leadership was listening when King spoke:

> The end we seek is a society at peace with itself. That will be a day not of the white man, not of the black man. That will be the day of man as man.[40]

≈ ≈ ≈

On June 4, 1965, President Johnson prepared to deliver a speech at Howard University. From the early drafts he had seen, Martin was convinced that this would be a historic speech. He had encouraged LBJ to consult with Roy Wilkins, Whitney Young, and other black leaders before delivering it. Sharing the president's limousine en route to Howard, Martin and Cliff Alexander listened as Johnson explained how he saw his role in civil rights. "People need a hero," Johnson told them, "a strong leader who they can believe in." The two men flanked the president as they walked into the crowded auditorium to the students' enthusiastic welcome. Johnson, enjoying the attention, was clearly at ease. In his speech he set the philosophical basis for what would later be called affirmative action as he called for equality not just as "a right and a theory, but equality as a fact and a result." He alluded to the more intractable racial problems and cautioned against expecting that legislation would bring an end to the struggle for equality:

You do not wipe away the scars of centuries by saying now you're free to go where you want and do as you desire and choose the leaders you please. You do not take a person who for years has been hobbled by chains and liberate him, bring him up to the starting line of a race and then say, you're free to compete with all the others. Negroes are trapped, as many whites are trapped, in inherited, gateless poverty. They lack training and skills. They are shut in slums without decent medical care.... We are trying to attack these evils.[41]

Martin noted: "No one who heard LBJ that day will ever forget him or the speech. It was a watershed in the civil rights struggle, and it cheered the hearts of the valiant band of freedom fighters in the South and gave impetus to the passage of the voting rights bill." [42]

Congress passed the Voting Rights Act and sent it to the White House for signing on August 4. The promise of decisive action that the president had made to Martin and to civil rights leaders was fulfilled two days later when Johnson signed the bill, which outlawed unfair electoral procedures and stipulated that the Justice Department supervise southern elections. The signing ceremony took place in the room where Lincoln had signed the Emancipation Proclamation. Speaking in the Capitol rotunda beneath a statue of Lincoln, President Johnson urged blacks to register and vote. "Your future, and your children's future, depend on it," he declared. "If you do this, then you will find, as others have found before you, that the vote is the most powerful instrument ever devised by man for breaking down injustice and destroying the terrible walls which imprison men because they are different from each other." [43] Johnson warmly acknowledged the hundred or so civil rights leaders present. "I was fortunate to be a witness to so much history in the making, fortunate also to be a participant in a process that brought this eventful day to dawn," Martin later reflected.[44]

Within a week, the Justice Department had filed suits in Mississippi, Alabama, and Virginia to end poll taxes, and suits in several states to suspend voter qualification tests. Local federal employees served as examiners to register black voters in Alabama, Mississippi, and Louisiana. At long last, the full political expression of the more than five million blacks of voting age in the Old Confederacy, where fewer than 20 percent of them had been registered, was becoming a real prospect. For Martin, it was the achievement of something he had been striving toward for thirty years.[45]

Johnson had pushed to have the two landmark bills passed as quickly as possible, in part because he feared that the more radical and strident black leaders then emerging might undermine support for the legislation. Rising younger leaders were growing more militant in their demands for action, and many were discarding King's Christian vow of turning the other cheek. Others were brushing away the traditional aid of white liberals and rejecting integration in favor of black nationalism.

Malcolm X, whose views on racial separatism had begun to change just before his assassination in 1965, put little stock in King's doctrine of nonviolent resistance. Speaking at a rally in Harlem in 1964, he argued that the white racist was a person who did not grasp the language of nonviolence: "Let's learn his language. If his language is with a shotgun, get a shotgun." Martin, who had little regard for black separatism and less for arming of the citizenry, was not so much shocked by Malcolm X as unimpressed. He felt that Malcolm's reputation as a revolutionary thinker was overblown, that in fact his strength was due simply to his being a "master at provoking people, and provoking the media." Roy Wilkins was more complimentary: "He was a mesmerizing speaker, the toughest man in debate that I've ever seen. None of us could touch him, not even Dr. King." [46]

The outlook of Stokely Carmichael was of more direct concern to the White House. Carmichael, a civil rights activist who had risen to the leadership of SNCC, was actively engaged in voter mobilization in the heart of rural Alabama in 1965. With armed Klan members in control of much of this territory, he had succeeded for the first time in getting significant numbers of rural blacks to register to vote by creating a third party, whose ballot symbol was a black panther. Unlike Malcolm X, he had effectively practiced nonviolence, but in the heart of Klan territory he, too, was now urging voters to carry guns to protect themselves. Carmichael had also become an outspoken opponent of the White House on Vietnam and repeated Mao Tse-tung's dictum that political power comes out of the barrel of a gun. [47]

LBJ and those close to him were deeply upset to see the newest generation of civil rights activists moving in this direction. Politically, Johnson was afraid of the white backlash these spokesmen could generate, especially among conservative congressmen. His greatest fear was that his Great Society programs would be stalled or rejected in favor of "get tough" approaches. Martin was upset as well. In his own life he had never shrunk from taking controversial, confrontational stands against unequal housing, job discrimination, and police brutality. But as an advocate of racial inclusiveness and electoral democracy, he was worried by the rising popularity of separatist philosophies and armed militancy. Speaking at Shaw University in Raleigh, North Carolina, in 1964, he said:

> There are a few Negroes who share the view that a separate state should be carved out of the United States in which Negroes would rule and build their own separate civilization. There are a few others who wish to take us all back to Africa and set up a new all-black empire. Here recently I read that at least one Negro is advocating what appears to be a shooting war against the 90 percent of Americans who happen to be born white.... The most unfortunate aspect of all this silly, wild talk is that so much of it is being taken seriously. Further, the voices of the sane, rational leadership among Negroes can hardly be heard above the noise and din raised by these emotionally disturbed, grown-up children who are masquerading as important leaders.[48]

Over the next couple of years, these "few" Martin complained about would multiply as it became clear that voting rights laws were not self-enforcing, that intimidation by rural whites and urban police had not ended, that in northern cities poverty would not melt away with a few federal programs, and that in comfortable suburbs all over America most whites were not ready for black neighbors. The administration's response to these realities was, generally, to create more programs and seek better enforcement of laws. But the response of young and increasingly radicalized students was often to urge separation from the body politic. By 1966, in reaction to continuing police brutality and the marginalization of black life, discontented black community activists in Oakland, California, had taken Carmichael's concept and transformed it into a militant separatist movement known as the Black Panthers. King's "Freedom Now!" slogan had begun to be replaced by "Black Power!"[49]

᎑ ᎑ ᎑

With the passage of the Voting Rights Act, the attention of the White House as well as of civil rights activists moved northward to the urban ghettos. By early 1966, King was in Chicago, leading rent strikes to force action on slum housing. Solving the southern problems of official segregation and disenfranchisement had been a clear-cut task—the problems of the inner city were far more complicated. Despite the Johnson administration's aggressive domestic agenda, much of it still in the making, urban unrest turned into riots in the summer of 1965. (Martin had warned Kennedy about this danger two years earlier, though his plea for major urban aid was more or less ignored until Johnson took office.) In early August, a riot broke out in the Watts section of Los Angeles. By the end of the week-long turmoil, which engulfed a vast area of southeast Los Angeles, more than 13,000 national guardsmen had been brought into the ghetto to stop the looting and arson, and thirty-one people had died. In what would become a familiar refrain throughout LBJ's presidency, L.A. police chief William Parker blamed the president and his liberal agenda. "We can only expect violence," he asserted, "when you keep telling people they are unfairly treated and teach them disrespect for the law." [50]

LBJ was taken aback by the Watts episode, reacting as though the rioters had launched a personal attack. "How is it possible," he asked his aide Joseph Califano, "after all we've accomplished? Is the world topsy-turvy?" Those who knew the black community better were much less surprised. A year earlier, smaller outbreaks had occurred in Harlem and other cities. Roy Wilkins noted that California voters had recently approved a statewide proposition rejecting fair housing and, more to the point, that Los Angeles treated its residents to a two-tiered system of justice. "Mayor Yorty was a law-and-order man—law for the white folks and plenty of orders for everyone else," he recalled. Wilkins could not disagree with what younger, more radical activists were also saying—that the system of law enforcement in Los Angeles was openly brutal and discriminatory. An editorial appearing in *The Nation* shortly after the riot summed up the cause of the riots this way: "The hatred and violence of race riots is triggered by contempt, and of all forms of contempt the most intolerable is nonrecognition, the general unawareness that a minority is festering in squalor." [51]

From his decades working in Detroit and Chicago, Martin was intimately familiar with these blights on urban life. His advocacy of the labor movement in the 1930s and 1940s was based on his belief that economic security was a vital component of a citizen's rights in a democracy. He vividly remembered the riots that had torn Detroit apart in June 1943, when lack of housing and economic insecurity had produced an atmosphere that needed only a minor confrontation to ignite. He was certain that if the recent attainment of full civil rights in law was to be translated into full equality of opportunity in practice, economic inequities would have to be addressed, and swiftly. For inner-city populations so little had changed, from slum conditions to joblessness to police brutality.

## WALKING THROUGH NEW DOORS

One small but swift step that Johnson took within his own administration was to streamline the handling of civil rights policy. Until now, much of the policy was worked out, as it had been under Kennedy, by a variety of special committees, two of them headed by Vice President Humphrey. Feeling that time did not allow for this arrangement and wanting more direct control, LBJ moved general responsibility to the Justice Department and made the other departments more directly accountable for civil rights–related policies. Humphrey, who for years in the Senate had been far ahead of Johnson on the issue of minority rights, was disheartened when LBJ told him he would lose his role in dealing with the issue. But he could not argue with the rationale when the president forcefully explained, "These programs will work better in the departments because these people will know they have to report directly to me then." [52]

༄ ༄ ༄

The turmoil of Watts was on LBJ's mind when he turned his attention a week later to his campaign commitment to provide home rule for the residents of the District of Columbia. The District had had no elected municipal government since 1874, when Congress took control of its affairs. Five times since the administration of President Truman, proposals to change this situation had been put before the Congress, and each proposal had been killed by the House's District of Columbia Committee, dominated by southern conservatives. Now Johnson was determined that after passage of the Voting Rights Act, the majority-black residents of the nation's capital had to be free to elect their own municipal government. Through the late summer of 1965, the White House worked around the clock to recruit congressional support. By the autumn, they had just enough supporters to force a vote, but meanwhile conservatives had put out a substitute bill to deny home rule. The substitute bill passed. [53]

Not ready to give up, the president turned to Martin and Califano to nominate new candidates for the city's appointed three-member board of commissioners, then headed by a white, Walter Tobriner. Residents were calling for a forceful black commissioner, and in a city that was majority black it seemed important to Martin and LBJ, as well, that the head of the triumvirate be black. The assignment was delicate. The city's white minority wielded nearly all the District's financial and political power, and as Martin recalled, the District of Columbia then felt like a southern town. "When we came here," he said, "one of the things that shocked me was that it was like going back to Savannah." Federal agencies (the city's largest employer) and municipal offices alike were studded with relatives of congressmen, so the new chief commissioner, whatever his skin color, would need excellent political skills and good connections. In May 1966, Martin and Califano recommended a black candidate to replace Tobriner. His name was Walter Washington, and as executive director of the National Capital Planning Authority he had already worked on the capital beautification effort with the first lady, who was solidly behind him.[54]

LBJ soon found that the city's major white business owners were frightened by the prospect of a black man heading up the board of commissioners and thereby governing the police force. Katharine Graham, publisher of the *Washington Post*, warned him of white flight. Martin stepped in with a compromise proposal: put Walter Washington into the number two position on the board, and then move him up to the top post later after Tobriner resigns. Martin thought he had Washington's agreement to this strategy, but when they met with LBJ, Washington insisted on the presidency of the board or nothing. This infuriated Johnson, who decided to clear the slate and start over.[55]

Johnson decided to replace the District's three-person board with a single appointed mayor and city council, a move that would not require the approval of the hostile House District Committee but would instead need the approval of the much friendlier Government Operations Committees of both the House and Senate. It took a year to secure the support of influential white business leaders and black District organizations, but by August 1967 they had come around. Meanwhile, Johnson had asked Califano to look specifically for white candidates. It turned out to be another LBJ ruse—a play for time. In late August, Johnson rejected Katharine Graham's white candidate, criminal lawyer Edward Bennett Williams, announcing, "He's white and I want a Negro. He doesn't have any experience running cities." He then turned around and named Walter Washington as his choice for mayor. By now Washington had taken a post as housing czar for the city of New York. When New York Mayor John Lindsay heard that his housing director was about to be stolen by the president, he flew to the capital and met with LBJ privately to tell him how unfair this was. But Walter Washington was delighted to return to the District and handed Lindsay his resignation the same day.[56]

Altogether it had taken Johnson more than two years, but with Martin's help, the District of Columbia had its first black mayor and was on the path toward home rule as well.

# WALKING THROUGH NEW DOORS

૨ૡ ૨ૡ ૨ૡ

In the spring of 1966, Martin advised Johnson that a civil rights dialogue was needed to put together a plan for achieving racial equality now that legislation addressing basic rights had been passed. He further argued that they would need to construct the plan with a view to gaining the broad popular support that a long-term effort would require. Johnson announced a White House conference of scholars, experts, government officials, and national leaders of all races to be held in the fall, and he put Martin in charge of planning the event. Martin worked on the project with Harry McPherson, the president's chief speechwriter. McPherson, a young white southerner who had been with LBJ since 1956, was not fully conversant with the civil rights movement or black leadership, though his acumen as a political strategist had kept him close to the president.[57]

The conference was immediately the subject of controversy. Johnson aide Daniel Patrick Moynihan had submitted a report on the causes of urban poverty that unleashed a torrent of criticism. Moynihan wrote that poverty in black ghettos was unlikely to abate as long as the number of single-parent households continued to grow. Floyd McKissick of CORE was among those who denounced the report as an example of cultural arrogance—a white middle-class man telling poor black families to adopt his preferred family structure. The backlash was further fueled by the report's semiclassified status—few could obtain a copy.[58]

Martin had known Moynihan since the 1940s, when Moynihan was a speechwriter for the Democratic party in New York, and thought him highly intelligent. Martin was more supportive of Moynihan's report than most blacks were, but he disagreed with its conclusion that the absence of fathers from black households was at the heart of the problem of widespread poverty. He recalled the debate: "I told Pat, 'Look, when I started business in Detroit, we were just revving up for the war. I saw blacks come out of the plantation to the new industrial plantation of northern industry. One relative at a time: father, wife, child, cousin, daughter, coming in one by one trying to get it together, to get a job. But once they got a job and that big money, the whole picture began to change. This migrant crowd started buying homes, dressing up their children, and moving immediately into a new kind of culture. I could see it happen.' " Martin recognized the importance of upbringing but felt that to place all the weight on family upbringing and argue against social spending was to defy the facts about poverty. "This is a money-oriented society," he would later say. "The whole business of educational opportunities and all that—it's unbelievable what happens when poor people finally feel that they are halfway financially secure. They take a new attitude toward life." [59]

In the end, LBJ took Moynihan's report seriously, including the recommendation that the opportunities for jobs and education needed to be shored up in the inner city, but he also sought alternative advice on his urban poverty initiatives from a number of distinguished social scientists. In this atmosphere, Martin worked with McPherson and LBJ's other aides to put together the conference as a first-rate symposium under the title "To Fulfill These Rights." Its aim was to tackle the larger issues of urban poverty as well as the finer points of policy. They assembled an advisory council largely made up of business and labor leaders, headed by railroad executive Ben Heineman. The idea was to entrust the agenda to centrists who believed in equal opportunity and also had the clout to do something about it. The council members were, in McPherson's estimation, far more understanding of urban issues than Congress was, and certainly no one could claim they were "revolutionaries or theorists." Martin made sure that Vernon Jordan was included in the planning as well. Jordan, a former NAACP activist from Georgia, had by 1965 become director of the revived Voter Education Project. Martin admired Jordan's work in the voter drives, and since hearing Jordan speak in South Carolina had been trying to recruit him to join the administration. [60]

The revolutionaries, of course, were not invited to the conference, though the participant list included civil rights leaders of all styles, including McKissick. A statement issued by Jesse Gray, a Harlem rent-strike leader, was not untypical of early reactions to word about the upcoming conference: "The black ghetto and the black South need no more conferences with the two-faced white power structure to understand its problems." [61]

Even while the planning continued, Johnson's advisors, anticipating pickets and other trouble, debated whether the president should attend. Martin was alert to the possible volatility of the event and designed every detail to minimize conflict. He made sure the conference was packed with members of the more established organizations, such as the NAACP and SCLC. Although SNCC and other radical groups had threatened disruptive demonstrations, the event went smoothly. [62]

The Heineman council's 100-page report of recommendations was reviewed, amended, and ultimately adopted by the conference's several thousand participants. Among the more aggressive ideas put forward but discarded was that General Motors be required to make its Chevrolet division a black-owned entity. Most of the accepted recommendations involved new or expanded federal programs, for example, the location of new federal buildings in poor sections of the nation's cities. Another recommendation was for the federal government to "assume responsibility for the quality of education in all parts of the United States." Another was that the Department of Housing and Urban Development should promote desegregation with all its resources. These recommendations reflected the conferees' optimistic yet somewhat naive view of federal authority (and federal efficiency). In fact, by law, public schooling remained under local and state control, and housing projects, too, were usually managed by nonfederal authorities.[63]

Although most of the conference's conclusions were never carried out, several of them were, and the hopeful mood these ideas reflected was heartening, especially given the antigovernment radicalism that was on the rise outside the White House. Martin had arranged a role reversal for the end of the conference: instead of giving the final address, the president introduced another speaker, Thurgood Marshall, then solicitor general of the United States. LBJ received an unexpected greeting of applause and cheers. Afterward he thanked Martin in a warm note: "Everyone I have talked with has spoken in the highest terms of your work in preparing for and carrying out the White House Conference. The consensus is, 'We don't know what we would have done without Louis Martin.' I share in that consensus, as I always have."[64]

After the conference, Johnson invited Martin to spend a few days at his Texas ranch. Vernon Jordan and Harry McPherson were there as well. Talking together over meals, they often touched on the topic of civil rights. On one occasion McPherson put forward the view that things weren't as bad as many blacks said they were, that in fact, much progress had been made. Jordan was startled to hear McPherson speak in these terms. "Vernon blurted out at him," Martin recalled, "and very vigorously took him to task on some of his statements."[65] While Martin felt McPherson was well meaning, he agreed with Jordan that this kind of self-congratulatory attitude had always made things worse. It was "a view that many blacks think is sort of illusory, in terms of racial progress," Martin later said. The next two years would serve to remove the rose-colored glasses from McPherson's eyes. By 1968, Martin would be escorting him on personal tours of the most deprived ghettos in America.

Meanwhile, Vernon Jordan had risen quickly in LBJ's estimation. During 1966, the president found an opportunity to do something about an injustice in the military that had been gnawing at him. The men serving in Vietnam were disproportionately coming from the have-nots and racial minorities, in part because at the time, the draft allowed young men whose families could afford to send them to college to avoid service. LBJ assembled a National Advisory Commission on Selective Service to review the system and recommend a way to fix it. Most of the commissioners were white. Among those who were not were John Johnson, the publisher of *Ebony* and *Jet*, and Vernon Jordan. The commission made several changes in the draft, the most dramatic of which may have been the elimination of college deferment, a change the commission passed by a narrow majority.[66]

☙ ☙ ☙

Despite Johnson's broad popularity among black citizens, by 1966 his relations with Martin Luther King, Jr., had become somewhat strained. No doubt some of Johnson's animosity was attributable to the nearly constant flow of negative reports on King coming from J. Edgar Hoover at the FBI. Hoover made no secret of his dislike of King, and he continued to communicate unflattering details of King's personal life supposedly collected from FBI wiretaps. He had sent similar messages to President Kennedy. Moreover, Johnson generally felt more comfortable with other civil rights leaders, such as Roy Wilkins and Whitney Young, than he did with King, whom he characterized as "vain, preachy, communist-influenced." Martin recalled that whereas King had been flattered and honored by invitations to the White House from President Kennedy, by the time he became a Nobel Prize winner he was less impressed by such invitations. With his fame firmly established, King now caused protocol problems at the White House by insisting on private meetings with Johnson and then canceling two appointments himself.[67]

Such snubs angered Johnson, especially after King had announced his opposition to the Vietnam War in the spring of 1967. Johnson was furious and denounced the civil rights leader as caring more about posturing than about helping his own people.[68] Martin, however, speculated that King's decisions derived from complex pressures exerted on him as a leader. He would write in his memoirs later:

I think King was under some pressure from the rising black militants.... His nonviolent concepts were being repudiated, and his leadership was slipping. The question arose, and it also arose with Wilkins and Young, about being too close to the president. More militant blacks began the snide attacks, claiming they were captives of the White House. In order to maintain their own leadership posture, they had somehow to indicate that while they agreed with the president on some things, they did not agree on others. In fact, Johnson told Wilkins once, "You can criticize me, you can hit me a little bit." He was worried about Wilkins's posture with his own people.[69]

By 1967, all of Johnson's social initiatives and other accomplishments and all the genuine change that had taken place in the civil rights arena could not stop the erosion of public confidence in the White House and in institutions of authority generally. In addition to the growing sore of Vietnam, urban unrest had intensified. In the summer of 1967, more cities blew up. The deadliest riots took place in Newark and Detroit in July, with the loss of sixty-six lives. Looting and arson on a large scale were carried out in these two cities by inner-city residents, almost all of them black. Most of the loss of life, however, was eventually traced to a different cause. In 1968, the Kerner Commission appointed by LBJ a year earlier to investigate the disorders and recommend preventive policies concluded that of the forty-three people killed in Detroit, *at least* twenty-seven were killed by the police or National Guard, and only two or three were killed by the rioters themselves.[70]

The Kerner Commission's report gave a detailed account of the deaths of three women, one a grandmother, who had died in the Newark riot. Young National Guard troops had been told that because of sniper fire they were to keep residents in a housing project away from windows. All three of the women had made the error of approaching windows, one to shoo her two-year-old out of danger, and had been shot by the guardsmen. If those facts were shocking to the white public, the commission's conclusion about the root cause of the disturbances was equally so:

> Race prejudice has shaped our history decisively in the past; it now threatens to do so again. White racism is essentially responsible for the explosive mixture which has been accumulating in our cities since the end of World War II.[71]

Roy Wilkins was a member of the largely white commission that reached this conclusion. Although it was hardly a radical group, LBJ found its report hard medicine to swallow. The report's statement that America remained a nation of two societies, one white and one black, still separate and unequal, struck the president as too extreme. When King read it he found it to be "an important confession of a harsh truth." [72]

What the Kerner report recommended was in many respects what Johnson and his aides had been seeking for two years and what Martin had always argued for—greater federal investment in housing and jobs. Indeed, despite the creative new programs started by LBJ's War on Poverty, actual funding authorized by Congress had fallen far short of the administration's requests. Congress was in no mood now to revisit a question of funding that might require a tax surcharge, and many members knew there was political hay to make with get-tough calls for law enforcement. Speaking on the floor of the Senate, Russell Long of Louisiana announced, "Mr. President, the people of this country are getting enough of that kind of thinking that lets our government be run by rioters." Moderate legislators also were hesitant to appear to be "rewarding" urban unrest with new social programs. By 1968, Congress was refusing to renew funding for a number of LBJ's urban initiatives. [73]

The charge was already being made—and has been often repeated since— that the Great Society's social programs were a failure. But many of them did succeed even though few were ever funded at the originally intended levels.

By this time it was also clear that the escalating cost of the war in Vietnam left dwindling resources for the domestic agenda. Referring to the recent White House conference on civil rights, McPherson later stated, "We had all these thoughtful recommendations coming out of the conference. Some of them we were able to put into effect. Most of them we weren't because the Vietnam War came along and took all the money." Moreover, Johnson's public confidence about winning his twin wars—against poverty and against the Vietcong—did not square with the images Americans saw on their television sets, a discrepancy leading to what was called "the credibility gap." Even within the Democratic party, the president began to lose support. Senator Eugene McCarthy of Minnesota started a campaign for the Democratic presidential nomination based chiefly on opposition to the war and attracted thousands of idealistic young people. In March, Martin's friend Bobby Kennedy also became an announced candidate. [74]

On March 31, 1968, Lyndon Johnson shocked the nation with his televised announcement that he would not seek another term as president. Vice

## WALKING THROUGH NEW DOORS

President Hubert Humphrey was suddenly and unexpectedly a candidate for the party's nomination.

ta ta ta

The spring and summer of that year brought a succession of tragedies. The assassination of Martin Luther King, Jr., on April 4, in Memphis, Tennessee, where he was supporting a strike by sanitation workers, abruptly changed everything. President Johnson declared Sunday, April 7, a day of national mourning. For Louis Martin and his family, April 4 was a day of mixed emotions. The wedding of Martin's second daughter, Anita, had been scheduled for that day. It was a simple wedding, but getting to and from the ceremony and then to the Mayflower Hotel was a logistical nightmare played out with a leitmotif of grief over King's death and foreboding over what might follow it. Their fears were justified. The assassination immediately triggered riots in cities across the country.

By the end of the week, 20,000 federal troops and 34,000 National Guardsmen were mobilized. Forty-six people had been killed, 2,600 had been injured, and 21,000 had been arrested.[75]

The president offered to fly King's father to a special memorial tribute to be held at Washington's National Cathedral on April 5, but the elder King was too sick to attend. When told that the president's prayers were with him, Daddy King responded, "Oh no, my prayers are with the president." The evening of the assassination, Johnson drew up a list of the most senior civil rights leaders, asking that they all come immediately to the White House to join ranks and attend the memorial service with him. A. Philip Randolph, Clarence Mitchell, Whitney Young, Bayard Rustin, Roy Wilkins, Dorothy Height, and Thurgood Marshall were asked to come, as were two black men whose recent elections to political office showed how far the nation had progressed in opening up voting opportunity: Mayor Carl Stokes of Cleveland and Mayor Richard Hatcher of Gary, Indiana. When the group arrived the day after King's death, smoke could be seen rising above the roofs just blocks from the Capitol.

Califano phoned Martin with the president's request that he join them and expect to spend all day and evening there. When Martin arrived at the gate, however, the guards did not recognize him and checked his car trunk. Finding golf clubs and other equipment, they suspected he might be a looter who had somehow wandered in from the rioting. After all, he was black. Once that was straightened out, Martin joined the group in the Cabinet

Room with the president. LBJ asked everyone for advice on how he should respond to the upheavals outside the window and across the country and also urged them to use their own influence to condemn violence. It had not helped matters that two days earlier Stokely Carmichael had publicly stated, "When white America killed Dr. King last night, she declared war on us." The leaders present readily agreed to speak out against rioting, although Mayor Hatcher expressed the anger he felt along with so many blacks at the racism still prevalent in the nation's institutions.[76]

While they were meeting, Martin received a call from the west basement gate explaining that Secret Service agents would not admit Floyd McKissick, then national director of CORE, and Roy Innis, his successor. Martin called the agents, but they still refused to admit McKissick and Innis since only one person from each organization had been invited and checked by the FBI. Martin was suspicious of the pair's motives. Both had become vocal in their criticism of Johnson, and it appeared that McKissick was angry because Stokely Carmichael had not been invited to the gathering.[77]

Martin went into the meeting and whispered to his old friend Roy Wilkins, "I've got a problem. Innis is acting up, and I don't know what the problem is. I don't want to mess this thing up because you fellows are supposed to go with the president over to the service at the cathedral."

"Well, keep him out of here," Wilkins replied. "We don't want any confusion." Meanwhile, the Secret Service agents discussed over their two-way radios what to do about the "package" (their code word for McKissick and Innis) in the basement.

Martin left the Cabinet Room to talk with the controversial pair. "I'm not going to the meeting without Roy Innis," McKissick fumed. By this time, the other civil rights leaders and the president were en route to the cathedral, a fact that Martin was careful not to mention. "Suppose every guest insisted on bringing an associate, how could we have a meeting?" he asked, appealing to the enraged McKissick for reason. "Look, let me check on the meeting."

Wheeling around, Martin hurried upstairs, tarried momentarily, then returned to tell the two the meeting was over. Thoroughly annoyed, McKissick threatened to call a press conference. Martin carefully talked him out of the idea, all the time concealing his frustration that the two men were causing him to miss the entire tribute to King. He had feared admitting the two because of Innis's tendency to be disruptive. Martin suspected that once Innis was seated with Young, Wilkins, and others in the Cabinet Room, he would seek the spotlight. That was because, in Martin's words, Innis was "on the make."

Martin later explained. "I thought about it. A perfect occasion for a headline would be for Innis to blast everybody during a formal ceremony with the president of the United States memorializing Martin Luther King, Jr. As a matter of fact, I was afraid McKissick was going to do it, but I was more afraid of Innis." [78]

When the group of eminent civil rights leaders returned from the cathedral, several gathered with LBJ in the Oval Office to continue their discussion. Roy Wilkins argued for additional civil rights measures, Whitney Young spoke about the need for jobs, and Leon Higginbotham talked about the courts. The conversation was inconclusive, and in the midst of it Walter Washington, who had been mayor of the District for just a year, kept leaving the group to receive updates on the riot. That afternoon, at the mayor's request, the president ordered federal troops to enter the city, under strict orders to avoid shooting at all costs. [79]

For the next three evenings the view from the White House, where crisis meetings went on continuously, was of a city under siege. According to McPherson's notes, the president's advisors had a hard time agreeing on what to do next. National Security Advisor Walt Rostow said that the people living in inner cities must be given the means to do for themselves and that Congress must pass legislation to that effect. Clifford Alexander pointed out that existing federal programs did little for the rioters themselves—"We help their neighbors," he said, "but not the people with the guns and firebombs." Martin added a more pessimistic note concerning the actual conditions of life in the ghetto: "Human misery—it's still there, and it has hardly been touched." [80]   A day after King's funeral in Atlanta, the House approved the Civil Rights Act of 1968, which had been passed by the Senate a month earlier. The next day, Johnson signed it into law. The legislation strengthened the 1964 Civil Rights Act, prohibited racial discrimination in the sale or rental of approximately 80 percent of the nation's housing, and protected civil rights workers from intimidation or injury while engaged in activities to promote equality in housing, education, and voting. Reflecting its context, the law also included anti-riot provisions, with stiff federal penalties for violators. The housing portion of the bill represented the end of a long and bitter fight. LBJ had been trying for two years to get nondiscrimination in housing enshrined in law—he considered Kennedy's earlier executive order on housing vulnerable to future dismantling—but even moderate congressional representatives had been afraid of the votes they might lose by unlocking the invisible gates of their all-white suburban neighborhoods. Califano recalled that after the president first proposed the measure in 1966, "it prompted some of the most vicious mail LBJ received on any subject, and the only death threats I ever received as a White House assistant." [81]

The 1968 legislation marked major progress on a problem Martin had been talking about for more than twenty-three years, even before the day he had led protests in Detroit over the barring of blacks from the Sojourner Truth Housing Project. The discrimination blacks suffered in renting and buying had been the topic of many editorials during his decades with the *Chronicle* and the *Defender*. A month after King's death, Martin, Alexander, and McPherson took a tour of Harlem to get a first-hand look at conditions and gain some sense of how people there felt. They had made similar forays into Chicago, Cleveland, Baltimore, and other cities.

McPherson informed LBJ that the influx of federal funding, "good police work," the growth of black business ownership, and even the vested interest that businessmen and numbers racketeers alike had in maintaining civil order all worked to make riots less of a likelihood in New York. However, he also described in painful detail the conditions that could still lead to a conflagration. The main conditions were the insufficient number of blacks on the city's police force, the high unemployment among young blacks, and inadequate housing. Time would show his prediction of no riots that summer in Harlem to be correct. [82]

⁂

The year 1968 held yet another tragedy for the nation and for Louis Martin personally. In June, triumphant in the California Democratic primary, Bobby Kennedy was thanking his supporters at the Los Angeles Ambassador Hotel. Just after midnight, as he left the crowd and walked through the hotel kitchen, he was shot, and five others were wounded. In less than two hours, Bobby Kennedy was dead. The nation had yet another assassinated leader to mourn, and Louis Martin had lost another old friend. Just the night before, he had gotten a phone call from the candidate, asking him to help out in the campaign.

Richard Nixon won the 1968 presidential election by only a half-million votes—or 2.3 million votes fewer than he had drawn in his 1960 loss to John F. Kennedy. Noting that Alabama governor George Wallace, running as a third-party candidate, had taken 13.5 percent of the popular vote and 45 electoral votes, carrying five southern states, analysts later concluded that Wallace's presence on the ballot took away enough votes from Humphrey to swing a few key states over to Nixon. It marked the beginning of a shift to the political right and a partisan realignment. As President Johnson realized when he signed the 1964 Civil Rights Act, the Democratic party would pay a serious political price for having swept away the legal underpinnings of racial discrimination.[83]

After the election, Martin accepted an offer to return to Sengstacke Publications as vice president and editor-in-chief of its newspapers. He was delighted at the thought of being a journalist again. After eight years working feverishly but often unrecognized behind the scenes, he relished the prospect of putting out his own paper again and expressing his viewpoints boldly in editorials and columns. In his letter of resignation to DNC chairman Larry O'Brien, Martin wrote:

> The contributions of the Democratic leadership to the political, social, and economic development of black Americans make me proud. A magnificent beginning has been made. The Negro in the deep South is walking through new doors to find power and prestige because Johnson fought for and won the Voting Rights Act of 1965. History has been made with black representation in the Cabinet, the Supreme Court, and other important federal agencies.... In the big cities, black mayors have proven that the political ladder by which other groups have climbed to power can work for Negroes despite entrenched racism.[84]

Even after his party's loss of the White House and five summers of rioting, Lyndon Johnson was able to speak with pride and warmth as he, too, spoke of the Voting Rights Act in a farewell address to black appointees a month after the election:

> I asked the attorney general the other day to tell me about the election and how it worked. He said, "We had over 600 observers out over this land— less than three years after that Act was passed—and we went to the worst places. We went where we thought we were bound to see intimidation and violations." He said, "Those 600 observers that went out have been unable to find one man to prosecute because it is a pretty well-accepted fact that Negroes can vote in this country." So if that can happen in three years—oh, think about what a marvelous future we have got ahead of us if we will just use our time—not bide it, but use it.

The outgoing president ended his remarks with these words: "I think the most merited tribute that I can pay to anyone who has not held any official position in this administration, but who has been one of the wisest and the most tireless counselors I have had…. a fighter for social justice, and a practical man of public affairs—on behalf of every man and woman in this room, and every black man and woman and boy and girl in this land and in the world, I think we ought to be very proud of Louis Martin…. I don't know what trouble Louis is going to get into. He got me into a good deal." [85]

⁌⁂ ⁌⁂ ⁌⁂

In interviews conducted with him after that time, Martin was repeatedly asked to compare the two presidents he knew so well. He felt Jack Kennedy lacked Johnson's ability to dominate Congress, to get legislation passed, to twist arms to get things done. Kennedy did use his bully pulpit to present civil rights to the public as a four-square issue of morality, Martin believed. "I think this is what we lacked in earlier years," he recalled, "particularly under Eisenhower, who refused or failed to give his personal view on the morality of the issue…. Although [Kennedy] did not live to actually make the moves, he did help create a receptivity to them." [86]

Of course, John Kennedy had driven Martin to frustration with his calculated attempt to wait for Congress to become receptive to civil rights and his willingness to bargain with the southern Dixiecrats.[87] Lee White, who served both presidents, later said, "If I had one criticism of Kennedy, it would be that he took a little too seriously the narrowness of his victory. He assumed he would have a second term and could do a lot of things then." [88] Martin had reached the same conclusion. While he was just as calculating, Johnson was much more aggressive. He took on the unfinished civil rights agenda as a personal crusade. LBJ's understanding of what it meant to start life disadvantaged was visceral.

For all their personal privilege, however, Martin thought the Kennedys' experience with discrimination as Catholics in the Protestant world of Harvard, and their knowledge of the country's earlier treatment of the Irish, made them quick learners. He noticed the speed with which Robert Kennedy was transformed from a reluctant attorney general to an angry fighter against southern injustice.

Both Kennedys were buffeted by circumstances—especially by the persistent pressure of the civil rights movement—to live up to their well-meaning campaign promises. Executive actions were politically the easiest and came most quickly: the promise of judicial appointments that JFK had made at the Harlem rally in 1960 was acted on immediately. So were other appointments that marked the beginning of genuine integration at the top of the federal bureaucracy.

"After the 1960 election," Martin recalled, "in the beginning, Jack, Bobby, and several others met one day and they said to me, 'What the hell are you going to do?' And I said, 'One thing I'm going to do is this: We're going to put a black in the Cabinet and a black on the Supreme Court.' We didn't name anybody, but I said we were going to do these things. John Kennedy started the job—Lyndon Johnson finished it. Kennedy was threatened by southern congressmen—Johnson threatened them back, and got his way."

But serious legislative action on civil rights, action that every civil rights leader had been calling for since 1957, came only in 1963 after George Wallace threw down the gauntlet of defiance, and television viewers around the world saw black children being firehosed in the streets of Birmingham. Martin's role in helping to change Kennedy's mind is evident when one considers the vacuum of support for civil rights even within the White House. As Burke Marshall later said of the decisive presidential actions finally taken in the spring of 1963: "Every single person who spoke about it in the White House—every one of them—was against President Kennedy sending up that bill, against his speech in June, against making it a moral issue, against the March on Washington." The sole exception, Marshall said, was the president's brother Bobby, the man who by 1963 was leaning on Martin for his most reliable day-to-day advice on the needs of the black community.[89]

Johnson inherited the civil rights bill and Kennedy's promises, and he inherited Kennedy's advisors as well. But everything had begun to change, and LBJ was afire with his determination to make racial justice a reality. "President Johnson was far more experienced and was basically an achiever," Martin observed. "Kennedy could inspire and motivate. They were not far apart at all on objectives and ideals, but in cold, practical terms, Johnson was able to accomplish far more on civil rights and poverty issues than Kennedy did, or could have done had he lived. We needed both."[90] "We got the civil rights legislation," Martin said of his days with Johnson. "I was with him in those periods when it was rough. He used to say, 'We don't have much time.' He knew the country's mood was not going to remain that way. I had my problems with Johnson, but nevertheless it was a happy period for me."

Of Martin's two objectives—black political participation and economic opportunity—the first had become a genuine reality. His confidence that the nation would achieve the second goal in the course of time was based on his faith in the power of political representation. As he said later, "After the Voting Rights Act, we learned that we could mobilize our own power through the electoral process and that the most successful march a person could take was to the ballot box." [91]

❧

# .8.

## RESCUING THE
## GEORGIA BRIGADE:
## THE CARTER YEARS

*It was quite a new thing then for
a president to seriously consider
black nominees to be federal
judges. I appointed more, with
Louis Martin's help, than all of
the other presidents in history
together.*

*—Jimmy Carter*

In August 1978, nearly a decade after leaving the Johnson White House, Louis Martin found himself once again in the Oval Office. Just eight months earlier, he had retired from Sengstacke Publications and moved to Washington, D.C., to take a position as a legislative aide to his friend, Illinois Senator Adlai Stevenson III. The week before, he had been summoned to meet with Jimmy Carter's White House staffers, who showed him a list of black candidates for the position of assistant to the president. Although he knew each of the candidates well, Martin explained that he could not choose among them because he was not sure what the position entailed and what the staff had in mind. All the candidates seemed so highly qualified, he pointed out, that it would not be a mistake to choose any of them. He further suggested that they consider running political operations out of the Democratic National Committee rather than out of the White House, an arrangement that he had found very effective under Kennedy and Johnson, since it had allowed him to run a freewheeling operation while still enjoying the privileges of a White House aide. The meeting ended without a decision.

Now, one week later, he was back at the White House, invited there to discuss the same list of candidates and help the staffers make a final selection. Hamilton Jordan, Carter's chief staff aide, suggested that Martin talk to the president directly. The two of them walked into the Oval Office, where to

Martin's surprise, Carter immediately asked him, "What did you do for Presidents Kennedy and Johnson?"

"That's a long story," Martin replied. "I did a number of things for them."

"Whatever you did for them, I want you to do for me." [1]

Carter, who had been in office a year and a half, intended his recruitment of Martin to mend what had become a badly strained relationship between his administration and the black community. Although Martin was surprised by the president's offer—no one had mentioned that he was being considered for the job—he accepted it. His appointment was set to begin when he returned from a Labor Day weekend vacation at the summer home in Wisconsin that he and Gertrude shared with her sister and brother-in-law.

≈ ≈ ≈

In the 1976 election campaign, Carter had vigorously pursued the black vote, and he had done so by bypassing black Democratic officials and appealing directly to black ministers. The list of endorsements from influential blacks in his home state of Georgia included Coretta Scott King, "Daddy" King, and Congressman and former SCLC member Andrew Young. Support from such stalwarts of the civil rights movement, coupled with the solid Democratic allegiance of both northern and southern blacks, helped Carter win 94 percent of the black vote in November. This gave him the narrow victory margins he needed in such key states as Missouri, Pennsylvania, Ohio, Louisiana, Texas, Mississippi, and Maryland. The new president later acknowledged that no southerner could have defeated Republican incumbent Gerald Ford without the kind of massive black support he received.

Martin, who had closely followed the campaign of this improbable candidate from Georgia, attributed Carter's success among blacks partly to his understanding of the black church. "I don't think any white in America was better prepared to handle a black congregation than Carter," Martin later commented. "He was absolutely unbelievable. He not only could quote the Bible at will, but he knew all the hymns, and there was a certain humility about his approach in a black church. He knew all the right words. He would sing 'Amazing Grace' or something else and everybody would just respond. The average white politician going into a black church talks friendly. But he normally does not understand that there are some biblical references, some code words that, if you're familiar with the Protestant church—and Carter was—got automatic feedback." [2]

When he first took office, the ever-smiling Carter brought many blacks a glimmer of hope. His talk was reminiscent of Lyndon Johnson, whose concern for fair and equitable government and sensitivity to minorities and the poor had not been forgotten. Many were heartened as well by Carter's efforts to bring back down to earth what had become under Nixon an "imperial presidency." Carter had promised to reestablish integrity and credibility in an executive branch devastated by the Watergate scandals, and his amnesty for Vietnam War protesters early in his term indicated that he meant to heal the divided nation's wounds. Many blacks were inspired as well by the president's elevation of human rights to a priority concern in American foreign policy and were heartened by the respect with which he treated black Africa's aspirations. Even Carter's status as a born-again Christian was a plus, particularly in the South. In the black community, political and spiritual leadership had traditionally been linked.

But before Carter's first year in office had ended, the hopes of many had soured as they found themselves at odds with the administration's domestic priorities. The new president's attention seemed focused on the energy crisis, government reorganization, and budget cutbacks, to the neglect of worsening economic conditions in the black community. By mid-1977, Vernon Jordan, still head of the National Urban League, was not alone in his conviction that an unexpectedly conservative Carter administration was neglecting black interests.

In a blistering keynote address at the 1977 National Urban League convention, Jordan charged:

> The administration has formulated a new foreign policy, a new defense policy, and a new energy policy. But it has not adequately addressed itself to a new domestic policy. We have no full employment policy. We have no welfare reform policy. We have no national health policy. We have no urban revitalization policy. We have no aggressive affirmative action policy. We have no national solution to the grinding problems of poverty and discrimination.[3]

Although stung by such criticism, Carter officials responded cautiously. In February 1978, they submitted to Congress a reorganization plan to strengthen the EEOC's enforcement of fair employment rules and to consolidate the government's scattered authority to ensure nondiscrimination in federal hiring and contracting. This would streamline the enforcement activities carried out by eighteen federal departments and agencies. The plan, however, was only partially implemented, and critics charged that it contained nothing new and merely promised better enforcement of inadequate existing laws.[4]

Carter hoped the White House staff position which he was now offering Martin could help improve political relations with blacks. Before he offered it to Martin he had offered the post to Mayor Richard Hatcher of Gary, Indiana. Hatcher declined, citing urgent problems in his city that demanded his attention. He was also influenced by the fact that in this post he would report to the chief of staff rather than directly to the president. To Hatcher and other blacks, such lack of access suggested that the post was to be used more as political appeasement than as a position of substance.

The position Hatcher turned down was already held by a former Gary resident, Martha ("Bunny") Mitchell. Her appointment had disappointed many of Carter's black supporters, who had hoped that the new White House post would go to an African American with far more political experience. Mitchell's political experience had been limited to her chairmanship of the District of Columbia Women's Political Caucus and her work as part-time consultant to government agencies. By the summer of 1978, White House officials decided they had made a mistake in appointing Mitchell. "We decided that we needed some gray hair and somebody slightly more senior," recalled Jordan.[5]

          **❧ ❧ ❧**

Martin was the obvious choice. Not only had he served in this capacity with two previous Democratic administrations, but even during the two Nixon administrations he had continued to work on behalf of blacks' full participation in the political system. Beginning in 1967, before Johnson left office, he had joined with black elected officials, intellectuals, and activists in a series of meetings that led to the creation of the Joint Center for Political Studies, an organization designed to meet the needs of black politicians and administrators, whose numbers were rapidly growing.

Empowered by the 1965 Voting Rights Act, blacks throughout the nation, and particularly in the South, had registered and voted in unprecedented numbers, often electing candidates of their own race. Martin and other leaders were aware that many of the newly elected black politicians lacked the skills and experience required of successful officeholders. More to the point, many of them needed to play catch-up with their established white colleagues. According to Martin, "There was no institution that could provide factual data and political analysis. There was not a place in Washington that a black mayor from a small southern town could call to get the answer to the question: Where can I find some money to pave my streets?" [6]

Another compelling reason to form such an institution was to affirm that black Americans could achieve racial justice and economic equality by working with, not against, the political system—an idea that embodied Martin's personal philosophy. At a time when the nation was being rocked by urban riots, and with a number of black militants advocating separation from the body politic, mainstream political participation and advocacy needed a home.

In 1969, after a number of conferences and meetings with black leaders, a task force appointed by the Metropolitan Applied Research Center (MARC) proposed the creation of a research and training institution for black officials. Funded by a two-year grant from the Ford Foundation, the new organization, to be jointly administered by MARC and Howard University, was named the Joint Center for Political Studies. It would offer educational services for leaders in public affairs, operate an internship and fellowship program enabling young blacks to learn about politics, and provide research, information, training and technical assistance for black elected officials. Martin was selected as the first chair of the Joint Center's five-person board of directors. [7]

Dubbed the "godfather of black politics" by the *Washington Post* a few years later, Martin possessed the political acumen, commitment, and sensitivity that were essential to steer the new organization through its formative years. A coalition builder, forever drawing larger circles of inclusion, he ensured the support of both Democrats and Republicans for the organization. Under the guidance of Martin and Frank Reeves, the Joint Center's first chief executive officer, the organization began to prosper.

In 1972, Reeves retired because of ill health. The board decided that the best candidate to succeed Reeves was Eddie Williams, then vice president for public affairs at the University of Chicago. A journalist by profession, Williams had worked with the Senate Foreign Relations Committee and had first encountered Martin years earlier as head of the State Department's Equal Opportunity Office. Martin was given the task of persuading Williams to agree to head up the fledgling organization. In the Chicago Press Club high atop the St. Clair Hotel, he successfully pitched the idea to him. Martin said later of the meeting, "I took him to the mountaintop and showed him the future." He often described his recruitment of Williams as "one of the best things I ever did in my life." [8]

A year earlier, Martin had been called on to help select the leadership of another major national organization. He was asked to chair the committee to select a new president for the National Urban League to replace his friend Whitney Young, who had drowned in a swimming accident in Nigeria. Martin's association with the National Urban League went all the way back to his early days in Detroit, when the group had been headed by Lester Granger. Martin suggested to the committee a man he had unsuccessfully tried to recruit for the Johnson administration—Vernon Jordan. Although Jordan had not been active in the Urban League and would, therefore, be somewhat of an outsider, his record as an NAACP official and his prominent role in national issues were well regarded. The committee approved the nomination unanimously.[9]

Thus, in the summer of 1978, when members of the Carter administration were pondering who could help them repair their relationship with blacks, Martin's stature in the black community was unparalleled. There was not an important figure in black politics whom he did not know, and many owed their success to his efforts. This also meant that he enjoyed close relationships with some of the administration's more vocal critics, Vernon Jordan among them. Looking back on the selection, Carter explained: "When I searched for someone to come in and be my right-hand person in the White House, typically we went through a long list of names. There wasn't any real competition when we got down to Louis and a few others; it was obvious that Louis Martin would be the one." [10]

મ. મ. મ.

The flap over Martin's appointment began even before he set up his office in the West Wing of the White House. His family had hardly arrived at the summer house in Wisconsin before telephone calls started coming in from angry black women across the country who had heard rumors that Martin was replacing Bunny Mitchell. He denied it. Mitchell was both intelligent and pleasant, he told them, and her problems with the Congressional Black Caucus and other critics merely reflected the attitudes of many of Carter's appointees, black or white, who were generally insensitive to congresspersons.[11] Martin had gotten the impression that his entry into the White House would not require Mitchell's exit, that she would be moved over but not out. There was certainly plenty of work for the two of them. Her title, special assistant to the president for *special projects*, suggested responsibilities different from his own as special assistant to the president. But this was not what the White House had planned, and Martin argued unsuccessfully with Ham Jordan and others that there was room for both Mitchell and himself.

Thus his tenure with the Carter White House began on an acrimonious note, hardly auspicious for an assignment aimed at overcoming African American disenchantment with the administration. The dissension increased when his appointment was announced. Critics who had lobbied for a black advisor at the level of Stuart Eizenstat, Carter's chief domestic policy advisor, charged that Martin's new post had no real authority. Indeed, Arthur Fletcher, who as assistant secretary of labor had been the highest ranking black official in the Nixon administration, expressed surprise that "a man with [Martin's] political savvy would accept a job with so little clout." [12]

A spokesman for the Congressional Black Caucus soon charged that Martin's post was toothless, watered down, and without direct access to Carter. With Martin's broad experience, extensive knowledge of Washington politics, and nationwide contacts, many of his supporters believed he was qualified to be White House chief of staff. Instead, as a special assistant, a notch below full assistant, he was ineligible to attend the president's senior staff meetings in the Oval Office. The absence of any black person at these daily meetings, critics charged, was a major mistake.[13]

Martin was not concerned about his title. He had always preferred to work in the background. As a newspaper reporter and editor, he had often operated behind the scenes because he thought that was the way to keep his objectivity. In his political work with the Kennedy and Johnson administrations, being in the background at the DNC gave him the flexibility to expand his responsibilities. He was confident that he could be an effective advisor to the Carter administration as long as he had the access to the president he had been promised. His foot was in the door, which he could always open wider. He kept his sights on the larger goal: having another chance to make a difference for millions of his people.[14]

At first, Ham Jordan was dubious about appointing the 66-year-old Martin to the relatively young staff. He soon realized that adding someone with a little gray hair and prior White House experience to the group proved very helpful, commenting: "There are not many people who are as good as they're advertised. Louis turned out to be every good thing that we heard about him. He made a tremendous first impression on all of us and that never changed. President Carter felt at ease with him and took an immediate liking to Louis, who not only had credibility and contacts but also had a history.

Looking at a problem, he often told us how Lyndon Johnson might have handled it." [15]

Martin dedicated himself to helping the president, who later described Martin's role as "very broad-ranging and very constructive." [16] The list of his responsibilities that Martin gave to the Reagan transition team in 1980 indicated the breadth of his job: He might be called on to help write part of a speech for the president or a member of the Cabinet. He responded to requests for information on topics that concerned blacks and organized and conducted special events for black constituents. Whenever there was an event at the White House, he made sure African Americans were included. He attended funerals of national leaders, particularly in Africa, and escorted the first lady to many events. He undertook special assignments for the president. But his most important function was far less specific than these routine tasks: he represented the views and interests of the black community to the president and his staff; conversely, he represented the president and his policies to the black community.

With a small staff of two professionals and three secretaries, Martin put together an efficient operation. Julia Dobbs, a Harvard-educated lawyer, helped with the case work, which mostly concerned contracts, grants, awards, and appointments. Karen Zuniga, who held an MBA from the University of Chicago, helped with a myriad of assignments. [17]

જ જ જ

Though he was not among the handful of senior aides who met with the president each morning, Martin was a regular at the larger staff meetings, which gave him a close-up view of White House policy and program planning. He had worked at the White House daily when he served under Kennedy and Johnson, but this was the first time he was involved in the day-to-day aspects of running an administration. The morning meetings gave him a chance to learn about the other members of the staff—their personalities, their ways of working, their ideas.

They were casual and friendly gatherings. Frank Moore, in charge of congressional liaison, began with a status report on the Hill, followed by Zbigniew Brzezinski, head of the National Security Council, with a summary of world events that affected the United States. Then Eizenstat from the Domestic Policy Council would report and Charlie Schultz from the Council of Economic Advisors. Anne Wexler, who was in charge of publicity, usually had something to say. Phil Wise, the appointments secretary for the president, would talk about the president's activities, Dick Moe would report on Vice President Mondale's schedule, and Mary Hoyt would update everyone on the activities of the first lady. Finally, those who represented special constituencies—blacks, labor, women—had an opportunity to talk.

Martin's challenge as a newcomer was to fit into a staff that had worked together for at least two years. Many staffers went back even further, having participated in the campaign or worked for Carter when he was governor of Georgia. At first, the Georgia advisors struck Martin as a very close-knit, secretive, smug group, but this perception changed as he came to know them. He found working with Ham Jordan, Frank Moore, and secretary to the Cabinet Jack Watson much easier than working with Stu Eizenstat or press secretary Jody Powell. Powell was unhappy that Martin kept inviting to the White House Congressional Black Caucus members who had publicly criticized the president's policies. "Martin wants to bring all these bastards in here, and as soon as they get out, they kick our asses," Powell complained. "They are going to do that anyhow," Martin countered. "You can make some friendships and get to know them." [18] Eizenstat struck Martin as cool and stand-offish. When they chanced to meet in the corridors of the White House, Eizenstat never spoke first. Moreover, while Eizenstat seemed always armed with facts to support his views, Martin felt that he often added them up wrong. He admitted that Eizenstat's remoteness may have added to his doubts about Eizenstat's domestic policy views. "Stu never seemed to have any doubts about anything and seemed to direct the Domestic Policy Staff with great authority," Martin recalled. "He seemed such a cold fish that I think his manner and attitude clouded my perception of his ability."

Martin often expressed his doubts about particular policy matters to David Rubenstein, Eizenstat's top aide. He found Rubenstein easy to talk to and more respectful of his experience. Rubenstein would often ask him in the middle of a policy discussion: "How did you do it in the Kennedy and Johnson administrations?" or "Do you think we are doing the right thing?" Martin particularly enjoyed the company of two of the president's economic advisors, Alfred Kahn and Charlie Schultz, although he found that their analyses of the economy and their priorities rarely squared with what he saw in the real world. Carter's staff were awed by Kahn's successes in deregulation, particularly in the airline industry. Martin was less excited about deregulation. As a businessman, he felt that some regulation was necessary to keep prices reasonable. But he enjoyed Kahn and Schultz's company, especially their warm, ready sense of humor.

Martin, who was not awed by people with money or power, worried that others in the administration were too deferential to wealthy business leaders. Even the Kennedy brothers, with all their family wealth, had been in Martin's experience much less inclined to give special treatment to big business. He recalled how Bobby Kennedy had once cut short a conversation with him, explaining that he had to get to a White House meeting with major CEOs and help his brother "kick ass." When Martin later mentioned this to another Kennedy staffer, the staffer told him that when it came to big business tycoons, the working rule was that it was better to "kick ass than kiss ass."

Along with this oversensitivity to business leaders, Martin quickly found that the Carter White House had the opposite attitude toward political leaders. Too many in the administration made enemies of potential allies through thoughtless, gratuitous slights. This lack of sensitivity seemed to permeate the White House's dealings with Congress. Complaints poured in to Martin's office that calls from important congresspersons to White House aides were not returned. On one occasion, the wife of a congressman complained to Martin that although the presidential box at the Kennedy Center was rarely occupied, members of Congress had not been offered the seats for themselves or their constituents. Calls to the White House requesting them had received no response at all.[19]

Martin set out to change the perception of insensitivity, first of all by establishing some regular communication with the black community. He began publishing a bulletin on White House letterhead bearing his name, which described administration initiatives and accomplishments of interest to blacks, including tidbits from every federal department. The bulletin, which bore the simple title, *Fact Sheet*, was mailed to every prominent black person in the country. The original mailing list of 4,000 eventually swelled to 20,000. It was quite a success. Shortly after Martin initiated the project, Ham Jordan remarked at a staff meeting that while he was pleased with the black turnout in a recent Florida election he was surprised that the only pamphlets black voters seemed to have were copies of Martin's bulletin. Andrew Young, speaking at his father's funeral, to which Martin escorted Rosalynn Carter, noted that his father had read the bulletin's every issue.[20]

Martin also made it his business to invite blacks to the White House to meet the president and participate in lectures, tours, and other events. These visitors included black artists, businesspeople, and professionals as well as organization representatives. He arranged for an administration official to talk to these visitors about a topic of concern to them, and then after spending some time with them himself, he would have the president come by to greet them. "I didn't pick just Democrats," he later explained. "I brought in people I thought would be helpful, who would need to know what Carter was doing, what he thought, and what the administration was about." During the three administrations he served, he brought in thousands of minority visitors from all over the nation.[21]

Eighty years after Theodore Roosevelt raised hackles by inviting Booker T. Washington to a White House dinner, Martin was making sure it was standard protocol to include blacks at every White House affair. A January 1979 Salute to American Poets, organized by the first lady, included two of Martin's black literary friends, poets Gwendolyn Brooks and Robert Hayden. Brooks, a Chicagoan who had made urban poverty a legitimate subject of serious verse, had been the first black to receive the Pulitzer Prize, awarded her in 1949 for her volume *Annie Allen*. Hayden, whose first book of poems Martin had published himself when Hayden was a reporter for the *Chronicle*, had since taught at Fisk University and the University of Michigan and won numerous awards. Both Brooks and Hayden had also held the prestigious post of poetry consultant to the Library of Congress.[22]

Martin made certain that blacks with expertise relevant to major foreign and domestic issues under discussion by the administration were able to share their views. Experience had taught him that black experts, especially those from academic circles, were generally unknown to the white political establishment. On one occasion, when Carter was seeking advice on how to handle the faltering economy, Martin suggested he consider what some distinguished black experts might have to say. When Carter agreed, Martin put together a private luncheon with the president to which he invited a group of black educators, administrators, and policy experts. Among the guests were two men whose presidential appointments Martin had helped secure under Kennedy and Johnson: Andrew Brimmer, who had since left the Federal Reserve Board for private practice, and former ambassador Clifton Wharton, then president of the New York State University system. Also present were Bernard Anderson, a Rockefeller Foundation economist; William Julius Wilson, a distinguished sociologist who then chaired the department of sociology at the University of Chicago; Jewel Plummer Cobb, a cancer researcher and dean at Rutgers University; Walter Massey, a physicist and director of Argonne National Laboratory; Walter Leonard, president of Fisk University; and Bernard Watson, vice president of Temple University.

During the luncheon, Carter remarked with a laugh that he had never been in the company of so many people with doctorates. Contributing their various expertise to the discussion of the economy, the guests reached a consensus in arguing that the twin evils of unemployment and inflation should not be separated but be addressed simultaneously. Carter took this advice seriously, and Martin noted that for their part many of the academics left the meeting impressed by the president's command of economic data.

Carter's contact with black academics was not limited to such meetings. He made a concerted effort to strengthen historically black colleges and universities by expanding their participation in federal programs. In January 1979, he asked Martin and Joseph Califano, then secretary of Health, Education, and Welfare, to monitor the results of a directive he had issued six months earlier, instructing department and agency heads to ensure that historically black colleges were getting a fair opportunity to receive federal grants and contracts. As a result of this effort, these institutions received a $15 million increase over the previous year's allocations. Martin also persuaded Carter to serve as an active co-chairperson of the United Negro College Fund drive, which raised $64 million that year.[23]

When Howard University was slated by the Office of Management and Budget (OMB) for a $2 million cutback in federal funding, the university's president, James Cheek, and board member Asa Spaulding came to Martin to plead their case. The $2 million had been earmarked for foreign students, mostly from Africa. Cheek charged that the government had encouraged Howard to train more foreign students and was now cutting funds necessary for the job. Martin took up Howard's cause. He pointed out to James McIntyre, director of the Office of Management and Budget, that a public battle with a nationally recognized black university over $2 million was ridiculous. While McIntyre investigated the matter, Martin lobbied other administration officials who might have some influence with the director. Within days, the funding for Howard was restored.

Among Martin's more intense encounters with Carter was an episode involving the new Department of Education, whose establishment Carter had announced at the beginning of 1979. By the fall of that year, Carter was ready to nominate the head of the new department. Ever since Robert Weaver had become secretary of Housing and Urban Development under Johnson, there had never been more than one black serving in the Cabinet at a time. Martin wanted Carter to break this tradition. A campaign was already under way to have Mary Frances Berry, a historian and early civil rights activist whom Carter had brought in as assistant secretary for education in HEW, appointed to the post. But along with her many fans, Berry had also made many enemies at HEW. Moreover, Arnie Miller, the head of personnel at the White House, seemed opposed to her nomination. Martin argued that even if she weren't acceptable, another black should be considered. Despite assurances from Miller that no nomination was imminent, Martin heard rumors that Shirley Hufstedler, a California judge, was being considered for the job. In late October, before Martin had the time to work on the matter, Hufstedler's name was submitted to the Senate for approval. Furious, Martin immediately confronted Miller. This time he asked for Miller's word that the number-two position in the department would definitely go to a black candidate. Although he received firm assurances that his viewpoint was being considered, he soon heard from a friend that Hufstedler had recommended a white colleague for the position. Martin decided that it was time to take his case to the president. Carter listened thoughtfully to Martin's argument, and then promised him that he would recommend a black appointee.[24] Carter kept his promise. Not long afterwards, Steven Minter, whose experience as the commissioner of welfare for Massachusetts more than qualified him, was appointed as undersecretary of education. Mary Berry, meanwhile, was appointed as a member of the U.S. Civil Rights Commission.

Carter's most generous attention to black appointees, and the area in which he later credited Martin's influence most strongly, concerned his appointments to the federal judiciary. The sheer number of Carter's black appointments was perhaps most striking. Presidents Nixon and Ford had named a total of ten black judges, all of them at the district court level, during their eight years in office. In four years, Carter named thirty-seven, expanding the number of those serving at the appellate level alone more than fivefold.

Characterizing Martin's role in these selections, Carter later stated: "If the attorney general, for instance, or if the senator from Arkansas couldn't come up with a qualified candidate who happened to be African American, then Louis would get on the phone or use his reservoir of knowledge and come up with names to be considered." Out of Carter's thirty-seven appointments, nine were to appellate court judgeships (at that level Nixon and Ford had appointed none), including two whom Martin had helped bring into the federal judiciary under Johnson: A. Leon Higginbotham and Damon Keith. The other seven were Theodore McMillian, Amalya Kearse, Joseph Hatchett, Jerome Farris, Nathaniel Jones, Cecil Poole, and Harry Edwards.[25]

For the first time, federal district courts in the South included black judges (Carter appointed nine). This was very significant for the enforcement of civil rights laws and for the signal it sent to southern whites. Carter made this emphasis clear early in his administration by recruiting two blacks to sensitive and significant posts: Attorney Drew Days III, from the NAACP Legal Defense and Educational Fund, to head the Justice Department's Civil Rights Division, and Appellate Judge Wade McCree to be solicitor general. Affirmative action received top billing as one of the most contentious issues of the administration, as represented by court challenges to school busing and to the active recruitment of minority students for university enrollment. The White House was partly successful. The Supreme Court upheld busing and, in its *Bakke* v. *Regents of the University of California* ruling, upheld affirmative action as broadly defined, although it knocked down the use of enrollment quotas. Concerning the *Bakke* decision, Martin proudly informed readers of his *Fact Sheet*:

> After the Supreme Court's decision in that case, the President in a personal handwritten note ordered all departments of the federal government to continue to vigorously implement affirmative action programs.[26]

Aside from his day-to-day tasks and routine, Martin represented the interests of African Americans in the formulation of domestic and foreign policy. As had happened under Kennedy, Martin sometimes had to fight with White House staff over the civil rights agenda. When his administration colleagues congratulated themselves for an occasional civil rights success, Martin usually punctured their complacency with the bittersweet observation: "Well that's good, but we still have a long way to go."

❧ ❧ ❧

Throughout the Carter years, rescuing the economy was the main focus of domestic policy. This became a continuing source of friction between the administration and black leadership. The economy suffered from what was termed *stagflation*—a period of poor economic growth and high unemployment complicated by rising prices, some of them driven up by the cost of foreign oil. Beginning in 1973, the oil-producing nations of the Middle East had begun imposing an oil embargo and soon formed a powerful cartel. Many Americans recognized for the first time how much they depended on foreign countries to supply their energy needs. Because of price constraints, the production of domestic oil and gas had not kept pace with demand, and by the time Carter took office, half of all the oil used in the United States was imported. Martin noted in his memoirs, "U.S. dependence on imported oil was in many ways the most dynamic and uncontrollable force operating on the domestic economy."

As the economic situation worsened, administration economists began to insist on severe cuts in the budget. Black leaders feared that blacks who were already feeling the brunt of economic bad times would be especially hurt by the austerity measures. The criticism expressed earlier by Vernon Jordan and other leading black citizens about the administration's lack of new domestic programs was resurfacing.

To combat the criticism, someone on the White House staff suggested that aides who represented special constituencies should call together leaders from their groups to make suggestions about how the budget could be cut. Dissatisfied with this approach, Martin argued vehemently that black Americans were already at the bottom of the economic ladder and would be hurt by any cut in programs affecting them. To alleviate his fears, James McIntyre and his aides at OMB prepared a list of all the programs that would not be touched. Most social programs were on the list. Thus when Martin called in black leaders to discuss budget cuts, he was able to forestall much of their criticism by telling them exactly which programs would be spared. Most of these leaders, he felt, were resigned to government cutbacks, but with the media playing up the new austerity program, many were still concerned that blacks might be hurt by the new budget.

By 1979, unemployment had begun to rise rapidly, and budget cutting became even less popular. Leaders from the Congressional Black Caucus, NAACP, and the National Urban League denounced the budget cutting as "balancing the budget on the backs of the poor." *New York Times* columnist Roger Wilkins, who was a nephew of Roy Wilkins and had served in the Justice Department under Johnson, reported that even some federal administrators agreed off the record that Carter's proposed 1980 budget would increase defense spending at the expense of social spending.[27]

In March 1979, Martin outlined for Carter several "critical black concerns." Carter's austere anti-inflation budget, which cut summer youth jobs and accepted 35.5 percent black youth unemployment, led Martin to warn:

> I think it is important to try to defuse some of the defeatism in the highly charged black communities. The looting that occurred in Baltimore and the

recent looting in Washington during the snow emergency—when hundreds of blacks reported for snow shoveling jobs that had already been filled—emphasize the need for attention.[28]

Martin hoped the president would put together a jobs program to address inner-city unemployment. He had been a champion of such government efforts ever since the Depression years of the first Roosevelt administration, and as a labor activist he was well aware of how important jobs with decent wages and benefits were. By the end of the year, Martin and others at the White House were putting together what would prove to be Carter's last major social initiative. The bill, which Carter submitted to Congress early in 1980, included new funding for vocational training, support for urban schools, and the expansion of existing youth programs. Though it passed easily in the House in August 1980, it never reached the Senate, killed in part by the political opposition typical of an election season.[29]

❧ ❧ ❧

During the summer of 1979, a troubled President Carter gave a national address in which he declared that the nation's problems were deeper than gasoline lines or energy shortages, deeper than inflation or recession—that the nation was suffering from a "malaise." Initially addressing the energy shortage, the president drifted into a somber discussion about what he called a national crisis of self-confidence. He traced the problem back to the assassination of President Kennedy, the "agony of Vietnam," the "shock of Watergate," and, finally, a culture in Washington, D.C., which, he asserted, had become "an island" separated from the American people and their concerns. Carter declared that the loss of national purpose threatened to destroy America's social and political fabric.

The speech was met with withering criticism. Many charged that the crisis of confidence was basically the president's invention, his way of explaining away political problems. "The American public was sick and tired of the administration's inability to handle the issues," Martin recalled, "and I think that malaise thing was a mistake, period. Anytime you expose your own weakness publicly, you're asking for it. Carter was groping for some answers that should have come out of his own leadership." Martin remembered how President Roosevelt handled difficulties with humor, but he saw little humor in Carter: "The American public just does not buy so much seriousness and deadpan approaches to things. You have got to give them a little blarney." [30]

In any case, the problems Carter saw were serious enough for him to decide, at the last minute, to hold a summit gathering in July at Camp David. His purpose was to solicit advice from businesspeople, labor leaders, teachers, ministers, governors, mayors, and private citizens on the direction his administration ought to be taking. In all, the list of those invited to the sessions ran to 150 people. Martin noticed that Rev. Jesse Jackson was not among the initial invitees. "I decided that since Jesse was one of the biggest preachers in the country, he should be invited," Martin later recalled. He had made a special effort to bring Jackson to the White House earlier to meet Carter, since Jackson had been virtually ignored during the first two years of the administration. At Martin's instigation, Jackson was invited to a small White House dinner party with the president and several other leaders, all of them white. Ham Jordan later informed Martin that the president was particularly taken with Jackson, that he found him one of the most articulate and lucid leaders he had met.

At the Camp David sessions, Carter held additional discussions after dinner in his own cabin, giving them an informal and intimate quality. However, the atmosphere became tense one evening when Jackson began to echo criticism of the ability and loyalty of the president's staff that had recently appeared in a newspaper column. Martin could feel the looks directed at him by the other staffers present, who clearly thought it had been a mistake to invite Jackson. Ham Jordan finessed the situation by suggesting that the White House staffers leave the cabin so the president and his guests could speak freely. The next morning, when Martin met the president and Jackson fresh from an early morning jog, it was clear to him that the two of them had developed a solid rapport. Martin was relieved. He was convinced that Jackson could be useful to Carter in the political battles that lay ahead.

He had expected that other black leaders might be upset that Jackson had been chosen as the first one to meet with the president at this important Camp David session, but the size and intensity of the protest from black organizations caught him off guard. In particular, Benjamin Hooks, executive secretary of the NAACP, told Martin that his members had been calling to express their outrage. Martin immediately pressed Jordan to invite other leaders, especially Hooks. But Jordan cited Hooks's recent criticism of the president as a reason not to bring him into the meetings. Edie Draper, who handled Jordan's correspondence, was the only staffer to agree with Martin that Hooks could not be excluded if others were being invited. Jordan finally gave in, and Martin called Hooks along with other black leaders and extended the invitation to come to Camp David.[31]

As a result of the Camp David retreat, Ham Jordan soon asked all staff members to submit their resignations to the president so that he could have a free hand at reorganizing the White House. Martin thought the idea was merely a cover, a gimmick, for getting rid of Joseph Califano, secretary of Health, Education, and Welfare. Carter named six new department heads—four of whom were already members of the administration. Martin received private assurances that his own job was not on the block.

The reorganization had mixed results for Martin. Jordan acquired an administrative aide, making him much more efficient but considerably less accessible. Martin wondered how this would affect his own ability to have the president's ear since he had always relied on Jordan, with whom he had a good working relationship, for that purpose. One good result of the reorganization, Martin felt, was that Lloyd Cutler joined the staff. Cutler was an old-timer like Martin and, as Martin put it, a pro. Cutler's arrival brought on board more experience and also led to a more formal, structured approach to the staff meetings as well, something Martin appreciated.

The reorganization also led to a shuffling of offices. Martin and his staff, along with the other special constituency liaisons, were moved to the East Wing. Martin agreed reluctantly to give up his West Wing office to Jack Watson and Watson's aide, but he argued that he must continue to maintain an office in the West Wing, which was more public. He took his case directly to Jordan. Arguing that blacks should not have to come in the back or side door to see him, Martin reminded Jordan of the country's history, which until recently prevented blacks from coming in the "front door." And, after all, Martin was their representative. Jordan agreed, giving him an additional small office there to receive visitors while the rest of his operation was run out of the East Wing. Others who had been forced out of their West Wing offices were, naturally, somewhat resentful.[32]

The summer of 1979 presented Carter with another crisis for which he sought Martin's help—Andrew Young's resignation. Young, the first black U.S. ambassador to the United Nations, was a close friend of the president, a fellow Georgian who had worked vigorously for his election. Because they trusted each other, Carter had given the outspoken civil rights leader wide rein as the U.S. representative to the UN, a position Carter had elevated to Cabinet rank. Calling Young's unexpected departure one of the most troubling events of his administration, Carter later described the situation this way: "Louis Martin was the one I called on to help me resolve that. He called together all of the top African American public servants in Washington—thirty or forty at a time as I recall it—and explained to them what had happened and let Andy meet with the key ones to tell them that he had indeed made a mistake."[33]

The event that led to Young's resignation occurred in July. For nearly a year now, Carter had been leading delicate peace negotiations on the Middle East. UN Security Council members were now proposing a resolution calling for the establishment of a Palestinian state. Since the United States opposed the resolution, Young suggested to some of the UN's Arab delegates that it would not be in the best interests of the United States, Israel, or the Arab world to have a debate and vote on the issue at this time. What happened next has received varied accounts. Carter, interviewed for this book, described the development this way: "He [Young] had a lot of problems with the State Department, [though] he thought the secretary of state should make all the policy decisions. But Andy met in his apartment at the Waldorf-Astoria with the PLO leadership, which violated a commitment—unfortunately I think—that Henry Kissinger had made on behalf of the country." According to other accounts, Young met with the PLO representative not at his own apartment but at the home of the Kuwaiti ambassador, who wanted to give Young a chance to reiterate his case concerning the vote on Palestinian statehood to a group of delegates from various Arab nations. In either case, Young had made clear that he would not be presenting official U.S. policy.

Young notified the Israelis about his meeting, according to Carter. Nevertheless, Young soon received a call from *Newsweek* magazine asking for his comment on Israeli government complaints about "secret meetings" with the PLO. The Israelis were outraged and demanded Young's resignation. U.S. State Department officials were also angry with Young, arguing that before meeting with the PLO he should have cleared the idea with them first.[34] In short, the incident had embarrassed the administration. Young resigned in the interest of the U.S. government and the fragile Arab-Israeli relationship. When he went before the White House staff to tell his story, he stressed that his departure was consistent with his long-standing promise to resign if he ever felt his actions brought more harm than help to the administration. Martin saw tears in the eyes of the usually cool Eizenstat, who had worked with Young in Atlanta when the latter ran for Congress. Eizenstat asked Young to reconsider and give himself more time to think about what he should do, but Young explained that he had agonized over the decision already and was sure the time had come for a clean break. Martin later arranged a large gathering of black appointees in the Roosevelt Room to hear Young's explanation of the controversy. Young repeated the story he had told the White House staff. Most of his listeners were sympathetic, but some wanted to know how they should handle rumors that he had been pushed out because of pressure from the American Jewish community. Young flatly denied the rumor.

Young's close friendship with Carter continued despite the public uproar. Indeed, during informal Oval Office conversations, Martin was struck by the president's continued loyalty to Young and his frankness about the UN crisis. Carter was convinced that Young would not have had to resign if a certain unnamed official had not complained. "I never had any problem with Andy," Carter later said, "because most of [his views on] the things around the world were compatible with what I believed." [35]

Young's replacement as UN ambassador was Donald McHenry, a black career foreign service officer. After the resignation, Martin accompanied Young on a two-week farewell trade mission through ten African countries. He felt that few had done more to strengthen the bond between Africans and African Americans than Young in his position as UN ambassador. Ever since his year in Nigeria, Martin had maintained a special interest in Africa. The trade delegation would be Martin's third journey to the continent since joining Carter's staff. He had been in the delegation led by Treasury Secretary Michael Blumenthal to the funeral of Algerian president Houare Boumedienne, and he had accompanied Supreme Court Justice Thurgood Marshall and Jeff Carter, the president's youngest son, to the funeral of President Jomo Kenyatta in Kenya. Later he would serve on the board of TransAfrica, the lobbying organization that contributed greatly to the eventual U.S. boycott of South Africa and to the downfall of apartheid there. [36]

Young had always been warmly received by African heads of state. Now, as the former UN diplomat returned to bid them farewell, African officials seemed anxious to show their regard. In Cameroon, U.S. ambassador Mabel Smythe, a friend of both Martin and Young and one of a dozen black ambassadors appointed under Carter, made advance preparations for the delegation's arrival. When Young reached Cameroon, flag-waving crowds in the streets welcomed him. Many African governments had broken relations with Israel over Young's resignation, but despite his personal experience Young continued to promote the U.S. position, urging leaders to resume relations with Israel. At the delegation's first stop in the Cape Verde Islands, a former Portuguese colony, Martin learned that Young not only sought business there for American firms but also a commitment from the island nation's president to recognize Israel.[37]

ﻙ ﻙ ﻙ

To the surprise of administration economists, over the next year the recession deepened, and unemployment rose despite the austerity measures. By the summer of 1980, there were calls for a stimulus package to reinvigorate the economy. Martin was among those at the White House calling for this radical change in course. At a briefing for staff held at campaign headquarters before the 1980 Democratic convention, he asked when the president would announce the stimulus package, reminding the others that Carter had told the National Urban League he would soon take action. David Rubenstein replied that it was in the works, but they were not yet ready to go public.

The media buzzed with speculation that some new economic move was imminent. In his address at the convention, Carter again promised that he would announce a new economic program soon. Not long after that, he held a ceremony in the East Room to introduce leaders from Congress, big business, and labor to his administration's new reindustrialization program, designed to restore American economic preeminence. A tax cut was part of the program.

Again the staff wanted Martin to meet with black leaders to get their ideas on the new economic package. Martin felt that these "exercises in participatory democracy," as he called them, did more harm than good. Although many black leaders were pleased to be asked for their opinions, some interpreted the solicitation of their advice as an admission that the administration did not know what to do. Martin raised this criticism with Jack Watson, but Watson overruled his objections and the assignment went forward.

In a similar vein, Alfred Kahn, the administration's top inflation fighter, called Martin about Carter's proposal for a two-tiered minimum wage law. Although a reduced minimum wage for students was already in effect, a lower minimum wage for youth in general, it was hoped, would lead employers to offer more jobs to the legions of youth in the ghettos. Kahn asked Martin to find out what the black community thought about the idea. Martin found that people were solidly opposed to any change in the law. Many maintained that a double standard for blacks and whites already existed. The National Urban League had studied the issue as well and also

.193.

recommended against any change. In the end, Carter never submitted the two-tier proposal to Congress.

Once the stimulus package was ready to be announced, Martin urged that Carter make a television address to the nation. That way, he argued, the president could take his message directly to the people without the filter of the press, which was unlikely to do it justice. Martin remembered being so emphatic about this point that "one staffer asked what I had eaten for breakfast." Again, however, his advice did not prevail. Instead, members of the administration were instructed to go to key cities to explain the program themselves. Unwilling to give up on the matter, Martin continued to insist that a national address would be more effective. Landon Butler, a top aide to Ham Jordan, finally silenced Martin's criticism with the startling assessment: "The program is not that good anyway."[38]

Martin sometimes found himself at odds with his young fellow White House staffers over foreign as well as domestic affairs, although he generally confined his advice to domestic issues. As an expert in public relations, he felt confident in expressing his opposition to the Rose Garden strategy, the term used to describe Carter's response to the Iran hostage crisis. On November 4, 1979, the U.S. embassy in Iran had been taken over by Iranian student extremists protesting the U.S. decision to allow the Shah of Iran—who had been ousted in January—into the United States for medical treatment. Embassy personnel had been taken hostage. The administration immediately froze Iranian assets in the United States and undertook other measures to get the hostages released. But the crisis turned into a stalemate when the Ayatollah Khomeini, Iran's new fundamentalist leader, backed the students, in effect making the embassy personnel hostages of the Iranian government. Carter followed the advice of staffers who believed the president should appear to stay riveted to the crisis so that it would seem he was doing all he could to resolve it. Martin thought otherwise—the strategy seemed to make the president yet another hostage. His suggestion that Carter continue with business as usual and focus the attention of the press and the public on other issues lost out against the competing advice.[39]

❧ ❧ ❧

One of Martin's most difficult assignments under Carter was tending to the badly strained relationship between the White House and the Congressional Black Caucus (CBC). Martin had become well acquainted with all the members of the CBC, both through his work during the Kennedy and

Johnson administrations and through his chairmanship from 1970 to 1978 of the Joint Center's board of governors. Some of the members accused Carter of not supporting the Humphrey-Hawkins full-employment legislation with sufficient vigor. Bitterness over economic issues had been so intense in 1979 that the CBC had refused to invite the president to address its annual dinner.

In the early spring of 1980, Senator Ted Kennedy's entry into the Democratic presidential primaries accelerated the anti-Carter campaign on Capitol Hill and complicated Martin's task. Several of the most influential caucus members, including the chair, Rep. Cardiss Collins of Chicago, had joined the dump-Carter movement. Most Caucus members knew of Martin's closeness with the Kennedys, but some might not have known of the faith he had in Carter's integrity. For Martin, there could be no question about his loyalty to the president. He believed that if Carter's record were properly communicated, it would carry as much weight with rank-and-file black Americans as Senator Kennedy's. When the senator first told him of his plan to run, Martin had urged him as firmly as he could not to, but to no avail. Now Martin had to persuade the black political leadership to coalesce behind Carter and, if possible, to build enthusiasm for the president's programs.

To smooth the relationship, Martin planned a White House reception for Caucus members to take place in September 1980, just after the Democratic National Convention. With 2,000 invited guests, it would be the largest social event the Carters held at the White House. In preparation, Martin visited each member in advance, offering as the reason for his visits that he wished to introduce Ray Miller, a new member of his staff. This ploy gave him a chance not only to hear the members' complaints firsthand—mostly about the White House's failure to keep promises—but also to try to resolve misunderstandings, all before the upcoming convention and the later White House reception.

Attitudes were, somehow, beginning to change. At the Democrats' convention in New York City, Cardiss Collins joined hands with the president in a show of unity. With the president's renomination, the infighting subsided, and the caucus seemed to be back on board. Martin's White House reception was a great success despite the fact that rain forced the 2,000 guests inside the mansion, which was supposed to accommodate no more than 1,000. In addition to the regular guest list, Martin had invited members of the diplomatic community and two special guests, the presidents of Sierra Leone and Rwanda. At the request of the State Department and the National Security Council, he had arranged for President Carter to meet the president of Rwanda just before the reception. The president was in good form, and the members of the caucus left the event in a cooperative mood. "We really won them over," Martin recalled, "but it took a lot of time." [40]

ঌ ঌ ঌ

In late 1979, a Soviet-backed coup had taken place in Afghanistan, and Soviet troops began streaming into the country, prompting what would become a prolonged civil war. Carter called immediately for international sanctions against Moscow, including a grain embargo and a boycott of the 1980 Moscow Olympics. Obtaining cooperation on both these matters from sovereign nations required the White House to take advantage of every resource. Heavyweight boxing champion Muhammad Ali had publicly condemned the Soviet invasion—referring to it as the killing of his Muslim brothers. As editor-in-chief of the *Chicago Defender*, Martin had met Ali several times before, so the State Department urged him to contact Ali in New Delhi, India, and persuade him to head a delegation to Africa to promote the boycott. Martin succeeded and was then asked to accompany the Ali mission. Officials at State assured Martin that by the time he caught up with Ali's eight-man delegation in India, U.S. embassy officials would have briefed Ali on the problems to expect in Africa. When Martin arrived, he discovered to his disappointment that this had not been done.

In Dar Es Salaam, Tanzania, a crowd estimated at close to 10,000 people greeted Ali at the airport, but his pride was hurt because President Julius Nyerere was not among them. On the first day in Tanzania, State Department officials warned Martin that they believed Ali was almost ready to cancel the tour because a group of black American expatriates had urged him to do so. At a press conference in Tanzania, Ali defended his decision to make the tour in front of a hostile press.

Martin and other delegation members thought the boxer did a creditable job, but stateside viewers of the press conference thought it was a disaster. Martin learned that in the United States, Ali's press coverage had been fragmented and edited in such a way as to make him appear simple and out of place in a role suited for a professional diplomat. After the delegation returned home, critics charged that Ali had failed to win over countries opposed to the Olympic boycott, although they admitted that he had strengthened the resolve of its supporters. For his part, Martin concluded that Ali had been an excellent ambassador in a mission that called for people-to-people diplomacy as well as negotiations with heads of Olympic delegations, not, as the media claimed, with heads of state.[41]

ૐ ૐ ૐ

As the 1980 campaign got under way, Martin found that new ethics laws severely hampered his role in the campaign. The sudden departure of Ham Jordan because of alleged ethics violations alerted the entire staff to the seriousness of the new reforms. Even though many of the staffers, including Martin, were not subject to the Hatch Act, which forbade political activity by certain federal employees, all were forced to operate in what Martin described as "a legal thicket." A log had to be kept of phone calls made on White House phones for political purposes. White House stationery could not be used for correspondence about political matters. Staffers were not allowed to raise or even handle funds for political events.

In particular, Martin recalled that during the primary campaign, the Kennedy forces filed complaints charging that the White House staff was engaged in political activity in violation of the new ethics and reform laws. Although these complaints were thrown out, Martin believed they inhibited political activity by all members of the staff. It especially angered him since he had been involved in so many past political campaigns, and wanted to be more involved in this one. He felt hemmed in.

To Martin, it seemed that the new laws governing federal financing of campaigns were designed to wipe out Democrats, an ironic twist since the laws had originally been drafted to prevent the kind of activities Nixon's staff had engaged in during the Watergate scandal. Under the new system, each candidate received a fixed sum of money from the federal treasury and was limited in the additional amount he could raise. However, there was no limitation on the activities or funds raised by independent political action committees as long as they purported to act independently of the candidate. Martin called it "an engraved invitation" for big business to funnel money to Republican candidates.[42]

On November 4, 1980, when Carter lost his bid for a second term to Ronald Reagan, Martin felt the country had turned a sharp corner. He took some small gratification from the fact that blacks had voted overwhelmingly for Carter. Nevertheless, Carter's defeat was crushing, and the word *transition* dominated headlines about the outcome, which was accompanied by the loss of thirty-three Democrats in the House and eleven in the Senate. Some of the Senate losers were big-name liberals—Frank Church of Idaho, Birch

Bayh of Indiana, George McGovern of South Dakota among them. The atmosphere at the White House was funereal.

The day after the election, Martin stopped by the Oval Office to thank the president for the opportunity to serve as his special assistant for two years. He had no appointment, but Nell Yates, the president's secretary, urged him to go in. Wearing his familiar cardigan sweater and drinking coffee with his friend Charles Kirbo, Carter got up to greet Martin. As Martin began to express his thanks, Carter smiled broadly. "You did a good job," the president told him, adding, "We still have two and a half months." Tears welled in Martin's eyes. He shook hands with Kirbo and walked out.

The next day's senior staff meeting in the Roosevelt Room was unusually well attended. Jack Watson, Ham Jordan's replacement, outlined steps for the transition. He said that an agreement had been worked out with Reagan's transition chief, Edwin Meese, and that they would each be getting an official list of the persons with whom to coordinate the transfer of their offices. Watson asked each of the staff members to produce two briefing papers— one for the incoming Reagan person and another listing their achievements for the record. Watson emphasized that President Carter wanted the transition to be a "class act."

As he left the meeting, Martin was already thinking about the future. He stopped by Mondale's office to find out who would now head up the committee and to ask whether the rumor that Mondale would run in 1984 was true. The vice president waved him in but was reluctant to talk when he saw another staff member seated in front of the desk. After an exchange of pleasantries, Mondale explained that he was leaving for a brief vacation and wanted to talk when he returned. But he suggested that Martin talk to Dick Moe, his aide.

After lunch, Martin told Moe of his concerns about the future of the DNC. Martin had been in touch with Joe Califano and Berl Bernhard, Secretary of State Ed Muskie's confidential aide. Bernhard had been emphatic about getting "the Georgians" out of positions of influence in the DNC. Martin asked Moe if he was interested in the job. When Moe declined to be considered, Martin asked him what he thought about Muskie. Moe indicated he thought Muskie would be acceptable, emphasizing as well that he thought Mondale was serious about campaigning for the nomination in 1984. Further, he said that he was getting in touch with the Kennedy people to try to work out a moratorium on political activity until they could all recover from the

GOP landslide. Martin's political status inside the party was intact, since blacks had again voted overwhelmingly for Carter.

Martin was apprehensive about the country's move to the right, though he understood Reagan's popularity, something that seemed to puzzle so many blacks and white liberals. "Sunshine and shadow," he called it in one interview. Despite his age, Reagan managed to seem energetic and optimistic, a decided contrast with Carter's somber, introspective persona. During the campaign debates, Reagan's repeated comeback to Carter—"There you go again"—conveyed to many voters that he did not take Carter very seriously, and neither should they. Martin also felt that the Carter campaign staff had not been nearly as good as Reagan's in presenting their candidate. Reagan's people knew, for example, that physical impressions matter. Because Carter was a short man, audiences were often disappointed that they could barely catch a glimpse of him. Reagan, a former actor, was accustomed to presenting himself in the best light.[43]

Martin felt that Carter had already been maligned by the media when he entered the White House and carried with him liabilities accumulated during the 1976 campaign. Some of the Washington press corps assumed that a southerner was not sufficiently sophisticated to cope with the seasoned insiders who pressure presidents for various special interests. A newcomer to Washington, Carter lacked ties to congressional leaders and did not exhibit much desire to develop relations with the social and political insiders whom Lyndon Johnson had cultivated. Washington media practitioners were especially skeptical of his religious convictions. After all, no one had ever heard of a "born-again Christian" in high office. With the cynicism so often found among the Washington media, they assumed that Carter did not really believe in the morality he preached. In their experience with politicians, scoundrels were more common than saints.

Martin attributed Carter's problems in governing to inexperience and to his faith in aides who had served him well in Atlanta but were misplaced among Washington's insiders. "He was slow to take people into his confidence on major matters," Martin noted. "In his campaign, he had been highly critical of Washington, and he seemed to fear being deceived by the very people he had denounced."[44] Although Martin was skeptical of the sincerity of those who called themselves born-again Christians, he conceded that if ever anyone deserved such a label, it was definitely Carter. "He had a good head and he had a good heart," Martin noted, recounting an incident that he thought spoke volumes about Carter. "One day when he was preparing to make a speech, I saw him in a corner, and I saw his lips moving, and there was nobody there. I went over. He was praying. You know, I just couldn't—really couldn't believe that would help him. I'd never heard of a Washington power praying. The guy really had a heart." [45]

Along with many political pundits, Martin viewed Ted Kennedy's challenge for the nomination as the final blow, compounding Carter's problems by fragmenting the party and weakening Carter in the general election. He wondered, too, as many people did, how the election would have turned out had the administration secured the release of the hostages in Iran.

ᕗ ᕗ ᕗ

At 68 years of age, Martin could have retired, but he was never one to sit on the sidelines. He rejoined the board of the Joint Center, became the first African American to sit on the board of Riggs Bank, and accepted a position at Howard University as assistant vice president for communications. Howard's president, James Cheek, was delighted to offer him this post, which would use Martin's network of influential friends to the university's advantage. "We frankly did not have a vacant position, so we created one because we knew he would be a mine of information," recalled Roger Estep, Howard's vice president. "Only once in a lifetime could we find a person of that stature and experience to come and help us leverage Howard University and open doors where we could not." [46]

As Martin prepared his list for the Reagan transition team and packed up his office, he mulled over the amazing changes he had seen in three administrations. When he first moved to Washington to serve the Kennedy administration, Jim Crow was still the rule in the South. Across the country, blacks were regularly prevented from exercising the most basic privileges of citizenship and treated as second-class citizens. Martin felt tremendously proud that he had contributed in his own way to his people's march toward political empowerment and economic opportunity.

Martin had experienced the best and worst: the exhilaration of hearing John Kennedy declare civil rights to be a moral cause, of seeing Lyndon Johnson sign into law the Voting Rights Act of 1965, of watching as Thurgood Marshall was sworn in as a justice of the United States Supreme Court. But the stunning successes of those years had been accompanied by sorrow—the losses seemed endless as Medgar Evers, John Kennedy, Martin Luther King, Jr., and finally Bobby Kennedy were all assassinated and the 1960s closed in a sequence of urban riots.

Carter had done much to repair the political disillusionment left by the tragedy of Vietnam and the cynicism of Watergate, though with his defeat, Martin feared the country had taken the turn to the right that Lyndon Johnson had warned him about a dozen years earlier. What this might mean for black Americans concerned him. But despite all, Martin was not a pessimist. He had witnessed real progress. The words he had spoken thirty years earlier seemed apt:

> I think we are fortunate to live in a democratic society which provides the tools with which we can build our brave new world. I take my stand with the optimists. Things may get worse in some quarters before they get better, but the winds of change are blowing inexorably across the land.[54]

❧

## .9.

### MOVING THE MOUNTAIN: THE LEGACY OF LOUIS MARTIN

*Thurgood Marshall probably would not have been appointed to the Supreme Court nor Andrew Brimmer to the Federal Reserve, nor Robert Weaver to President Johnson's Cabinet, but for Louis Martin.*

*—Vernon Jordan*

In September 1992, Ron Brown, the first African American to chair the Democratic National Committee (DNC), presided over ceremonies in Washington, D.C., honoring Louis Martin and eight other Democrats. Each received the first annual Lawrence F. O'Brien Democratic Party Award, named after the DNC's late chair, with whom Martin had worked so closely, for services to the party that Brown described as "far above the call of duty."

"Mr. Martin was responsible more than anyone else for removing old barriers and creating opportunities in America," declared Brown, who since his boyhood days in Harlem had looked up to Martin as one of his heroes. "He made an extraordinary contribution to American politics." As the first black to hold the position of deputy chair of the DNC, Martin had helped pave the way for the man who now led the ceremonies honoring him.

Despite the many tributes and awards Martin received over the years, his legacy is not as well known as it should be. His political work in Washington was mostly behind the scenes, pushing others to the forefront, letting them take the credit. An important factor in his success was this willingness to remain in the background in an arena where egotism and self-aggrandizement are common.

Over a span of more than five decades, Martin pursued racial justice and economic opportunity through every means available to him—as a crusading newspaperman, labor activist, and political operative, as well as White House advisor. Many of his achievements are easy to document, such as his influence on the appointment of black Americans to senior government positions previously held by whites only. In other areas—his advice to presidents and his linkage of the black community and the white establishment during the civil rights movement—Martin's legacy is perhaps less tangible and therefore more difficult to measure. The confidential nature of his role made it essential that he be trusted by all sides and that he be discreet.

Ꮹ Ꮹ Ꮹ

Martin joined the movement to guarantee black Americans full access to the political system the moment he gained the leverage to do so in 1936, as the publisher of the *Michigan Chronicle*. At the same time, he helped build an important coalition between blacks and labor, which not only brought black workers greater equality in the workplace but helped them gain political influence. First as a pro-New Deal journalist and then as deputy chair of the DNC, he helped to convert traditional black loyalty to the Republican party to a new identification with the Democratic party.

Today this identification is taken for granted, but that was not the case in the world Martin knew as a young editor. The newspapers read by black Detroiters before World War II reflected the political orientation of most of the city's black middle and upper class—loyalty to the party of Lincoln and gratitude to employers like Ford. Even though his parent paper, the *Chicago Defender*, had consistently supported Republicans before the 1936 election, Martin began a conscious crusade to support Franklin Roosevelt's New Deal and the burgeoning labor movement that Roosevelt tacitly supported. He had decided, simply, that these two forces could bring real change to the lives of ordinary black people.

The coalition Martin helped to forge between the black community of Detroit and the United Auto Workers in the early 1940s came at a time when most black community leaders were suspicious of the labor movement. Yet this coalition quickly became crucial in solving many of the immediate problems blacks faced in that city, as elsewhere: insufficient housing, job discrimination, police brutality, and racial strife. On these issues, the black community found that labor could provide strong allies. This partnership extended well beyond the borders of Detroit, leading to the development of a strong bond between labor and the NAACP and generally playing a role in civil rights progress over the next several decades. During this period, Martin began to develop the large network of contacts that would prove so useful to him in the future, including Robert Weaver, Thurgood Marshall, Charles Diggs, William Dawson,

Walter White, Lester Granger, Roy Wilkins, and George Edwards, as well as Walter Reuther and Mildred Jeffrey of the UAW.

Martin was an optimist. Although white city officials and business leaders in Detroit labelled him a radical, he believed devoutly in the American political system and its capacity to deliver on the promises of the Constitution. By 1944, when he worked on his first presidential campaign, he had fallen in love with what he described as "the crazy, unpredictable interplay of forces" that makes up American politics. "This is the reason he got along with John Kennedy," Harris Wofford explained, years later, "because the President's game in life was also politics." [1] Perhaps this was what Wofford recognized when he and Frank Reeves recruited Martin to join them on John Kennedy's election campaign in 1960.

Martin's profound understanding of the power of the black vote was crucial to Kennedy's election. It is sometimes forgotten that at the start of the campaign many blacks felt Richard Nixon had a stronger civil rights record than the young senator from Massachusetts, who was actually once booed during the campaign by civil rights supporters who had favored Hubert Humphrey in the primary. That changed in the last two months of the campaign, as Nixon's silence on civil rights issues and Kennedy's solicitation of the black vote became public. Martin contributed heavily, perhaps decisively, to that turnabout in black support in an election so close that if Kennedy had lost just one vote per precinct in Illinois, he would have lost the state.

Martin was also a vital force in shaping the character of his party. In his role as deputy chair, he ceaselessly recruited black voters and supporters. As blacks became an increasingly important component of the Democratic vote, they gained influence within the party, whose leaders frequently had to walk a tightrope between courting the black vote and losing the support of southern Dixiecrats. Even FDR, despite his philosophy of opportunity, had avoided taking action on civil rights issues out of fear that he would lose the party in the South. Under Kennedy and Johnson, the party gradually gave up trying to placate segregationist leaders and moved instead toward supporting civil rights and appealing to black voters. As liaison with the black community, Martin made sure that its voice was heard. Equally important, he added his own voice to steer the party toward greater advocacy on behalf of the poor, the dispossessed, and the disadvantaged. By the time Jimmy Carter became president, the liaison role that Martin had created while deputy chair of the DNC was elevated to an official position on the White House staff. Since then, all presidents, Democrats and Republicans alike, have had special assistants whose responsibilities include maintaining communication with minorities.

ꝛ ꝛ ꝛ

Before Louis Martin, no African American had been granted regular, direct access to the president of the United States. Frederick Douglass had counseled President Lincoln, Booker T. Washington had advised Theodore Roosevelt on an irregular basis, and the Taft administration had employed black assistants, though they served no official policy function. Franklin Roosevelt did have a large team of black agency advisors with well-defined roles; but these advisors, although they were both visible and active, lacked regular access to the Oval Office. Even E. Fredric Morrow, the first black presidential advisor to receive an official White House staff appointment, left the Eisenhower administration feeling that his counsel, especially on civil rights matters, was entirely ignored.[2]

President Kennedy broke this tradition. Although he was not ready to appoint a black to be the White House advisor on civil rights (Harris Wofford had tried to persuade him to name Martin), by making Martin deputy chair of the DNC Kennedy made it possible for him to shape his own role. Lee White, civil rights advisor to Kennedy and later to Johnson, described Martin as the White House's "stealth weapon."[3] Martin's work as liaison with the black community came at a crucial time—while activists engaged in direct action for major reform, Martin supported their efforts from within the apex of the federal establishment.

According to Ernest Green, the "Little Rock Nine" graduate who went on to become an assistant secretary of labor under Jimmy Carter, Martin was probably the most influential civil rights insider in the Kennedy, Johnson, and Carter administrations. "The outsiders—whether Martin Luther King, or the NAACP's Roy Wilkins or the National Urban League's Whitney Young— could not have wrung concessions from those administrations without Louis," Green concluded.[4] Carl Rowan, who under Kennedy became the highest-ranking black in the State Department, found that Martin wielded more influence through his ready access to presidents than he could have as an elected official or civil rights activist. "People get over-impressed by the guy who is in the streets marching and shouting and making bold speeches—but changing nothing." Rowan said. "He is in no way comparable to a Louis Martin, who understands that nothing much changes in America except as it is run through the political system. The guy who is on the inside, not compromising but understanding how the game is played, is the one who lifts the level of life for black America. That's what Louis Martin did."[5]

Sargent Shriver, who worked closely with Martin in the Kennedy campaign and during the transition, was unstinting in his admiration. Describing Martin as one of the most sensitive, dedicated, selfless, intelligent, and courageous persons he had ever known, Shriver added: "[Martin] was in positions frequently in Washington where he could have been pushing Louis Martin.... But he was always extremely modest, giving his advice quietly and sometimes without anybody even knowing that he was giving it to people in positions of influence. He never sought credit for himself and yet the suggestions that he made, as well as the way he made them, contributed significantly to political decisions that were made by others."[6] In his farewell remarks to black public officials who had served in his administration, Lyndon Johnson described Martin as "one of the wisest and most tireless counsellors I have had... a fighter for social justice... a practical man of public affairs."[7]

Martin was loyal to the presidents he worked with, but he was also honest in his criticism. In the early spring of 1963, with protests reaching a crescendo in Birmingham and elsewhere, he let the administration know just what he thought of its go-slow approach to civil rights legislation. His memos to the president and attorney general, as well as his passionate appeals during Cabinet-level meetings, made his a rare but unmistakable voice on the issue inside the White House. He was arguing against the overwhelming majority of Kennedy's advisors when he urged the president to bring a comprehensive civil rights bill before Congress and again when he argued that the White House should encourage the 1963 March on Washington. Ramsey Clark, who went on to become attorney general in 1966, credited Martin as a key factor in persuading Kennedy to include Title II, forbidding discrimination in public accommodations, in the civil rights bill that Congress finally passed in 1964.[8]

Of equal importance were Martin's efforts on behalf of the struggle for voting rights. Early in the Kennedy administration, he quietly helped persuade Martin Luther King and others of the value of the Voter Education Project, which made it possible for the Justice Department's voting rights enforcement efforts to take advantage of the registration work of courageous activists in the South. During the Selma protests in 1965, he was in constant communication with civil rights leaders and others in Alabama, passing along requests for federal intervention and making sure that the attorney general was accurately informed. For Martin, passage later that year of the momentous Voting Rights Act represented the culmination of a lifetime quest.

One important, very visible result of this legislation has been an explosion in the numbers of elected blacks at all levels of government. In 1960 Congress included only four black representatives, but by the time of Jimmy Carter's election in 1976, the Congressional Black Caucus had grown more than fourfold. Since then, progress has continued. While in the late 1980s, nearly all the black representatives in Congress came from urban districts in the North, most of the black members elected since then have come from sprawling, predominantly rural districts in the South. In 1992, five states of the old Confederacy—Alabama, Florida, North Carolina, South Carolina, and Virginia—sent blacks to Congress for the first time since Reconstruction.

A more recent development that particularly pleased Martin was the accession of blacks to positions of power within Congress. After three decades of growth, members of the Congressional Black Caucus reached sufficient seniority to chair several full committees and numerous subcommittees, including chairmanships of the House Armed Services, Government Operations, and Post Office and Civil Service Committees. Having witnessed under Kennedy how getting just a few distinguished black judicial appointees approved required tortuous fights with the southern segregationists who dominated the Senate Judiciary Committee. Martin was gratified to see blacks seated as heads of committees, knowing this was also good news for future minority appointments.

રેસ રેસ રેસ

In 1960, when Martin began compiling his list of 750 black candidates for Kennedy administration appointments, there were barely enough black professionals in the federal agencies in Washington to hold "a decent poker game," as Martin put it. Joining Sargent Shriver's team to review candidates for appointment, he helped mold the new administration into one that better reflected the ethnic and racial mix of the nation's citizens. His nationwide search for talented blacks broke new ground and proved so valuable that he continued this work under Johnson and Carter.

Martin's agenda was to put blacks and other minorities into positions where they could make public policy, not simply influence the decisions of others. He believed that political and economic equity would never become a reality until minorities were represented in all branches and at all levels of government. Lasting change had to occur within the system and become incorporated into it. Black appointees at the highest levels, he felt, would also spark greater enthusiasm among African Americans for voting and running for elected office. This was a sentiment that President Johnson shared as well.

"For one hundred years," Martin recalled, "Congressmen and others had recommended people for government jobs, and their recommendations would always be taken seriously. Nobody recommended any blacks." He followed every avenue to obtain these appointments. By 1967, when Thurgood Marshall was appointed to the U.S. Supreme Court, Martin had helped move hundreds of distinguished blacks into senior policy and judicial positions.

Many of the black officials who attained high posts during the 1960s and 1970s looked to Martin, by then a senior sage, for advice on what political buttons to push, which levers to pull, and how to survive the minefield of Washington politics. As with his White House work, Martin stayed in the background, avoiding cameras and microphones while keeping his eyes and ears open.

Nonetheless, Martin's gift for recognizing and promoting black talent earned him high praise and gratitude. To list all the senior appointments for which he lobbied would require more space than this book affords, but the names of those who were the first to break the all-white tradition at the government's most powerful institutions reveal the depth of the change. Among them were Thurgood Marshall, the first African American to sit on the U.S. Supreme Court; Andrew Brimmer, the first African American to serve as member of the Federal Reserve Board; Robert Weaver, the first African American to serve in the president's Cabinet; and Clifford Alexander, Jr., the first African American to serve as secretary of the army.

Martin also influenced Kennedy's appointment of a number of blacks to embassy posts and, more importantly, encouraged Kennedy to break with the tradition of limiting black ambassadors to Africa and the Caribbean, beginning with the appointment of Clifton Wharton, Sr., as ambassador to Norway and Carl Rowan as ambassador to Finland. Lyndon Johnson followed suit, appointing Patricia Roberts Harris as ambassador to Luxembourg. By 1966, blacks were representing the United States as ambassadors in six countries, and they had advanced within the foreign affairs establishment as agency directors and division heads.[9]

While the importance of these top appointments may be obvious, the significance of blacks in sub-Cabinet posts may be less so. When Martin began working for Kennedy, he was surprised to discover how influential the many sub-Cabinet positions were. Since the massive bureaucracy had the ability to thwart any new president's intentions, it was crucial to select appointees very carefully.

In 1961, there were about 3,000 political appointments in all agencies, yet the black presence within this group was almost nonexistent. Even among career civil service employees, there were few blacks in senior positions. In the Agriculture and Defense departments, for example, blacks were less than one percent of the senior level staff.[10] By the end of the Carter administration, the top ranks of the federal bureaucracy were fairly well integrated, partly as a result of continuous, active recruitment for which Martin had set the standard.

Perhaps the most lasting influence any president has is through his appointments to the federal courts. President Carter believed that one of his greatest achievements on behalf of blacks was in the area of judicial appointments, and in later years he spoke warmly of Martin's role in this achievement:

> I think the most tangible impact he made that is still being felt was the high number of black federal judges that I appointed.... I appointed more, with Louis Martin's help, than all of the other presidents in history together. I think that's a lasting legacy of my Administration in which I think Louis Martin played a very strong role.[11]

In all, Carter named thirty-seven blacks to federal judgeships, including the first ever to serve in U.S. district courts in the South.[12]

≈ ≈ ≈

Another memorable part of Martin's legacy was the establishment of an independent institution to help blacks continue the pursuit of political empowerment and, ultimately, of economic opportunity. The mission of the Joint Center for Political and Economic Studies, which Martin helped found and lead, dovetailed perfectly with his own political philosophy: to help achieve racial justice and economic opportunity through full participation in the political arena and to provide black officials with the information and technical support they needed to succeed in public office. The Joint Center became one more way for Martin to put into practice his vision of an inclusive American democracy, as well as a vehicle through which he could share his experience, insights, and wisdom with black leaders.

# MOVING THE MOUNTAIN

As the first chairman of the Joint Center's board of governors, Martin imbued it with his philosophy that one should "draw a bigger circle, include more people in the struggle and exclude nobody." Although he was himself a loyal Democrat, he knew that the institution needed to be nonpartisan, so he brought on board prominent Republicans, including Senator Edward Brooke of Massachusetts and attorneys Samuel Jackson and Wendell Freeland. In keeping with his lifelong efforts to build broad-based coalitions, he encouraged the Joint Center to seek coalitions and develop programs with other groups and organizations. The Joint Center's first contribution to the new cadre of black elected officials included training in the basics of governance and administration. As Martin often explained, many of the newest black public officials did not yet know how to seek federal funds for their municipalities or where to turn to get their roads paved. For providing this kind of information, as well as its published studies on election strategies and social and economic policies, the Joint Center became recognized as a unique resource for black elected and appointed officials and for the black community as a whole.

The Martin legacy is pervasive, embracing most of the political, social, and economic changes in the life of African Americans during the past six decades. From his labor advocacy in Detroit to his White House advisory role during the civil rights era, from his list of Cabinet candidates under Kennedy to his list of judicial candidates under Carter, from his hard-hitting editorial writing to his empowerment of black officials through the Joint Center, Martin broke racial barriers and pulled together lasting coalitions.

Louis Martin's ability to persuade others to do the right thing and to bring together the right people to get things done is legendary. Many of today's black leaders remember their pride at hearing him refer to them as "great Americans," knowing that it meant he expected great things of them. Martin once observed that he began his career as a journalist in the 1930s with the idea of using the position as "a lever to move this mountain of racism." While he labored toward this goal all his life, always believing that it could be done, he knew he could not do it alone. His greatest legacy may be that he inspired and empowered so many other "great Americans" to join him in the effort.

ॐ

# NOTES

ABBREVIATIONS

Edwin Interview
    Martin, Louis E. Interviews by Ed Edwin (April 1981–April 1987). Columbia University Oral History Collection.

Grele Interview
    Martin, Louis E. Interviews by Ronald Grele (March–May 1961). John Fitzgerald Kennedy Library Oral History Collection.

McComb Interview
    Martin, Louis E. Interview by David McComb (May 14, 1969). Lyndon Baines Johnson Library Oral History Collection.

DNC
    Democratic National Committee

JCPES
    Joint Center for Political and Economic Studies

WHCF
    White House Central Files

## 1. Learning About Race

1.  The details of Louis Martin's early life in this chapter are drawn entirely from interviews with Martin and his relatives, together with Martin's memoirs, particularly Memoir A.
2.  Dates and Barlow, *Split Image*, 355.
3.  The first break in Martin's journalism career came in 1959 when he spent a year in Lagos, Nigeria, as a consultant to the West African Press, although while in Africa he continued to write columns for the *Defender*. Upon his return to Chicago he was asked to join the Kennedy campaign, an invitation that ultimately led to his service with the Kennedy administration and then the Johnson administration. In 1969, Martin returned to the *Defender* and remained with the paper until 1978, shortly before he joined the Carter administration. In 1987, when he retired to Chicago, he was asked to write a column for the *Defender*, which he did until 1992.

## 2. Crusading in Detroit

1. Dates and Barlow, *Split Image*, 344–357.
2. *Chicago Defender*, June 15, 1935.
3. Memoir C.
4. Wilkins, *Standing Fast*, 132.
5. Memoir C.
6. Martin, "Blood, Sweat, and Ink," 37.
7. Communication from Gertrude Martin.
8. Martin, "Blood, Sweat, and Ink," 37.
9. Martin, "Blood, Sweat, and Ink," 38.
10. Memoir C; Memoir I.
11. Memoir C.
12. Author interview with Leroy Thomas.
13. Memoir C; Franklin, *From Slavery to Freedom*, 614. In 1996 the son of Charles Diggs, Jr., Douglas, was a candidate for Congress from Detroit.
14. *Michigan Chronicle,* June 10, 1939.
15. *Chicago Defender,* January 25, 1992.
16. Meier and Rudwick, *Black Detroit*, 9–11.
17. *Michigan Chronicle,* June 24, 1939.
18. Martin, "The Ford Contract," 284–285, 305; *Michigan Chronicle*, June 28, 1941; Memoir I.
19. Memoir I. The East St. Louis riot had turned into a pogrom against the black residents, 125 of whom died in the massacre.
20. Meier and Rudwick, *Black Detroit*, 32–33.
21. Meier and Rudwick, *Black Detroit*, 58; Wilkins, "Mind Your Own Business," 241.
22. Meier and Rudwick, *Black Detroit*, 55–59.
23. Meier and Rudwick, *Black Detroit*, 68–71, 86–87.
24. Memoir A; Meier and Rudwick, *Black Detroit*, 68–71.
25. Meier and Rudwick, *Black Detroit*, 66–71.
26. Martin, "Blood, Sweat, and Ink," 39.
27. Meier and Rudwick, *Black Detroit*, 84–107.
28. Martin, "The Ford Contract," 285.
29. Martin, "The Ford Contract," 284–285, 302.
30. Martin, "The Ford Contract," 302.
31. Meier and Rudwick, *Black Detroit*, 102.
32. Meier and Rudwick, *From Plantation to Ghetto*, 242–243.
33. Meier and Rudwick, *Black Detroit*, 108–109.
34. Franklin, *From Slavery to Freedom*, 578.
35. Meier and Rudwick, *Black Detroit*, 111.
36. *Michigan Chronicle,* June 28, 1941.
37. Franklin, *From Slavery to Freedom*, 579.
38. Meier and Rudwick, *Black Detroit*, 111–112.

39. Louis Martin to Walter White, October 2, 1941 (the letter is quoted in Meier and Rudwick, *Black Detroit*, 110).

40. Meier and Rudwick, *Black Detroit*, 120–136, 207–208.

41. *Michigan Chronicle*, January 13, 1940.

42. Meier and Rudwick, *From Plantation to Ghetto*, 240–241.

43. *Michigan Chronicle*, January 13, 1940.

44. Meier and Rudwick, *Black Detroit*, 175–183; Martin, "The Truth About Sojourner Truth," 113.

45. Meier and Rudwick, *Black Detroit*, 184–185.

46. *Michigan Chronicle*, February 20, 1943.

47. Martin, "The Negro in the Political Picture," 104–107, 137–139.

48. Meier and Rudwick, *Black Detroit*, 192.

49. Meier and Rudwick, *Black Detroit*, 169–171; Memoir A.

50. Memoir A.

51. Meier and Rudwick, *Black Detroit*, 194–196.

52. Marshall's report, which appeared in the NAACP's *Crisis* magazine (August 1943) is excerpted in Mitchell, *Race Riots in Black and White*, 129–131.

53. The cabdriver's remarks were published in the *Wayne Dispatch*, July 2, 1943, and are quoted in Mitchell, *Race Riots in Black and White*, 145.

54. Meier and Rudwick, *Black Detroit*, 192–197.

55. Memoir A.

56. *Michigan Chronicle*, July 24, 1943.

57. Memoir A.

58. Memoir A.

59. Hamilton, *Adam Clayton Powell, Jr.,* 168–173.

# 3. Drawing a Larger Circle

1.  Memoir E.
2.  Author interview with Louis Martin.
3.  Memoir E.
4.  Memoir A; Memoir E; Author interview with Louis Martin.
5.  Memoir A.
6.  Memoir E.
7.  Memoir A; Memoir E.
8.  Memoir E.
9.  Memoir E.
10. Weiss, *Farewell to the Party of Lincoln*, 37–40, 136–139, 145.
11. Weiss, *Farewell to the Party of Lincoln*, 71–74, 141, 148; Franklin, *From Slavery to Freedom*, 531–533.
12. Memoir G; Weiss, *Farewell to the Party of Lincoln*, 138–139.
13. Memoir G.
14. Memoir G.
15. Memoir A; Memoir D.
16. Weiss, *Farewell to the Party of Lincoln*, 158.
17. Memoir A; Memoir D; Memoir E.
18. Author interview with Louis Martin; Memoir A.
19. Memoir D.
20. Memoir D.
21. Memoir D.
22. Memoir E.
23. Dates and Barlow, *Split Image*, 356–57.
24. Memoir E; Weiss, *Farewell to the Party of Lincoln*, 92–93.
25. Memoir E.
26. Memoir D.
27. Memoir F.
28. Memoir E; Memoir D.
29. Memoir E.
30. Memoir D.
31. Author interview with Louis Martin.
32. Memoir A.
33. Memoir A.
34. Memoir C.
35. Memoir C.
36. Offiong, *Imperialism and Dependency.*
37. Memoir F.
38. Memoir F.

# 4. Rallying the Troops

1. Memoir F.
2. Memoir F; Memoir B; Branch, *Parting the Waters*, 342.
3. Memoir F.
4. Martin's speech, given on April 26, 1963, at Durham, North Carolina, is reprinted in Roy Hill, *Rhetoric of Racial Hope.*
5. Garrow, *Bearing the Cross*, 127.
6. Memoir F; Lewis, *King*, 124.
7. Wofford, *Of Kennedys and Kings*, 52–53.
8. Third Edwin interview, 48–49; Wofford, *Of Kennedys and Kings*, 57–58.
9. Wofford, *Of Kennedys and Kings*, 47, 60; DeFrancis interview with Mildred Jeffrey.
10. Branch, *Parting the Waters*, 313; *Chicago Defender*, May 18, 1991; Memoir F.
11. Memoir F.
12. Author interview with R. Sargent Shriver.
13. First Grele interview, 3; Wofford, *Of Kennedys and Kings*, 60; Branch, *Parting the Waters*, 342.
14. First Grele interview, 5, 24.
15. Branch, *Parting the Waters*, 342.
16. Third Edwin interview, 49; McComb interview, 9; Second Grele interview, 8.
17. First Grele interview, 4.
18. Memoir B.
19. Memoir F.
20. Memoir F; Memoir B.
21. Memoir B.
22. First Grele interview, 8; Author interview with Louis Martin; *Chicago Defender*, May 18, 1991.
23. Wofford, *Of Kennedys and Kings*, 60.
24. First Grele interview, 6–7; Morrow, *Black Man in the White House*, 292–247.
25. Guthman and Shulman, *Robert Kennedy: In His Own Words*, 90–91.
26. Memoir F; First Grele interview, 11–13.
27. Memoir F; Memoir B; First Grele interview, 12–13.
28. Memoir F.
29. Wofford, *Of Kennedys and Kings*, 61; Garrow, *Bearing the Cross*, 142.
30. McComb interview, 7; First Grele interview, 10; Bositis, *Blacks and the 1996 Democratic National Convention*, 13.
31. First Grele interview, 11.
32. Second Grele interview; Suggs, "Virginia" in *The Black Press in the South*, 379–421.
33. Second Grele interview, 14.
34. Second Grele interview, 10.
35. Second Grele interview, 11; Memoir B.
36. First Grele interview, 13; Memoir F.

37. Memoir B.
38. Memoir F; Wofford, *Of Kennedys and Kings*, 59. The press statement is recorded in *Freedom of Communications*, Part I, 68–70.
39. Memoir F.
40. Meier and Rudwick, *From Plantation to Ghetto*, 346; Memoir F.
41. Memoir F; First Grele interview, 16–18.
42. Memoir B.
43. Letter from D. Arnett Murphy to Congressman William Dawson, DNC files, John Fitzgerald Kennedy Library.
44. Letter from D. Arnett Murphy to Congressman William Dawson, DNC files, John Fitzgerald Kennedy Library; Memoir B.
45. Memoir F.
46. First Grele interview, 19–21; Author interview with Louis Martin; Memoir B.
47. Author interview with Louis Martin.
48. Memoir B; Memoir F.
49. First Grele interview, 22; Memoir B.
50. First Grele interview, 22–23; Memoir B.
51. Wofford, *Of Kennedys and Kings*, 62.
52. Memoir F. The Chicago speech, delivered at Lake Meadow Shopping Center on October 1, 1960, is on file with the John F. Kennedy Pre-Presidential Papers, Senate Speech Files, 1953–1960, Box 912, John Fitzgerald Kennedy Library.
53. First Grele interview, 26.
54. Quoted in first Grele interview, 27.
55. Memoir F; First Grele interview, 27.
56. Letter from D. Arnett Murphy to Louis Martin, October 18, 1960, DNC files, John Fitzgerald Kennedy Library.
57. Other participants at the National Conference on Constitutional Rights included New York senator Herbert H. Lehman, New York mayor Robert Wagner, former New York governor Averell Harriman, Oregon senator Wayne Morse, New York congressman Emanuel Celler, Michigan senator Philip Hart.
58. First Grele interview, 27–29; Wofford, *Of Kennedys and Kings*, 63.
59. Wofford, *Of Kennedys and Kings*, 63; Branch, *Parting the Waters*, 343–344.
60. Quoted in Memoir F.
61. First Grele interview, 27; First Edwin interview, 52.
62. Memoir F.
63. Second Grele interview, 3; Memoir F; Third Edwin interview, 20.
64. Memoir F.
65. Second Grele interview, 4.
66. Memoir F.
67. Memoir B; Second Grele interview, 3; Branch, *Parting the Waters*, 343.
68. Second Grele interview, 16–19.
69. Lewis, *King*, 125–126.
70. Author interview with Louis Martin; Garrow, *Bearing the Cross*, 146.
71. Lewis, *King*, 127.

72. Second Grele interview, 21.
73. Memoir A.
74. Second Grele interview, 20; Memoir A; Memoir B.
75. Author interview with R. Sargent Shriver; Wofford, *Of Kennedys and Kings*, 18–19, 27; Branch, *Parting the Waters*, 362.
76. Wofford, *Of Kennedys and Kings*, 19–20; Schlesinger, *Robert Kennedy and His Times*, 234; Garrow, *Bearing the Cross*, 147.
77. Garrow, *Bearing the Cross*, 147; Lewis, *King*, 128; Second Grele interview, 21.
78. Memoir A; Wofford, *Of Kennedys and Kings*, 23–24.
79. Wofford, *Of Kennedys and Kings*, 24–25; Garrow, *Bearing the Cross*, 149.
80. Branch, *Parting the Waters*, 369; Lewis, *King*, 129.
81. Lewis, *King*, 129.
82. Second Grele interview, 24; Wofford, *Of Kennedys and Kings*, 24–26; Branch, *Parting the Waters*, 368.
83. Branch, *Parting the Waters*, 374; Morrow, *Black Man in the White House*, 296.
84. Although the election was very close, the loss of Illinois alone would not have tipped the election to Nixon. However, the loss of Illinois *plus* one or two of the other states that were closely contested could easily have resulted in Kennedy's defeat; Memoir A.

# 5. A Voice for Civil Rights

1. *Chicago Defender,* July 10, 1991; Whalen and Whalen, *The Longest Debate,* xvii.
2. Strober and Strober, *"Let Us Begin Anew,"* 282; Schlesinger, *Robert Kennedy and His Times,* 309.
3. Wilkins, *Standing Fast,* 278–280; Third Grele interview, 63.
4. *Chicago Defender,* May 28, 1988; Third Grele interview, 10.
5. Wofford, *Of Kennedys and Kings,* 141.
6. Third Grele interview, 16, 29; Author interview with Louis Martin; First Edwin interview, 61.
7. Ruffin interview with Louis Martin.
8. Third Grele interview, 20; McComb interview, 26; Wofford, *Of Kennedys and Kings,* 150
9. Rowan, *Breaking Barriers,* 97–170.
10. Rowan, *Breaking Barriers,* 172–173.
11. Memoir A.
12. Memoir A.
13. Author interview with Louis Martin; Third Grele interview, 65; Memoir C.
14. Second Edwin interview, 17–19; Eddie N. Williams, personal communication, December 1996.
15. Second Edwin interview, 17–21; Memoir C.
16. Second Edwin interview, 18–19, 21.
17. Wofford, *Of Kennedys and Kings,* 131–133; Cross, *The Black Power Imperative,* 330.
18. Memoir A.
19. Memoir A.
20. Lewis, *King,* 130.
21. Wofford, *Of Kennedys and Kings,* 136–138; Author interview with Harris Wofford.
22. Schlesinger, *Robert Kennedy and His Times,* 310.
23. Wofford, *Of Kennedys and Kings,* 139.
24. Wofford, *Of Kennedys and Kings,* 144–148.
25. Memoir A.
26. Wofford, *Of Kennedys and Kings,* 420; Third Edwin interview, 16, 45–46.
27. Strober and Strober, *"Let Us Begin Anew,"* 281.
28. Third Grele interview, 68.
29. Memoir A.
30. Memoir C.
31. Schlesinger, *Robert Kennedy and His Times,* 335; Wofford, *Of Kennedys and Kings,* 141.
32. Third Edwin interview, 47; McComb interview, 16–17.
33. Memoir C.
34. Author interview with Harris Wofford.
35. Branch, *Parting the Waters,* 404.

36. Branch, *Parting the Waters*, 405; Memoir C.
37. Memoir C; Branch, *Parting the Waters*, 407; Schlesinger, *Robert Kennedy and His Times*, 381.
38. Branch, *Parting the Waters,* 405–406; Memoir C.
39. Wofford, *Of Kennedys and Kings*, 159; Branch, *Parting the Waters,* 407; Memoir C.
40. Sixth Edwin interview, 38–39.
41. Lewis, *King*, 135–138; Schlesinger, *Robert Kennedy and His Times*, 324–325.
42. Wofford, *Of Kennedys and Kings,* 159; Garrow, *Bearing the Cross*, 163; Memoir C.
43. Wilkins, *Standing Fast*, 278.
44. Third Grele interview, 22; Schlesinger, *Robert Kennedy and His Times*, 334.
45. Third Edwin interview, 10–11.
46. Wofford, *Of Kennedys and Kings,* 150.
47. Wofford, *Of Kennedys and Kings,* 150–151.
48. Memo from Louis Martin to Robert Kennedy, May 9, 1961, DNC papers, John Fitzgerald Kennedy Library.
49. Williams, *Eyes on the Prize*, 144–161; Wofford, *Of Kennedys and Kings*, 151–158; Branch, *Parting the Waters*, 412–491.
50. Third Grele interview, 24.
51. Author interview with Thurgood Marshall; Davis and Clark, *Thurgood Marshall*, 224.
52. Author interview with Thurgood Marshall; First Edwin interview, 54.
53. Third Grele interview, 25; Memoir A.
54. Memoir A; First Edwin interview, 55; Memoir A.
55. First Edwin interview, 55.
56. Third Grele interview, 26–27; Author interview with Thurgood Marshall.
57. Schlesinger, *Robert Kennedy and His Times*, 330–331.
58. Davis and Clark, *Thurgood Marshall.* 223–240; Schlesinger, *Robert Kennedy and His Times*, 330–331.
59. Memoir A.
60. Schlesinger, *Robert Kennedy and His Times,* 344–346.
61. Williams, *Eyes on the Prize,* 216–217.
62. Third Grele interview, 50.
63. Branch, *Parting the Waters*, 685; Schlesinger, *A Thousand Days*, 950.
64. DeFrancis interview with Lee White; Memoir C.
65. DeFrancis interview with Lee White; Memoir C.
66. Memoir C.
67. Reeves, *President Kennedy*, 462.
68. Memo quoted in Reeves, 468.
69. Reeves, *President Kennedy*, 469.
70. Reeves, *President Kennedy*, 468.
71. Special Message to the Congress on Civil Rights, February 28, 1963, in *Public Papers of the Presidents: John F. Kennedy, 1963*, 222.
72. Wofford, *Of Kennedys and Kings*, 170.

73. D. Carter, *The Politics of Rage*, 115; Lewis, *King*, 174.

74. Lewis, *King*, 182–186, 192.

75. Lewis, *King*, 196–196.

76. Carter, *The Politics of Rage*, 125.

77. Carter, *The Politics of Rage,* 126–127.

78. Memo quoted in Wofford, *Of Kennedys and Kings*, 171.

79. Branch, *Parting the Waters*, 815–816.

80. Third Grele interview, 43.

81. Louis Martin, journal entry dated June 16, 1963, Martin family papers.

82. Louis Martin, journal entry dated June 16, 1963, Martin family papers; Third Grele interview, 45, 48.

83. Third Grele interview, 45.

84. Third Grele interview, 45.

85. Third Grele interview, 46–47.

86. Louis Martin, journal entry dated June 16, 1963, Martin family papers; Third Grele interview, 45–45.

87. Third Grele interview, 45.

88. Louis Martin, journal entry dated June 16, 1963, Martin family papers.

89. Third Grele interview, 55.

90. Ramsey Clark, undated letter to Louis Martin, Martin family papers; Third Edwin interview, 41–42.

91. Third Edwin interview, 42; Third Grele interview, 42.

92. Third Grele interview, 54.

93. Third Edwin interview, 42.

94. Ramsey Clark, undated letter to Louis Martin, Martin family papers.

95. Branch, *Parting the Waters*, 821.

96. Branch, *Parting the Waters,* 822–823.

97. Branch, *Parting the Waters*, 823; Schlesinger, *Robert Kennedy and His Times*, 369; Radio and Television Report to the American People on Civil Rights, June 11, 1963 (President's Office Files, Speech File, Box 45, John Fitzgerald Kennedy Library).

98. Third Grele interview, 60–61.

99. Garrow, *Bearing the Cross*, 265–269.

100. Reeves, *President Kennedy*, 529.

101. Memoir C; Memoir H.

102. Memoir C; Author interview with Louis Martin; Third Grele interview, 61–62.

103. Memoir C.

104. Memoir C.

105. Memoir C.

106. Memoir C.

107. Speech as reprinted in Friedman, ed., *The Civil Rights Reader.*

108. Memoir C.

109. Memoir C.

110. Author interview with Louis Martin; Memoir C.

# 6. Making History

1. McComb interview, 19.
2. Memoir C.
3. McComb interview, 12–18.
4. McComb interview, 17–18.
5. Author interview with Louis Martin.
6. First Edwin interview, 63.
7. Memoir C.
8. Cross, *The Black Power Imperative*, 347–348; Memoir C.
9. *Chicago Defender*, October 10, 1987.
10. Third Edwin interview, 4–5.
11. Author interview with Andrew Brimmer.
12. Califano, *The Triumph and Tragedy of Lyndon Johnson*, 109–111.
13. Third Edwin interview, 4.
14. Author interview with Louis Martin.
15. McComb interview, 27; Third Grele interview, 22.
16. Califano, *The Triumph and Tragedy of Lyndon Johnson*, 127; McComb interview, 22.
17. McComb interview, 22–23.
18. Califano, *The Triumph and Tragedy of Lyndon Johnson,* 128.
19. Califano, *The Triumph and Tragedy of Lyndon Johnson,* 129.
20. McComb interview, 23–25; First Edwin interview, 62; Third Edwin interview, 12–13.
21. McComb interview, 24–25.
22. Author interview with Thurgood Marshall; Davis and Clark, *Thurgood Marshall,* 244.
23. Author interview with Thurgood Marshall.
24. Author interview with Thurgood Marshall.
25. McComb interview, 27; First Edwin interview, 56–57; Third Edwin interview, 13.
26. Author interview with Thurgood Marshall.
27. Author interview with Thurgood Marshall; Davis and Clark, 265.
28. McComb interview, 30–35; Third Edwin interview, 14.

# 7. Walking Through New Doors

1. McComb interview, 18.
2. Address Before a Joint Session of Congress, November 27, 1963, in *Public Papers of the Presidents: Lyndon B. Johnson*, 1963–64 (Vol. 1), 9.
3. McPherson, *A Political Education*, 136.
4. Memoir C.
5. McComb interview, 13.
6. McComb interview, 14.
7. McComb interview, 22.
8. Califano, *The Triumph and Tragedy of Lyndon Johnson*, 53.
9. First Edwin interview, 51.
10. Third Edwin interview, 54.
11. Memoir C.
12. Third Edwin interview, 27.
13. Branch, *Parting the Waters*, 183, 221–22; McPherson, *A Political Education*, 142–144.
14. Third Edwin interview, 43–44.
15. Memoir C.
16. Memoir C.
17. Memoir C.
18. Memoir C.
19. Third Edwin interview, 45, 46.
20. Memoir C.
21. Memoir C.
22. Memoir C.
23. Memoir C.
24. Memoir C.
25. Memoir C.
26. Williams, *Eyes on the Prize*, 248.
27. Stone, *Black Political Power in America*, 51–52.
28. Memoir C.
29. Memoir C.
30. Memoir C.
31. *Michigan Chronicle*, June 24, 1939.
32. Third Edwin interview, 26.
33. Williams, *Eyes On The Prize*, 253.
34. Williams, *Eyes on the Prize*, 253.
35. Garrow, *Bearing the Cross*, 398–399.
36. John Cashin, letter to Ofield Dukes, August 11, 1996; DeFrancis interview with John Cashin.
37. March 8, 1965, HUr/ST, FG35, WI, WHCF, Lyndon Baines Johnson Library; Garrow, *Bearing the Cross*, 400–401.
38. Garrow, *Bearing the Cross*, 400–404.
39. Quoted in Rowan, *Breaking Barriers*, 250.

40. Lewis, *King*, 292.
41. Quoted in Rowan, *Breaking Barriers,* 251–52.
42. Memoir C.
43. Califano, *The Triumph and Tragedy of Lyndon Johnson*, 57.
44. Memoir C.
45. Califano, *The Triumph and Tragedy of Lyndon Johnson*, 58
46. Califano, *The Triumph and Tragedy of Lyndon Johnson,* 11; Malcolm X's December 20, 1964, speech as quoted in Mitchell, *Race Riots in Black and White*, 45; Fifth Edwin interview, 20–23; Wilkins, *Standing Fast*, 317.
47. Hampton and Fayer, eds., *Voices of Freedom*, 267–282.
48. Speech by Louis Martin, Shaw University, Raleigh, North Carolina, March 20, 1964.
49. Hampton and Fayer, eds., *Voices of Freedom*, 349–372.
50. Lewis, *King*, 314–317; McCone report, quoted in Mitchell, *Race Riots in Black and White*, 124; Califano, *The Triumph and Tragedy of Lyndon Johnson*, 59.
51. Wofford, *Of Kennedys and Kings*, 321; Wilkins, *Standing Fast*, 312–313; Editorial, *The Nation,* August 30, 1965, quoted in Mitchell, *Race Riots in Black and White*, 54.
52. Califano, *The Triumph and Tragedy of Lyndon Johnson*, 67.
53. Califano, *The Triumph and Tragedy of Lyndon Johnson*, 228–229.
54. Fourth Edwin interview, 23, 26–27.
55. Califano, *The Triumph and Tragedy of Lyndon Johnson*, 230–231.
56. Califano, *The Triumph and Tragedy of Lyndon Johnson*, 232–233.
57. DNC files Series 2, Box 276, 13–4033, John Fitzgerald Kennedy Library; McPherson, *A Political Education,* 347–348
58. McPherson, *A Political Education,* 335–339.
59. Third Edwin interview, 38–39.
60. McPherson, *A Political Education*, 345–346; Author interview with Vernon Jordan.
61. Quoted in McPherson, *A Political Education,* 346.
62. McPherson, *A Political Education*, 346–347.
63. McPherson, *A Political Education*, 351–352.
64. McPherson, *A Political Education,* 348; Lyndon Johnson to Louis Martin, June 7, 1966 (WHCF, Executive HU/MC, Box 23, Lyndon Baines Johnson Library).
65. Third Edwin interview, 31.
66. Califano, *The Triumph and Tragedy of Lyndon Johnson*, 196–197.
67. Lemann, *The Promised Land,* 185.
68. Author interview with Louis Martin.
69. McComb interview, 30.
70. From the Kerner Commission report, quoted in Mitchell, *Race Riots in Black and White*, 148.
71. The Kerner Commission report, quoted in Mitchell, *Race Riots in Black and White*, 137–138; Mitchell, *Race Riots in Black and White*, 51–52.
72. Quoted in Wilkins, *Standing Fast*, 327–328.

73. McPherson, *A Political Education,* 368–369; Mitchell, *Race Riots in Black and White,* 155.
74. Author interview with Harry McPherson.
75. Gertrude Martin, personal communication with Marc DeFrancis, JCPES, December 21, 1996; Califano, *The Triumph and Tragedy of Lyndon Johnson,* 274–275
76. Califano, *The Triumph and Tragedy of Lyndon Johnson,* 274–275, 278.
77. McPherson, *A Political Education,* 365.
78. Author interview with Louis Martin.
79. McPherson, *A Political Education,* 365–366.
80. McPherson, *A Political Education,* 366–368.
81. Califano, *The Triumph and Tragedy of Lyndon Johnson,* 276.
82. McPherson, *A Political Education,* 370–371.
83. Califano, *The Triumph and Tragedy of Lyndon Johnson,* 55.
84. Louis Martin to Larry O'Brien, December 10, 1968 (WHCF, Executive PL, Box 2, Lyndon Baines Johnson Library).
85. "Remarks at the Reception of Negro Presidential Appointees and Their Guests," Washington, D.C., December 17, 1968.
86. Third Grele interview, 65.
87. Davis and Clark affirm this deal in *Thurgood Marshall,* 235–36; Califano also alludes to such deals in *The Triumph and Tragedy of Lyndon Johnson,* 311–12.
88. DeFrancis interview with Lee White.
89. Wofford, *Of Kennedys and Kings,* 172.
90. Third Grele interview, 72.
91. Ruffin interview with Louis Martin.

# 8. Rescuing the Georgia Brigade

1. Memoir C; Author interview with Louis Martin.
2. Author interview with Louis Martin.
3. Jordan, "State of the Nation Report," National Urban League, 1977.
4. Robert Bohanan, Jimmy Carter Library, personal communication with Marc DeFrancis, January 1997.
5. Cross, *The Black Power Imperative*, 336; Author interview with Hamilton Jordan.
6. Quoted in Ruffin, "Louis Martin, the Godfather," 5.
7. The proposal was the work of task force members Frank Reeves, on leave from the Howard Law School faculty; Donald Stocks, a corporate executive; Eleanor Farrar, vice president in charge of MARC's Washington office; and Timothy Jenkins, a member of the Howard University Board of Governors.
8. Information about the formation of the Joint Center supplied by Eleanor Farrar, senior vice president of the Center until her retirement in 1996.
9. Memoir C.
10. Author interview with Jimmy Carter.
11. Author interview with Louis Martin.
12. *Chicago Tribune*, August 14, 1979.
13. Author interview with Hamilton Jordan.
14. Gertrude Martin, personal communication with Mary T. Garber, JCPES, November 1996.
15. Author interview with Hamilton Jordan.
16. Author interview with Jimmy Carter.
17. Memoir C.
18. Author interview with Louis Martin.
19. Memoir C.
20. Memoir C; Author interview with Louis Martin.
21. Second Edwin interview, 6–8.
22. *Chicago Defender*, February 10, 1992; Memoir C.
23. Memoir C; Louis Martin files, WHCF, Fed. Gov. Orgs., Boxes FG 62, FG 6-11, Jimmy Carter Library.
24. Memoir C.
25. Author interview with Jimmy Carter; U.S. Dept. of Justice.
26. Cross, *The Black Power Imperative,* 348; Martin, ed., "Minority Report," *Fact Sheet* 106, August 1979.
27. Memoir C.
28. Louis Martin files, HU1 LA2, FG 6-1-1, Jimmy Carter Library.
29. Robert Bohanan, Jimmy Carter Library, personal communication with Marc DeFrancis, January 1997.
30. Author interview with Louis Martin.
31. Memoir C.
32. Memoir C.

33. Author interview with Jimmy Carter.
34. Author interview with Jimmy Carter; Carter, *Keeping Faith*, 491.
35. Author interview with Jimmy Carter; public statement issued by Andrew Young, White House, August 14, 1979; Hamilton Jordan Papers, Box 57, Andrew Young file (CF64), 14 August 1979, Jimmy Carter Library.
36. Author interview with Louis Martin.
37. Author interview with Louis Martin; Memoir C.
38. Memoir C.
39. Memoir C.
40. Author interview with Louis Martin; Memoir C.
41. Author interview with Louis Martin; Memoir C.
42. Memoir C.
43. Memoir C.
44. *Chicago Defender*, March 10, 1990.
45. Author interview with Louis Martin.
46. Author interview with Roger Estep.
47. Martin, "The Emancipation Proclamation."

# 9. Moving the Mountain

1. Author interview with Harris Wofford.
2. Morrow, *Black Man in the White House.*
3. DeFrancis interview with Lee White.
4. Author interview with Ernest Green.
5. Author interview with Carl Rowan.
6. Author interview with R. Sargent Shriver.
7. "Remarks at the Reception of Negro Presidential Appointees and Their Guests," Washington, D.C., December 17, 1968.
8. Strober and Strober, *"Let Us Begin Anew,"* 274; Ramsey Clark, undated letter to Louis Martin, Martin family papers; DeFrancis interview with Lee White.
9. Franklin, *From Slavery to Freedom,* 648.
10. Wofford, *Of Kennedys and Kings,* 141.
11. Author interview with Jimmy Carter.

# BIBLIOGRAPHY

## Books

Aptheker, Herbert, ed. *A Documentary History of the Negro People in the United States,* vol 3. Secaucus, New Jersey: Citadel Press, 1973.

Bositis, David. *Blacks and the 1996 Democratic National Convention.* Washington, D.C.: Joint Center for Political and Economic Studies, 1996.

Branch, Taylor. *Parting the Waters: America in the King Years, 1954–63.* New York: Simon and Schuster, 1988.

Brisbane, Robert H. *The Black Vanguard.* Valley Forge, Pennsylvania: Judson Press, 1970.

Burns, MacGregor, William Crotty, Lois Lovelace Duke, et al., eds. *The Democrats Must Lead: The Case for a Progressive Democratic Party.* Boulder, Colorado: Westview Press, 1992.

Califano, Joseph A., Jr. *The Triumph and Tragedy of Lyndon Johnson: The White House Years.* New York: Simon and Schuster, 1991.

Carter, Dan T. *The Politics of Rage: George Wallace, the Origins of the New Conservatism, and the Transformation of American Politics.* New York: Simon and Schuster, 1995.

Carter, Jimmy. *Keeping Faith: Memoirs of a President.* New York: Bantam Books, 1982.

Cross, Theodore. *The Black Power Imperative.* New York: Faulkner Books, 1987.

Dates, Jannette L., and William Barlow. *Split Image: African Americans in the Mass Media.* Washington, D.C.: Howard University Press, 1990.

Davis, Michael D., and Hunter R. Clark. *Thurgood Marshall: Warrior at the Bar, Rebel on the Bench.* New York: Carol Publishing Group, 1992.

Fager, Charles E. *Selma, 1965.* New York: Charles Scribner's Sons, 1974.

Farmer, James. *Freedom—When?* New York: Random House, 1965.

Forman, James. *The Making of Black Revolutionaries.* New York: Macmillan Publishing Co., Inc., 1972.

Franklin, John Hope. *From Slavery to Freedom: A History of Negro Americans.* 3rd ed. New York: Vintage, 1969.

Friedman, Leon, ed. *The Civil Rights Reader: Basic Documents of the Civil Rights Movement.* New York: Walker and Company, 1967.

Garrow, David J. *Bearing the Cross: Martin Luther King, Jr., and the Southern Christian Leadership Conference.* New York: William Morrow and Company, Inc., 1986.

Gilliam, Reginald E. *Black Political Development: An Advocacy Analysis.* Port Washington, New York: Dunellan Publishing Company, 1975.

Gomes, Ralph C., and Linda Faye Williams, eds. *From Exclusion to Inclusion.* New York: Greenwood Press, 1992.

Guthman, Edwin O., and Jeffrey Shulman, eds. *Robert Kennedy— In His Own Words: The Unpublished Recollections of the Kennedy Years.* New York: Bantam Books, 1988.

Hamilton, Charles V. *Adam Clayton Powell, Jr.: The Political Biography of an American Dilemma.* New York: Macmillan, 1991.

Hampton, Henry, and Steve Fayer, eds. *Voices of Freedom: An Oral History of the Civil Rights Movement From the 1950s Through the 1980s.* New York: Bantam Books, 1990.

Harding, Vincent. *The Other American Revolution.* Los Angeles: Center for Afro-American Studies, UCLA, 1980.

Hill, Roy L. *Rhetoric of Racial Hope.* New York: McDaniel Press, 1976.

Holden, Mathew, Jr. *The Politics of the Black "Nation."* New York: Chandler Publishing, 1973.

Hughes, Langston. *Selected Poems of Langston Hughes.* New York: Vintage Books, 1959.

Jordan, Hamilton. *Crisis: The Last Year of the Carter Presidency.* New York: G. P. Putnam's Sons, 1982.

Kaufman, Burton I. *The Presidency of James Earl Carter, Jr.* Lawrence, Kansas: University Press of Kansas, 1993.

Lemann, Nicholas. *The Promised Land.* New York: Alfred A. Knopf, 1991.

Lewis, David L. *King: A Biography.* 2nd ed. Urbana, Illinois: University of Illinois Press, 1978.

McPherson, Harry. *A Political Education: A Journal of Life With Senators, Generals, Cabinet Members, and Presidents.* Boston: Little, Brown and Company, 1972.

Meier, August, and Elliott Rudwick. *Black Detroit and the Rise of the UAW.* Rev. ed. New York: Oxford University Press, 1976.

——. *From Plantation to Ghetto.* 3rd. ed. New York: Hill and Wang, 1976.

Mitchell, J. Paul, ed. *Race Riots in Black and White.* Englewood Cliffs, New Jersey: Prentice-Hall, Inc., 1970.

Morrow, E. Frederic. *Black Man in the White House.* New York: Coward-McCann, Inc., 1963.

National Advisory Commission on Civil Disorders. *The Kerner Report: The 1968 Report of the National Advisory Commission on Civil Disorders.* New York: Pantheon Books, 1988.

Offiong, Daniel A. *Imperialism and Dependency: Obstacles to African Development.* Washington, D.C.: Howard University Press, 1982.

O'Reilly, Kenneth. *Nixon's Piano: Presidents and Racial Politics From Washington to Clinton.* New York: The Free Press, 1995.

# BIBLIOGRAPHY

*Public Papers of the Presidents of the United States: Lyndon B. Johnson, 1963–64*, Vol. 1. Washington, D.C.: Government Printing Office, 1965.

Reeves, Richard. *President Kennedy: Profile of Power*. New York: Simon and Schuster, 1993.

Rowan, Carl T. *Breaking Barriers: A Memoir*. Boston: Little, Brown and Company, 1991.

Schlesinger, Arthur M., Jr. *Robert Kennedy and His Times*. New York: Ballantine Books, 1978.

———. *A Thousand Days*. Boston: Houghton Mifflin Co., 1965.

Sorensen, Theodore. *"Let the Word Go Forth": The Speeches, Statements, and Writings of John F. Kennedy*. New York: Delacorte Press, 1988.

Stokes, Carl B. *Promises of Power: A Political Autobiography*. New York: Simon and Schuster, 1973.

Stone, Chuck. *Black Political Power in America*. New York: Dell, 1968.

Strober, Gerald S., and Deborah H. Strober, eds. *"Let Us Begin Anew": An Oral History of the Kennedy Presidency*. New York: HarperCollins, 1993.

Suggs, Henry L. *The Black Press in the South*. Westport, Connecticut: Greenwood Press, 1983.

Thomas, Richard W. *Life for Us Is What We Make It: Building Black Community in Detroit, 1915–1945*. Bloomington: Indiana University Press, 1992.

U.S. Congress. Senate. *Freedom of Communications: Final Report of the Committee on Commerce, United States Senate—Part I: The Speeches, Remarks, Press Conferences, and Statements of Sen. John F. Kennedy, August 1–November 7, 1960*. Washington, D.C.: U.S. Government Printing Office, 1961.

Walters, Ronald W. *Black Presidential Politics in America*. Albany: SUNY Press, 1988.

Weiss, Nancy J. *Farewell to the Party of Lincoln: Black Politics in the Age of FDR*. Princeton: Princeton University Press, 1983.

West, Cornel. *Race Matters*. Boston: Beacon Press, 1993.

Whalen, Charles, and Barbara Whalen. *The Longest Debate*. Washington, D.C.: Seven Locks Press, 1985.

Wilkins, Roy, with Tom Mathews. *Standing Fast: The Autobiography of Roy Wilkins*. New York: Da Capo Press, 1994.

Williams, Juan. *Eyes on the Prize: America's Civil Rights Years, 1954–1965*. New York: Viking, 1987.

———. *The Joint Center: Portrait of a Black Think Tank*. Washington, D.C.: Joint Center for Political and Economic Studies, Inc., 1995.

Wofford, Harris. *Of Kennedys and Kings: Making Sense of the Sixties*. New York: Farrar, Straus, Giroux, 1980.

## Articles

Martin, Louis E. "Behind Detroit's Terror." *New Masses* (July 6, 1943).

——. "The Big Stick in Detroit." *The Crisis* (December 1937): 364, 378.

——. "Blood, Sweat, and Ink." *Common Ground* (Winter 1944): 37–42

——. "Detroit—Still Dynamite." *The Crisis* (January 1944): 8–10, 25.

——. "The Ford Contract: An Opportunity." *The Crisis* (September 1941): 284–285, 302.

——. "Minority Report." *Fact Sheet* 106 (Office of Louis Martin, The White House) (August 1979).

——. "The Negro in the Political Picture." *Opportunity* (July 1943): 104–107, 137–139.

——. "Revised Appointees List." *Fact Sheet* 115 (Office of Louis Martin, The White House) (August 1980).

——. "Tokyo Looked at Detroit." *New Masses* (March 17, 1942): 13–14.

——. "The Truth About Sojourner Truth." *The Crisis* (April 1942): 112–113, 142.

Ruffin, David. "Louis Martin, The Godfather." *FOCUS,* Joint Center for Political and Economic Studies (March 1990): 5.

Smith, Robert C. "Black Appointed Officials: A Neglected Area of Research in Black Political Participation." *Journal of Black Studies* (March 1984): 369–388.

——. "Black Power and the Transformation from Protest to Politics." *Political Science Quarterly* 96 (Fall 1981): 431–443.

Wilkins, Roy. " 'Mind Your Own Business.' " *The Crisis* (August 1937): 241.

Williams, Eddie N. "The Next 20 Years." *FOCUS,* Joint Center for Political and Economic Studies (March 1990): 2.

Williams, Juan. "The Joint Center: A Historical Portrait." *FOCUS,* Joint Center for Political and Economic Studies (April 1995): 3–4, 8.

## Newspapers

*Chicago Defender.* 1935–36; 1947–60.

*Chicago Tribune.* 1979.

*Michigan Chronicle.* 1939–44.

# BIBLIOGRAPHY

## Speeches

Johnson, Lyndon. Remarks at the Reception of Negro Presidential Appointees and Their Guests, Washington, D.C., December 17, 1968.

Jordan, Vernon. "State of the Nation Report." Comments made to the National Urban League's 67th Annual Conference, Washington Hilton Hotel, Washington, D.C., July 24, 1977.

Martin, Louis E. The 1984 Millender Memorial Lecture. Speech delivered at Wayne State University, Detroit, Michigan, February 28, 1984.

——. Address at the Pi Alpha Alpha Induction Ceremony, School of Business and Public Administration, Howard University, Washington, D.C., June 23, 1983.

——. "The Emancipation Proclamation: 100 Years Thereafter." Speech delivered at the 28th Annual Meeting of the Association of Social Science Teachers and the Annual Meeting of Sigma Rho Sigma Honorary Society, North Carolina College, Durham, North Carolina, April 26, 1963. (Reprinted in Roy Hill, ed., *Rhetoric of Racial Hope*).

## Interviews

### AUTHOR INTERVIEWS

The author's principal interviews with Louis E. Martin, Gertrude Martin, Lillian Calhoun, and Gertrude Elizabeth Martin Hatter were conducted in December 1991. All other author interviews were conducted during 1992. Subjects interviewed:

| | | |
|---|---|---|
| Clifford Alexander | William Gray | Carl Rowan |
| Lou Alexander | Ernest Green | John Sengstacke |
| Judy Andrews | Richard Hatcher | Sargent Shriver |
| Ben Bradlee | Alan Hermesch | Robert Smith |
| Andrew Brimmer | Benjamin Hooks | Adlai Stevenson III |
| Les Brownlee | Vernon Jarrett | Chuck Stone |
| Jimmy Carter | Hamilton Jordan | Leroy Thomas |
| James Cheek | Vernon Jordan | William Taylor |
| Kenneth Clark | Thurgood Marshall | Ronald Walters |
| William Clay | Harry McPherson | Harris Wofford |
| Henry Duvall | August Meier | Lee White |
| Stuart Eizenstat | Lu Palmer | Eddie Williams |
| Bob Elliot | David Palombi | Karen Williamson |
| Roger Estep | Joe Rollins | (formerly Zuniga) |
| Eleanor Farrar | | |

COLUMBIA UNIVERSITY ORAL HISTORY COLLECTION

Martin, Louis E. Interviews by Ed Edwin. As cited, interviews on the following dates:

First interview: April 17, 1981.

Second interview: December 7, 1984.

Third interview: May 2, 1985.

Fourth interview: July 18, 1985.

Fifth interview: October 16, 1985.

Sixth interview: January 23, 1986.

Seventh interview: September 18, 1986.

Eighth interview: February 6, 1987.

Ninth interview: March 11, 1987.

Tenth interview: April 30, 1987.

LYNDON BAINES JOHNSON LIBRARY ORAL HISTORY COLLECTION

Martin, Louis E. Interview by David McComb, University of Texas Oral History Project, May 14, 1969.

JOHN F. KENNEDY LIBRARY

Martin, Louis E. Interviews by Ronald Grele. As cited, interviews on the following dates:

First interview: March 14, 1966.

Second interview: April 7, 1966.

Third interview: May 11, 1966.

OTHER INTERVIEWS

Cashin, John. Telephone interview by Marc DeFrancis. September 9, 1996.

Jeffrey, Mildred. Telephone interview by Marc DeFrancis. January 30, 1997.

Martin, Louis E. Interview by David Ruffin for *FOCUS* magazine. October 9, 1992.

White, Lee. Telephone interview by Marc DeFrancis. September 20, 1996.

## Unpublished Manuscripts

UNPUBLISHED MEMOIRS OF LOUIS E. MARTIN

Memoir A. Untitled. Four notebooks, handwritten, 339 hand-numbered pages (photocopy). Undated (text indicates writing was begun February 17, 1977). Collection of Gertrude Martin.

Memoir B. Untitled. Typed, 45 hand-numbered pages (original typescript and photocopy). Undated. Collection of Gertrude Martin.

# BIBLIOGRAPHY

Memoir C. Untitled. Typed, 220 numbered pages (original typescript and photocopy). Undated (text indicates writing was begun November 4, 1980). Collection of Gertrude Martin.

Memoir D. Untitled. Typed, 22 numbered pages. Undated. Collection of Gertrude Martin.

Memoir E. Untitled. Typed, 39 numbered pages (photocopy; several pages missing). Undated. Collection of Gertrude Martin.

Memoir F. "Home From Nigeria." Handwritten, 61 hand-numbered pages (photocopy). Undated. Collection of Gertrude Martin.

Memoir G. Untitled. Handwritten, 7 pages, unnumbered (photocopy). Undated (text indicates writing was begun in 1972.) Collection of Gertrude Martin.

Memoir H. "March on Washington." Handwritten, 8 hand-numbered pages (photocopy). Undated. Collection of Gertrude Martin.

Memoir I. Untitled. Typed, 11 numbered pages (page 1 missing). Undated. Collection of Gertrude Martin.

# PHOTO CREDITS

# ACKNOWLEDGMENTS

In September 1991, Eddie N. Williams, president of the Joint Center for Political and Economic Studies, and Milton D. Morris, then senior vice president for research, queried me about writing Louis Martin's political biography. They expected the work to trace Martin's journalistic and political development by relating his career to post–World War II black politics; by sketching his views on the manner in which blacks influenced political decision making, despite their historic role as outsiders to the political system; and by appraising Martin's influence on the process by which African Americans accessed the political system.

As a journalist, I had followed Martin's distinguished career. Hence, the Williams/Morris invitation was an attractive opportunity. Honoring me as a Distinguished Scholar for 1991–92, supplemented by a MacArthur Foundation grant, the Joint Center also provided office space for my occasional work in Washington, supplied documents and taped interviews of Martin, and funded my visits to Martin's home in Diamond Bar, California, as well as to the John F. Kennedy Library in Boston, the Lyndon B. Johnson Library in Austin, Texas, and the Jimmy Carter Library in Atlanta.

Obviously, this political biography would not have been possible without the steadfast cooperation of Louis Martin, his wife, Gertrude, and their five daughters. Though paralyzed and wheelchair-bound by a 1988 stroke, Martin spent many hours with me, recalling in minute detail events spanning seven decades. Occasional gaps in his narrative were bridged by his wife, their oldest daughter, Trudy (Mrs. Terry Hatter), their second oldest daughter, Anita Martin, and Gertrude Martin's sister, Lillian Calhoun. Los Angeles Federal District Judge Terry Hatter, one of Martin's sons-in-law, was also helpful.

Among the numerous other persons whom I interviewed for the book, especially valuable were former President Jimmy Carter, Justice Thurgood Marshall, who received me in his Supreme Court chambers two months before his death in 1993, Vernon Jordan, who was in the midst of chairing Bill Clinton's 1992 presidential transition team, and of course Eddie Williams.

Additional interviewees—"Martin fans" might be more descriptive—included Clifford Alexander, former aide to LBJ and secretary of the army under Carter; Andrew Brimmer, former Federal Reserve Board member; James

## ACKNOWLEDGMENTS

Cheek, former Howard University president; Representative William L. Clay; William Gray, former U.S. representative; Eleanor Farrar, a founding board member and administrator of the Joint Center; Ernest Green, assistant secretary of labor under Carter; Benjamin Hooks, retired NAACP president; Carl Rowan, former State Department official and ambassador to Finland under Kennedy; R. Sargent Shriver, the first director of the Peace Corps; Adlai Stevenson III, retired U.S. senator; Chuck Stone, a Philadelphia newspaper columnist; Ronald W. Walters, former chairman of the Howard University political science department; and Harris Wofford, former Kennedy White House aide and close companion of Louis Martin in the 1960 presidential campaign.

Valuable information about Martin also came from retired Chicago banker Louis G. Alexander; Ben Bradlee, retired editor of the *Washington Post*; Les Brownlee, a Chicago journalism professor; Charles A. Davis, a Chicago publicist and insurance executive; Stuart Eizenstat, Carter's domestic policy advisor; former mayor Richard G. Hatcher of Gary, Indiana; Hamilton Jordan, Carter's chief of staff; Harry McPherson, former LBJ speechwriter and aide; August Meier, a Kent State University historian; Lu Palmer, a veteran Chicago journalist/activist; John Sengstacke, *Chicago Defender* publisher; William Taylor, a civil rights attorney in Washington; Leroy Thomas, a Chicago journalist; Lee White, former civil rights advisor to Kennedy and Johnson; and Karen Williamson, a former Martin aide.

I purposely single out my longtime friend and mentor, political science professor Charles V. Hamilton of Columbia University, whose wise and sensitive reading of the manuscript was just as helpful to me as when he wrote the foreword to my 1970 book, *Black Power, Gary Style: The Making of Mayor Richard Gordon Hatcher.*

Also helpful was the research assistance I received from professional staffers at the Carter, Kennedy, and Johnson presidential libraries, particularly from photo archivists David Stanhope, Alan Goodrich, and Philip Scott. I am grateful as well to Helene Berinsky for the generous donation of photographs of the 1960 Kennedy campaign. Others who helped greatly in the search for photographs were Eugene Scott at the *Chicago Defender* and Norman Currie at Bettman Archives.

Finally, I am deeply indebted to my colleagues at the Joint Center, particularly Eddie Williams, Milton Morris, and Eleanor Farrar. I am indebted as well to senior editor Marc DeFrancis; editors Mary T. Garber and Ruby Essien; indexer, photo researcher and production manager Theresa Kilcourse;

researchers Marland Buckner and Byron Spears; copyeditors Jane Lewin and Pat Tschirhart-Spangler, and proofreader Jerry Richardson; and assistants Pat Kaenel, Lisa Bell Gonzalez, and John Ulmer.

To my wife, Norma, retired director of Chicago's DuSable High School library, I owe special thanks for relevant research materials she unearthed and for putting up with the stress and strain that nearly always accompany an ambitious undertaking of this sort.

All these collaborators are responsible for whatever merit readers find in this political biography. But only the author deserves responsibility for its flaws.

—Alex Poinsett
Chicago, January 1997

# INDEX

# INDEX

# INDEX

# INDEX

# ABOUT THE AUTHOR

Alex Poinsett is an award-winning black journalist and author. As a contributing editor at *Ebony* magazine for 26 years, he logged more than one million miles on assignments in Haiti, Kenya, Liberia, Nigeria, and the Soviet Union. His other books include *Black Power, Gary Style* (1970), a political biography of former mayor Richard Hatcher, and, as contributing author with Leslie Dunbar, *The Common Interest: How Our Social Welfare Policies Don't Work and What We Can Do About Them* (1988). For his writing on urban and social issues for the Ford Foundation, the Carnegie Corporation of New York, and the Lily Endowment, as well as for his writing on minority topics generally, he has been honored by numerous institutions, including the University of Missouri Journalism School, Florida A & M University, and the PUSH Foundation. In 1991 he was appointed a distinguished scholar by the Joint Center for Political and Economic Studies to undertake the research and writing of this book.